BEING AGILE

YOUR ROADMAP TO SUCCESSFUL ADOPTION OF AGILE

Mario E. Moreira

Apress®

Being Agile: Your Roadmap to Successful Adoption of Agile

ISBN-13 (pbk): 978-1-4302-5839-1

ISBN-13 (electronic): 978-1-4302-5840-7

President and Publisher: Paul Manning
Acquisitions Editor: Robert Hutchinson
Editorial Board: Steve Anglin, Mark Beckner, Ewan Buckingham, Gary Cornell, Louise Corrigan,
     Jonathan Gennick, Jonathan Hassell, Robert Hutchinson, Michelle Lowman,
     James Markham, Matthew Moodie, Jeff Olson, Jeffrey Pepper, Douglas Pundick,
     Ben Renow-Clarke, Dominic Shakeshaft, Gwenan Spearing, Matt Wade, Tom Welsh
Coordinating Editor: Rita Fernando
Copy Editor: Laura Poole
Compositor: SPi Global
Indexer: SPi Global
Cover Designer: Anna Ishchenko

Distributed to the book trade worldwide by Springer Science+Business Media New York, 233 Spring Street, 6th Floor, New York, NY 10013. Phone 1-800-SPRINGER, fax (201) 348-4505, e-mail orders-ny@springer-sbm.com, or visit www.springeronline.com. Apress Media, LLC is a California LLC and the sole member (owner) is Springer Science + Business Media Finance Inc (SSBM Finance Inc). SSBM Finance Inc is a Delaware corporation.

For information on translations, please e-mail rights@apress.com, or visit www.apress.com.

Apress and friends of ED books may be purchased in bulk for academic, corporate, or promotional use. eBook versions and licenses are also available for most titles. For more information, reference our Special Bulk Sales–eBook Licensing web page at www.apress.com/bulk-sales.

Any source code or other supplementary materials referenced by the author in this text is available to readers at www.apress.com. For detailed information about how to locate your book's source code, go to www.apress.com/source-code/.

Apress Business: The Unbiased Source of Business Information

Apress business books provide essential information and practical advice, each written for practitioners by recognized experts. Busy managers and professionals in all areas of the business world—and at all levels of technical sophistication—look to our books for the actionable ideas and tools they need to solve problems, update and enhance their professional skills, make their work lives easier, and capitalize on opportunity.

Whatever the topic on the business spectrum—entrepreneurship, finance, sales, marketing, management, regulation, information technology, among others—Apress has been praised for providing the objective information and unbiased advice you need to excel in your daily work life. Our authors have no axes to grind; they understand they have one job only—to deliver up-to-date, accurate information simply, concisely, and with deep insight that addresses the real needs of our readers.

It is increasingly hard to find information—whether in the news media, on the Internet, and now all too often in books—that is even-handed and has your best interests at heart. We therefore hope that you enjoy this book, which has been carefully crafted to meet our standards of quality and unbiased coverage.

We are always interested in your feedback or ideas for new titles. Perhaps you'd even like to write a book yourself. Whatever the case, reach out to us at editorial@apress.com and an editor will respond swiftly. Incidentally, at the back of this book, you will find a list of useful related titles. Please visit us at www.apress.com to sign up for newsletters and discounts on future purchases.

The Apress Business Team

I dedicate this book to two fine ladies and grandes dames who have given life to me and my family and a raison d'être

—Floy and Sajida

I also dedicate this book to all of those agile enthusiasts who understand that they need to not only "do" Agile but eventually to "be" Agile to gain the business benefits that Agile can bring.

.

Contents

About the Author

Mario E. Moreira is an enterprise change agent who has worked in the Agile field since 1998. He is a certified Scrum Master (CSM) and Scrum Professional (CSP) with Scrum, XP, and Kanban experience in the context of enterprise-level Agile transformations, coaching, and team-building. He was Senior Director for Agile and Configuration Management at CA Technologies.

As an IT professional in the networking, communications, product, open source, and financial industries for over 20 years, Moreira has experience in software configuration management, project management, software quality assurance, requirements engineering, architecture, and IT governance. He served as Vice President of Engineering and Methodologies at Fidelity Investments.

Moreira is the author of *Adapting Configuration Management for Agile Teams*, *Software Configuration Management Implementation Roadmap*, and *Agile for Dummies*. He is a writer for *Agile Journal*, a columnist for *CM Crossroads Journal*, a blogger at *Agile Adoption Roadmap* (cmforagile.blogspot.com), and a regular speaker on Agile topics at US and European conferences.

Acknowledgments

I want to especially thank Robert Hutchinson, Rita Fernando, and Jeffrey Pepper at Apress for their encouragement, patience, attention to detail, and support in helping me make this book a reality.

To all of the many Agile champions who contributed to my surveys and provided feedback to my Agile articles—thank you for helping me understand Agile from so many points of view.

To all my readers—thank you for making a commitment to "be Agile" and for striving to adapt your culture toward an Agile mindset aligning with Agile values and principles.

To Ken Schwaber, who introduced me to Agile and Scrum—thank you for my Certified Scrum Master training and for continuing your mission to create a more adaptive world.

To Sherris Moreira—thank you for reviewing sections of my book and providing feedback.

And to my beautiful wife and daughters, who make my life so full and wonderful—thank you for being patient as I was writing this book.

Getting Started

Adapt or perish, now as ever, is nature's inexorable imperative.

—H. G. Wells

Throughout the history of the human species, people have learned to adapt to the environment. When the weather got too cold during the ice ages, Northern Hemisphere peoples either migrated south or adapted their clothing to live in the cold. People have adapted their eating habits, tools, and resistance to certain germs. Theories of physical and cultural evolution postulate that successful human populations and processes continuously adapt to their environments.

As a complex process practiced by a specialized subpopulation in a rapidly changing technological and business environment, we are under constant adaptive pressure to evolve. Somewhere along the way, however, many of us in the world of software development have grown content with fixing long-term goals, and we resist adaptive pressures to make corrective course changes. This conservative inertia has definitely gotten in the way of how we do business, clogging it with unwieldy upfront requirements and inflexible planning. The good news is that companies are seeing the benefits of moving back to a more adaptive approach.

Agile has secured its place within the software development community where it originated and evolved, and now Agile is spreading into many other areas of the professional workplace, where its embrace of adaptive feedback can help businesses thrive. Many are seeing that a more iterative approach allows them the flexibility to adjust to the changing needs of customers and the continuous churning of market conditions. Many others would like to apply Agile effectively because they are hearing it from all corners of their professional life.

No matter how prevalent and popular the adoption of Agile has become, getting started with Agile and then continuing to apply its methods and practices remain significant challenges. This is what I call "doing Agile," by which I mean mechanically applying Agile methods and practices—whether they are Scrum, eXtreme Programming (XP), Kanban, Test Driven Development (TDD), or any of the many other variants. More important than the selection of a particular style of Agile, however, is the art of learning how to live Agile values and principles to transform Agile mechanics into Agile mindset. This is what I call "being Agile."

Purpose of This Book

The purpose of this book is to help you and your organization not only apply Agile methods and practices ("do Agile") but transform yourselves to an Agile mindset and live in an Agile culture ("be Agile") grounded in Agile values and principles, customer value, continuous customer engagement, and employee engagement.

The more you empower teams within your organization to self-organize and draw out valuable employee knowledge, the more integrally and continuously you incorporate customer feedback into your development process; the more responsively and sensitively your product team and organization adapt to customer needs and changing market conditions; the more your organization will thrive and profit from the benefits of Agile.

Throughout this book, I offer guidance, lessons, and tips regarding the adoption of Agile. Some of these might seem obvious and derived from the principles and values, yet they often are missed, neglected, or glossed over. Commonsense considerations about adopting and implementing an Agile culture change are often the elephant in the room. Individuals in any company are generally reluctant to expose themselves to embarrassment if they point out things that might seem blindingly obvious or ask questions that might reveal an embarrassing knowledge gap. A prime example is knowledge of Agile itself.

Many people pretend or imply by their silence that they know what Agile is, but they really have only a vague idea. If they don't understand what Agile is, they can't understand its benefits. Certainly if they don't understand how to *do* Agile, they can't understand what it means to *be* Agile. Another example is that some folks suppose that introducing Agile is a minor change. They fail to see the elephant in the room (see Figure 1-1): adopting Agile requires significant organizational change in order to transform their culture and produce major benefits.

Figure 1-1. Agile elephant in the room. Agile requires a culture change, but most only want to apply tool and process changes

What You Will Learn

This book is a roadmap designed to help you consider, understand, deploy, and adapt Agile methods and practices within an organization and on an Agile team. More important, it will help you understand the Agile mindset to not only "do Agile" but "be Agile" to truly achieve a transformation and the business benefits it can provide. It is intended to be a pragmatic guide, and as such is neither exhaustive nor prescriptive. The guidelines in this book apply equally to situations when a team is embarking on new product development following Agile or to existing legacy products that are introducing Agile. With new product teams, the material in this book can help the team prepare for activities to achieve an Agile transformation. With legacy product teams, aspects of this book may be used to help examine current thinking and then adapt current mindsets and processes. These guidelines are also meant to apply to the whole organization, because "being Agile" requires buy-in across the enterprise.

This book will help you embrace Agile values and principles, adopt the methods and practices of Agile and, more important, enable you to cross the chasm between "doing Agile" to "being Agile." In particular, *Being Agile*:

- Presents a methodical yet adaptable approach toward Agile transformation, encapsulated in a ready–implement–coach–hone (RICH) model that can be easily understood and followed.

- Advocates a framework in which values, customer engagement, employee engagement, and an Agile process can lead to an increase in sales and productivity, incorporated in the Agile Value to Incentive Differentiator (AVID) framework.

- Provides a mechanism for evaluating your level of alignment to the Agile values and principles, encapsulated in the Agile Mindset, Values, and Principles (Agile MVP) Advisor.

- Promotes a special focus on value-added work (VAW) that features customer work as valuable and an accompanying value capture metric.

- Models how to implement Agile at both the product team level and the organizational level.

This book maps the path for adopting and adapting Agile in such a way as to gain the full benefits that you desire from the Agile transformation. The topics that this book focuses on include:

- Business benefits

- Mindset, values, and principles

- An adaptable approach for deploying Agile

- Suitability for applying Agile

- Stakeholder buy-in and support

- Team willingness and capability

- Overview of Scrum, XP, Lean, DSDM, and Kanban

- Roles and responsibilities

- Frameworks and practices

- Scalability such as Scrum-of-Scrums

- Education

- Agile community

- Success measures

- Writing user stories

- Backlog and grooming

- Story point sizing techniques

- Velocity and burn-downs

- Sprint 0 and Agile Release Planning

- Done criteria

- Customer validation vision

- Agile tools and infrastructure

- Agile assessments
- Grooming in-house talent
- Performance reviews in Agile world
- Agile organizational governance
- Agile adoption case studies

Who This Book Is For

The primary readers for this book are:

- executives and senior management
- Agile Coaches and consultants
- Scrum Masters and Agile project managers
- Product Owners, product managers, business analysts
- cross-functional engineering/scrum teams including developers, quality assurance (QA) analysts and testers, technical writers, user experience (UX) engineers, configuration management (CM) engineers, and more

Others who will benefit from using this book include:

- development, functional, and QA management
- sponsors and customers

How to Navigate This Book

You can read this book in various ways depending on your purpose and prior knowledge. Of course you are welcome to read the book consecutively from beginning to end. However, you can also customize your path through the book to suit your knowledge level or the specific challenge you are trying to solve.

For those that are more experienced in Agile but seeing challenges in "being Agile," I encourage you to pay particular attention to the discussions on crossing the Agile chasm, achieving the Agile mindset, business benefits, and the importance of customer engagement and employee. You may find the RICH deployment model, the AVID framework, and Agile MVP Advisor particularly useful. When you have not seen the Agile transformation you have been hoping for, trawl the RICH readiness activities suggested throughout this book for insight into your particular question or challenge.

Agile Pit Stop Pay particular attention to the Agile Pit Stops throughout the book. They illuminate ideas with examples or highlight important points, cautions, or tips.

Following is a list of chapters or chapter clusters to consult for particular topics and needs.

- Reasons to move to Agile: Chapter 3 ("Business Benefits of Being Agile") and Chapter 8 ("Motivations for Moving to an Agile Culture").

- What it really takes to gain the Agile mindset: Chapter 2 ("Crossing the Agile Chasm"), Chapter 4 ("Importance of Customer Engagement"), Chapter 5 ("Importance of Employee Engagement"), and Chapter 9 ("Achieving an Agile Mindset").

- Review of Agile processes and methodologies: Chapter 6 ("Foundations of Agile") and Chapter 15 ("Constructing a Scalable Agile Framework").

- Deployment and planning for an Agile transformation: Chapter 7 ("RICH Deployment Framework"), Chapter 10 ("Evaluating Executive Support and Team Willingness "), Chapter 14 ("Establishing Measures of Success"), and Chapter 11 ("Treating Agile as a Transformation Project").

- Key deployment activities: Chapter 12 ("Adapting to Agile Roles and Responsibilities") to Chapter 21 ("Considering Agile Tools within an ALM Framework").

- How to establish a strong Agile community: Chapter 16 ("Establishing an Agile Education Program") and Chapter 22 ("Implementing, Coaching, and Honing Activities").

- How to adapt organization level processes: Chapter 23 ("Adapting Governance and Performance Reviews").

- Case studies: Chapter 24 ("Three Case Studies in Adopting Agile").

Crossing the Agile Chasm

Anything can be achieved in small, deliberate steps. But there are times you need the courage to take a great leap; you can't cross a chasm in two small jumps.

—David Lloyd George

Adopting a new concept often proves harder than it seems at first. Adopting Agile is definitely a case in point. Although Agile is still relatively new, having been formally defined by a meeting of seventeen signatories in February 2001 in their "Manifesto for Agile Software Development," it has gained significant adoption over the past decade.[1] At first glance, it appears that many software development–related companies have adopted Agile at some level. However, on further investigation, it appears that only some parts of Agile are being adopted and often in a spotty manner. A few data points that help us understand Agile's current adoption levels include the following. A 2012 study on product team performance done by Actuation Consulting indicates that 71 percent of surveyed organizations self-reported using Agile to some degree.[2] This sounds significant, right? However, that study showed that only 13 percent reported that they are using "pure" Agile in the sense that Agile values and principles were being followed and iterative incremental techniques were not being mixed with other methodologies. A 2009 study indicated that

---

[1]See Kent Beck, et al. "Manifesto for Agile Software Development," (2001), http://agilemanifesto.org.
[2]Actuation Consulting and Enterprise Agility, "The Study of Product Team Performance, 2012," http://www.actuationconsultingllc.com/whitepaper_request.php.

35 percent of surveyed organizations said that Agile in one form or another best describes the way they build products.[3] Although such evidence reveals significant levels of self-identification by information technology (IT) firms with Agile methodologies and their deployment of some Agile practices, only a small minority of companies have adopted and implemented "pure" Agile. Penetration of Agile practices and even more the adoption of pure Agile programs still have a long way to go in the industry.

Agile Is Really a Culture Change

When we discuss Agile adoption, we are talking about a change to the organizational culture. Culture disruption is never painless. This is because adopting Agile is not a matter of learning skills or understanding a procedure, it is about adopting a set of values and principles that require change in people's behavior and the culture of an organization.

Generally, a skill change is easier than a procedural change, and a procedural change is easier than a culture change. A skill change is limited to how an individual operates or maintains an asset and is fairly mechanical. A procedural change is a change in the steps to get something done and can also be fairly mechanical but is of a higher order than a skill change because a chain of employees needs to deploy complementary skills in a coordinated and effective way. A culture change implies a behavioral change in people in response to a change in the values and assumptions of their organization that is expressive of a new way of thinking. This kind of culture change takes time. This is why I suggest that you think of your change to Agile as a *journey*.

Getting people to change their outward behavior is notoriously difficult. Getting them to change their mindset is even tougher, because they must come to endorse, internalize, and really believe in the change. Figure 2-1 graphically represents the relative magnitudes of change and adjustment periods for changes in skills, procedure, and culture. The further up the change type axis you go, the greater the magnitude of change and the more time is needed to implement that change. Culture change is a transformation that involves the most change and requires the most time for an organization to adjust.

---

[3]Forrester-Dr. Dobb's Global Developer Technographics Survey, Q3 2009.

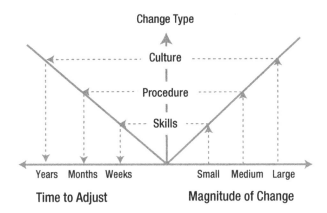

Figure 2-1. Dynamics of organizational change (*source: adapted from Paul S. Adler and Aaron Shenhar, "Adapting your Technological Base: The Organizational Challenge," Sloan Management Review, 2, no. 1 (Fall 1990), figure 2, 36*)

Imagine for a moment that you are in Italy. You learn to drive a Ferrari and enjoy driving it around. Does this make you an Italian? Of course not. You have learned an exciting new skill on an Italian machine, but it doesn't mean you can interact as an Italian with locals around you.

Now imagine that you have learned enough Italian that you can walk into a café in Rome and order a *fette biscottate* and *caffè e latte* for your *colazione*. Does being able to order breakfast make you an Italian? Of course not. You know the procedure and vocabulary for ordering breakfast, but it doesn't mean you can interact as an Italian with the locals. To the Italians around you, you stick out like a sore thumb.

Now imagine that you have lived in Italy for several years, immersed yourself in the language, and adopted the local customs (instead of shaking hands, you air-kiss on both cheeks). You have achieved a sophisticated understanding of Italian wines and the precise weight of the cloth needed for your clothing to hang elegantly. You engage in animated discussions with the locals about the various regions and subcultures within Italy. Does all this make you an Italian? It won't right away, but the Italians around you will credit that you are making an honest effort to change your behavior and are really attempting to understand not only how Italians do things but why they do things. Over time, your own culture will change enough that you start internalizing the Italian culture. There's the key correlation: a culture change of large enough magnitude to be internalized and recognized as "being Italian" will take you a lot of effort expended over a long time.

Many who have implemented Agile think that it is a procedural change that can be layered into their organization with little change to their current culture. I believe the contrary: if you don't think Agile should fundamentally change your culture, then your half-measures will block the business benefits you are looking for.

To gain an appreciation of the full potential of Agile within your company, read the rest of this chapter and the next four chapters. Culture change in Agile isn't just for the engineering department but for the whole organization. The Agile journey isn't just an option for the self-selected few; everyone must sign on to adapt their behavior in alignment with Agile values and principles.

Technology Adoption Lifecycle

Agile is already a mainstay in the software product development arena, even if we are seeing uneven adoption. However, because of its relative newness, Agile adoption continues to be embraced by innovators and early adopters in context of the classic technology adoption lifecycle model advanced by sociologists Joe M. Bohlen and George M. Beal in 1957, shown in Figure 2-2.[4] This life cycle model describes the acceptance of innovation according to the demographic and psychological characteristics of defined adopter groups. The successive groups include *innovators*, *early adopters*, *early majority*, *late majority*, and *laggards*.

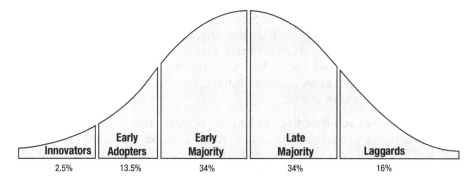

Innovators	Early Adopters	Early Majority	Late Majority	Laggards
2.5%	13.5%	34%	34%	16%

Figure 2-2. Technology adoption lifecycle

In this model, innovators are described as educated risk takers who enjoy innovation, are willing to try out new ideas, and are more tolerant of mistakes. They require little guidance and actually enjoy spending hours figuring out how to adopt the innovation. Innovators are helpful critics who are ready to invest the time and effort to get the innovation to work. The early adopters are described as educated community leaders who are constantly seeking

---

[4] Joe M. Bohlen and George M. Beal, "The Diffusion Process", Special Report No. 18, Agriculture Extension Service, Iowa State College, May 1957, 1:56–77.

better ways and looking to gain visibility and credibility, while accepting some level of risk. Both the innovators and early adopters have seen the intrinsic benefits of going Agile and are fairly sincere in their efforts to change their behavior and culture for the better.

The early majority are described as more pragmatic, open to new ideas, and avid for ways to become more successful. Whereas innovators and early adopters are willing to struggle to make the new innovation work, the early majority are looking for guidance on how to adopt it so they can manage the change more carefully. The late majority and laggards await the results of those who blaze the trail and are often pushed, sometimes grudgingly, into the new world. These last two groups are the ones least interested in changing their culture.

Agile Cultural Chasm

In 1991, Geoffrey Moore refined the classic technology adoption model with an additional element he called the "chasm."[5] He advanced a proposition specific to disruptive innovation that there is a significant shift in mentality to be crossed between the early adopter and the early majority groups. Disruptive innovation is the development of new values that forces a significant change of behavior to the culture adopting it. In this case, Agile is that disruptive force that insists on applying a set of values and principles within a specific culture of "being Agile" to be successful and for the organization to realize the full business benefits of Agile.

At first glance, it would appear from the adoption statistics cited at the beginning of this chapter that as of this writing Agile is solidly in the early majority stage of its adoption life cycle—or perhaps the late majority stage. I believe, however, that this perception is specious, in view of the further observation that the majority of companies that are "doing" Agile at some have not actually adopted the new values and made the cultural shift to actually "being" Agile. Such companies look at Agile as a set of skills, tools, and procedural changes and not the integrated behavioral and cultural change it truly is. In other words, they think they have crossed the chasm, but they have not made the significant change of behavior required to make the leap.

---

[5]Geoffrey A. Moore, *Crossing the Chasm* (New York: Harper Business Essentials, 1991).

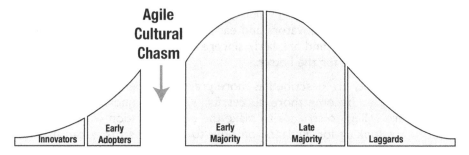

Figure 2-3. Crossing the Agile chasm requires that you apply a new set of values and a significant shift in behavior

My experience in the field leads me to posit a refinement on Moore's chasm concept as applied to Agile. First, there is the real Agile chasm between those on the left side who have made the organic behavioral changes consistent with the values of being Agile—and those on the right side who are just doing" Agile mechanically. Second, there is a fake chasm, which many organizations pride themselves on having crossed by virtue of adopting some mechanical features of Agile, whereas they have not been willing or able to make the behavioral changes and adopt the values required to cross the real chasm. Although many companies say that they are doing Agile in some form, a large proportion of these are actually doing Fragile ("fake Agile"), ScrumBut ("I'm doing Scrum but not all of the practices"), ScrumFall ("I'm doing mini-waterfall in the sprints or phase-based Agile"), or some other hybrid variant that cannot deliver the business benefits of pure Agile.

Agile Pit Stop   There is a "fake chasm" crossed by those unwilling or unable to make the behavioral changes to cross the real Agile chasm. This is exemplified by such practices as Fragile, ScrumBut, and ScrumFall prevalent in the software industry.

I cannot overstate this point: many companies and teams within companies are mechanically doing some form of Agile without having actually crossed the Agile chasm, discarding the behavioral baggage that is keeping them from being Agile. Until a team attains the state of being Agile, the business benefits that Agile can provide will be elusive. I contend that the industry has barely entered the early majority of true Agile cultural transformation, and many companies continue to struggle to leap the Agile chasm or, in many cases, even recognize that they have only crossed a fake Agile chasm.

Agile Pit Stop   Many are only mechanically "doing" Agile and have not yet really begun to "be" Agile (i.e., actually applying the values and principles of Agile).

Looking through the lens of the adoption lifecycle model, let's review the results of the surveys on Agile's adoption levels mentioned at the beginning of this chapter. The 2012 study referenced earlier indicated that 71 percent of organizations self-reported using Agile to some degree. This level of adoption would seem to suggest that Agile has reached the late majority stage. But the same study indicated that only 13 percent said they were using "pure" Agile. This statistic would seem to suggest that Agile is still in the early adopter stage. The 2009 study mentioned earlier indicated that 35 percent of respondents follow one form of Agile or another. This fact would seem to suggest that Agile is in the early majority. Although both studies report significant levels of adoption, those levels are sufficiently low as to be consistent with the proposition that crossing the Agile cultural chasm is proving a tough challenge for a majority of companies.

Key to meeting this challenge is identifying ways to bridge the communities of the early adopters and the early majority. While the early adopters are very willing to take risks and try new things, the early majority are less risk-tolerant and look for guidance that will help them reduce the disruptive stresses of Agile adoption. They have seen the benefits of Agile around them, but they need more help in its adoption. In some cases, prospective adopters may be pushing the boundaries of Agile. A good example is that early adoption of Scrum focused on small collocated product teams. However, as folks saw the success of Scrum, the industry has learned to adapt it for larger, more distributed product teams. In short, companies seek a solid foundation of information and guidance to help them cross the chasm.

This book lays the foundation for those who want to cross the Agile cultural chasm, understand the behaviors that need to change, and gauge progress along the way. It provides an Agile transformation roadmap to the destination of Agile: business benefits.

Business Benefits of Being Agile

Profit in business comes from repeat customers that boast about your project or service and that bring friends with them.

—W. Edwards Deming

In my experience, the ultimate business benefit of going Agile is that it ... can ... make ... the ... company ... more ... money. Did this get your attention? I find that few people will actually say this out loud. However, to make money, you need to delight your customers by building customer value and harness the brainpower of your employees.

Think about it for a moment:

- If you are truly committed to building customer value, then you will be building what the customer wants and the customer will be delighted, *ergo* they will buy the product or buy more of the product, while increasing the likelihood of remaining loyal to you.

- If you are truly committed to empowering your employees, then you will provide a work environment where they feel ownership of the work and can make their own decisions, and they will be more motivated to activate their brainpower, improving morale and increasing the likelihood that they will go the extra mile to create a quality product.

The employees are the company's greatest assets for success, and the customer represents the greatest potential for company revenue. Isn't this what you really want?

Although executives/senior management in companies may have some sense of the business benefits of Agile, I suggest that a major reason Agile is being implemented in many organizations is because they see it as the trend in the industry, so they think they better do it as well. In other words, they may be introducing Agile for the sake of jumping on the bandwagon, and most of their employees are then not sure why they are doing it but are mechanically following the process.

A mistake I often see when Agile is first rolled out is that only the mechanical aspects are introduced. For example, "this is a Scrum team," and "this is Continuous Integration." This is particularly harmful when senior management is introduced to Agile this way. They then interpret this as "Agile is something the engineering team should do" and don't really see their role in Agile.

Agile Pit Stop   Do not introduce senior management to the mechanical aspects of Agile first. Instead, introduce them to the agile principles, business benefits, and their role in the agile transformation. This way they realize that Agile helps their business opportunity and that they have a role to play.

Instead, when you introduce Agile to executives/senior management, they should be educated in the agile values and principles, business benefits, and their role in an agile transformation. Then they will realize that Agile is about helping their business opportunity and that they have a role to play.

There are supplementary reasons teams or organizations are turning toward Agile. In general, many software development projects have a poor track record of delivering on time, on budget, with high quality, and what the customer wants. The question then becomes, what are the reasons for this track record? Some reasons include:

- Cannot possibly know everything or most things upfront.
- Schedules are defined with little information about the work.
- Software development is complex.
- Processes are often lengthy, with a lot of rigid ceremony.
- Defining requirements in detail is difficult.
- Customer needs change, and so do market conditions.
- Testing gets abused and minimized at the end as schedules get tight.

The good news is that applying an adaptive framework like agile methods can reduce many of these problems. For example, if you reach every scheduled release date, you bring the project in on budget, and you build it with quality, but you do not build features that customers want, they will not buy it and you have failed. This is why I contend that if you align your culture and processes around building customer value (e.g., what customers need and when they need it), then you will be successful and have increased your chances of making money.

Agile Pit Stop   If you finish within the schedule, bring the project in on budget, and build it with great quality, but do not deliver what the customer wants, they will not buy it and your business may fail.

In addition, I see Agile often focused on the engineering side of the company because there is a lack of understanding that Agile will help an organization's bottom line. Although Agile will benefit the engineering side, particularly eXtreme programming (XP) practices, Agile should really be driven by strong business reasons. If you look at Agile as a business tool to make more money for the organization, you will gain greater buy-in from senior management, who are often the sponsors of agile programs and are looking for a business edge.

Show Me the Money

Though there are many benefits for going Agile, it occurred to me that to get serious executive/senior management attention is to get them to understand that Agile is really there to increase revenue—in short, to help them make money.

One way to help them is to provide an illustration in which Agile is their dashboard, with dials and levers that can help their organization (see Figure 3-1). I ask, what do they think occurs when they step up the level of customer engagement? What happens when you move up the level of employee engagement?

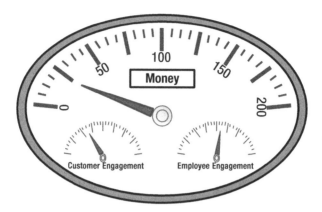

Figure 3-1. Gauges for your agile dashboard: adjust your levels of customer and employee engagement to see the changes to your profits

I leave executives to ponder whether they think these sincere actions can lead to making more money. In my experience, this gets them to actively listen, versus the passive listening they may exhibit when they think Agile is an engineering method or something the engineering team and others must do.

Yes, Agile can increase productivity. Yes, it may reduce your time to market. Yes, it can improve employee morale. Yes, it can help you manage change. Yes, it can help you increase project visibility. Yes, it can help you improve quality. Yes, it helps in many other ways. And yes, Agile can lead to an increase in customer sales, *ergo* an increase in profits. This is all true *if* Agile is implemented correctly.

Agile Pit Stop   Attention all executives/senior management types: Agile is really there to help make you more money!

There I said it: *if* Agile is implemented correctly. This is a big and important *if*. The *if* means that Agile must be implemented sincerely, aligned with agile values and principles, and with a special focus on the customer and employee. This is where I contend that an organization really has to "be Agile" to get to the point of affecting their profits. It does not mean that a company can do anything to make money, and it particularly implies that you have to think and act differently to achieve the results you are looking for.

Engaging Your Customers and Employees

I have narrowed down what I believe are the two success factors in creating a thriving business. To achieve making more money, you have to have a culture where customers and employees really matter. I'm not talking about the lip service that is prevalent today. In some cases, we see quite the opposite, where employees are disenfranchised and customers are rarely engaged. Instead, the goal is to have a culture and practices in place that truly gain the benefits of engaging with customers and employees. Through the customer and employee, a company draws their power within an agile culture and, I contend, within any thriving company.

■ **Agile Pit Stop**   It is through the customer and employee that you draw your power within an agile culture and within any thriving company.

When you have a riveting focus on the customer and you believe that an engaged customer matters, then you have the basis for a relationship where you can truly understand what the customer wants. When you have a sharp focus on employees and provide them the space to make decisions and own their work, then you will begin to understand the value an engaged employee base can provide.

Agile Value to Incentive Differentiator (AVID)

Let me introduce you to a concept I call the Agile Value to Incentive Differentiator (AVID). This is a framework where the values of the organization or company convey the importance of customers and employees (i.e., that "customers and employees really matter"). If the values are sincerely translated to organizational objectives and agile approaches are applied, then it can act as a differentiator between the success of your organization compared to the success of other organizations. Of course, every company likes to say that employees and customers matter, but are their objectives and actions really aligned with these values?

Upon closer inspection, the values should translate into objectives focusing on customer engagement and employee engagement.

- Customer engagement focuses on establishing meaningful and honest customer relationships with the goal of initiating continuous customer feedback to truly identify what is valuable to the customer. This includes establishing all of the activities involved in attaining this.

- Employee engagement focuses on empowering employees so they can self-organize into teams and can own and be a part of the decision-making process at their own level.

Then we add the "secret ingredient" of applying a continuous and adaptive approach (a.k.a. agile processes, methods, practices, and techniques). If done properly with the ability to adapt, this can lead to an increase in customer sales and an increase in team productivity. This finally leads to your incentive, which is an increase in company profits (more money).

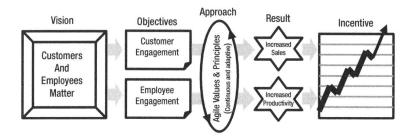

Figure 3-2. Agile Vision to Incentive Differentiator (AVID)

I know this is both simplistic and difficult, but if implemented and if the vision is sincere, it may be achieved. The goal of this book is to help you adjust your mindset to achieve the vision and objectives. How true you are to the vision and objectives is up to you. Please note that you will have a dependency on your sales and marketing practices, but if you are building customer value (i.e., what your customer wants), then marketing and selling should be easier. Because customer value is so important, let's take a closer look at understanding this concept.

Elusive Customer Value

The value of an idea lies in the using of it.

—Thomas A. Edison

As you may know, a key focus of Agile is to deliver customer value. Value is the benefit a customer will get from your product or the functionality if you align with their needs. Customer value should be specified from the perspective of the end customer or those receiving the value from a specific product. The authors of *Lean Thinking* put it this way:

> *Value can only be defined by the ultimate customer. And it's only meaningful when expressed in terms of a specific product (a good or a service, and often both at once), which meets the customer's needs at a specific price at a specific time.*[1]

Agile Pit Stop   Customer value = customer needs + right timing + right cost conditions. It is an elusive target that must be adapted to continually.

Customer value has both temporal and cost conditions. It is an elusive target that must be adapted to continually. What is considered valuable today may not be valuable tomorrow.

For example, in the 1980s, cellular phones were large and emulated the shape of a brick. In the 1990s and into the early 2000s, customers valued smaller and smaller phones. We saw evidence of this with the Motorola StarTac cellphones and the even smaller Pantech C300. But in the late 2000s and early 2010s, customers began valuing larger screen sizes on their phones due the advancement of smartphone technology (see Figure 3-3). We see evidence of this with smartphones now having 4.7-inch screens and larger. Build a great small phone for the wrong time, and few customers find it valuable.

---

[1]James P. Womack and Daniel T. Jones, *Lean Thinking: Banish Waste and Create Wealth in Your Corporation* (Productivity Press, 2003).

Figure 3-3. Evolution of the cellular phone—from larger to smaller to larger again

This provides us with more evidence as to why Agile and its continually adapting nature is so important in the effort to grasp the elusive customer value. From an agile perspective, this specification of what is customer value for a product should be a continuous activity to ensure you align and adapt with the ever changing needs of the customer and sporadic changing conditions within the marketplace.

Agile Pit Stop   To grasp the elusive customer value for a product, there should be continuous customer engagement to ensure we align and adapt with the changing needs of the customer and changes within the marketplace.

Agile Business Strategy

The primary intention of the AVID model is for companies to craft a business strategy that incorporates the customer and employee engagement objectives and agile values and principles that can help drive the mission of a company. This strategy should focus on elusive customer value, support continuous customer validation, and apply prioritization and minimum viable product techniques that lead to greater financial gain. A strategy that truly understands the advantages of employee engagement—including empowerment, self-organizing teams, and ownership—may gain the benefits of increased productivity and stronger company performance.

If customer and employee engagement are not woven into the company strategy, it sends an unwritten message that these factors do not really matter and can lead to substandard financial results. By incorporating these agile elements into your business strategy, you can set the levels of customer and employee engagement to see how they affect customer value and employee empowerment and eventually your profits.

With this in mind, let's take a closer look at what the vision of "customers and employees matter" really means. Let us start by discussing the importance of customer engagement (Chapter 4) and then the importance of employee engagement (Chapter 5).

Importance of Customer Engagement

No plan survives contact with the customer.

—Variation on Helmuth von Moltke

In Agile, delivering customer value is key. As discussed in the preceding chapter, what the customer finds valuable, changes over time, and so do the market conditions. This is why applying big upfront methods, such as waterfall, can be unwieldy. When you fix customer needs up front and plan the path to delivery without continuously engaging with the customer, you might stick to the plan, but you will be incrementally veering away from what the customer finds valuable. The moment you engage with customers on a continual basis, the plan will not survive. So the question becomes: Is it better to deal with a changing plan and deliver something the customer actually wants, or is it better to stick to the plan and not end up delivering functionality the customer wants? Keep in mind that if you are not listening to your customers, your competitors will be.

■ **Agile Pit Stop**   The moment you engage with customers, the plan will not survive. But what is more important: the precious plan or meeting customer needs?

This is why it is critical to have effective customer engagement. If you have effective customer engagement, you should be building product and functionality that customers want, therefore increasing the likelihood of making more money for the company.

Identifying the elusive customer value is challenging. There have been several studies estimating that a majority of new products launched into the software product marketplace fail. More than 65 percent of new products built by established companies fail.[1] When you look further at startups, the failure rate of new products takes a huge leap to 90 percent. Based on the percentage of new products that fail, $260 billion is lost annually in the United States. If we extend this to companies around the world, we may be talking about more than half a trillion dollars of lost money. More important than the lost investment is the lost opportunity: this is half a trillion dollars that could have been spent building valuable products, which in turn would make the company more money.

To add to this, new functionality is being built into new or existing successful products that few want or end up using. Jim Johnson, chairman of the Standish Group, quoted two studies that highlight the amount of unused features.[2] A DuPont study found that only 25 percent of a system's features were really needed and used by the user. A Standish study found that 45 percent of features were never used, and only 20 percent of features were used often or always. These findings are further supported by a Department of Defense (DoD) study, which found that only 2 percent of the code in $35.7 billion worth of DoD software was used as intended; 75 percent was either never used or was canceled prior to delivery.[3] Adding the initial and maintenance cost (paid by customers) of unused functionality of successful software products to the cost of failed software products (paid by sellers) brings us into the realm of a trillion dollars of lost money across the global market. Stanching this trillion-dollar hemorrhage is a major driver of the movement we see toward Agile and the agility and adaptability it brings.

Non-Agile Pit Stop   An analogous predicament that many individual consumers experience is with cable TV service. Cable TV providers offer subscription channels only in big, expensive, one-size-fits-all bundles without reference to the individual customer's needs, use patterns, or preferences. A result of this that customers are compelled to pay each month for hundreds of channels that they could not be paid to watch. No wonder millions of cable customers have cut the cord (or are itching to do so).

---

[1]Rob Adams, *If You Build It, They Will Come* (Wiley, 2010), 1–2.
[2]Jim Johnson at Third International Conference on Extreme Programming, May 2002.
[3]Theron R. Leishman and David A. Cook, "Requirements Risks Can Drown Software Projects," *CrossTalk: The Journal of Defense Software Engineering* (April 2002).

Of the many reasons for new product failures, two stand out. First, many companies are not as in touch with their customers as they believe they are. Second, many companies aim to build a global set of features for any new product that will be imposed on every customer willy-nilly. They ignore the Agile approach: start out with a minimal set of core features based on customer prioritization and feedback, get the new product to market sooner, and build out the product based on ongoing and specific customer input.

As an exercise, ask yourself:

- What percentage of products have you built that have failed?

- What percentage of functionality of your released products is unused or has low usage?

It can be painful to answer these questions, because you may not want to hear the bad news. However, to avoid repeating the mistakes of the past, it is good to understand how you arrived at this situation and then, more important, how you can mitigate or avoid the same mistakes moving forward. Understanding and acting on the twin notions of continuous customer engagement and feedback and minimum viable product can help you build products customers want and value.

Continuous Customer Engagement

Catch-phrases in the software industry such as "customer is king" and "the customer is always right" are mostly noticeable when they are *not* observed. The actual time spent engaging with customers, understanding their needs, and continuously eliciting and processing their feedback is deficient. True customer management discipline to ascertain what is valuable to customers in the ever-changing conditions of needs and the marketplace is glossed over. Some of this complaisance is driven by the false assurance of some within a company that they already know what their customers need and want. Some of this neglect is because people like to lay out and then follow a precise and inflexible plan. Some of this neglect occurs because of a lack of consciousness of what true customer engagement means and a lack of continuous customer engagement strategy and practices therein.

Agile Pit Stop   What the customer sees as progress is not project documents, project plans, and more status reports. Rather, customers see progress as tangible working product functionality.

We need to think like the customer. What the customer sees as progress is not the standard project documents, a project plan that indicates the task completion, or more status reports. Rather, customers see progress as tangible working product functionality. They purchase working software, not the plans, status reports, and other intangibles. Customers delight in seeing working software in action and the inspect-and-adapt approach allows customers to reconsider and adjust their needs until they are transformed into a valuable working product. Progress is not advanced until a piece of functionality is built with quality, meets the customer acceptance criteria, and is available for review by the customer in the demonstration.

Functionality equates to value for the customer and ultimately means delivering that business value. Of course, this implies that you have to continuously engage with the customer to get there. Engaging with customers only during the requirements-gathering phase and approaching product launch phase is not enough. We need to *continuously* engage with customers as we are actively building the product throughout the project life cycle.

Agile Pit Stop Engaging with customers only when gathering requirements and before product launch is not enough. We need to continuously engage with customers as we are actively building the product.

As discussed in the preceding chapter, the needs of customers change, and so do the market conditions. More traditional methods, such as waterfall (or hybrids of waterfall), apply a phase-based approach to product development. These methods postulate a fixed set of requirements up front as the first or second phase. Typically, some kind of change control or change management process is built into a waterfall model. However, these processes either tend to have strong teeth used to prevent change from occurring, or have no teeth and add new scope without taking much existing scope away. In an Agile model, change to requirements occurs on a continuous basis, applying a methodical prioritization and rank ordering throughout the project (Figure 4-1).

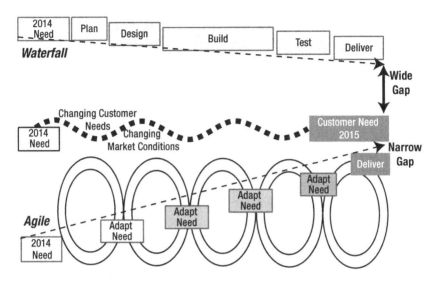

Figure 4-1. Agile adapts to changing customer needs and market conditions. The gap between what gets delivered and what the customer needs will be much smaller in Agile than in waterfall

For a waterfall-based project, the longer the time from the initial need (a.k.a. requirements phase) to the release of the product, the greater the risk (a.k.a. gap) of delivering unwanted functionality. As you will recall from Chapter 3, part of the definition of customer value is the timing. If you define requirements up front in the beginning of the year, inhibit the changes throughout the year for the release, when you get to the end of the year, the gap between what you delivered and what the customer needs may be quite wide.

In Agile, we follow a continuous build-inspect-adapt model so that requirements are continually validated with the Product Owner and customers during each iteration review (a.k.a. Sprint Review). This practice ensures there are continuous customer engagement and, more important, a continuous customer feedback loop. At the end of the project, the result should be a narrow gap between what was delivered and what the customer now needs. The narrower the gap, the more money a company is likely to make.

Dedicated Team Business Representative

The Business Representative is critical to identifying customer value. A key environmental accelerator to Agile adoption and project success is "dedicated business expertise" on the team.[4] Scrum addresses this need by requiring a Product Owner. The Product Owner should be a dedicated part of the team who bridges the gap between the customers and the engineering team.

The mission of the Product Owner is to identify requirements on a rolling basis and gather feedback from continuous demonstrations of working software, all with the goal of narrowing the gap between what was delivered and what the customer now needs (Figure 4-1). It is also his or her job to reconcile the different views of customer value as seen by different customer target groups.

The Product Owner is responsible for identifying and characterizing in detail the customers who are valuable to the company. That information helps in segmenting the customers to better understand their specific needs and pinpoint who should attend the Sprint Review/demos of the working software to supply the most valuable customer feedback. You will learn more about the Product Owner role in Chapter 12.

Minimum Viable Product (MVP)

When prioritizing a set of product features, sometimes it is hard to determine what is acceptable as the minimal set of features. Continuous customer engagement can help you understand what a minimum viable product (MVP) is for the first and subsequent releases.

The concept of MVP specifies a strategy whereby you attempt to identify the minimum amount of features that customers find valuable for any given release of the product—and no more. To identify the minimal set of features, a strong customer feedback loop (via Sprint Reviews/demos) is needed to ensure you are building the minimal features based on what customers deem valuable.

---

[4]Scott Ambler, "Agile Adoption Strategies: November 2011 Survey Results," http://www.ambysoft.com/surveys/agileStateOfArt201111.html.

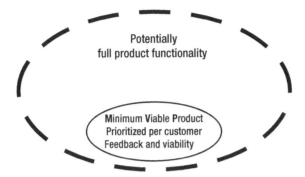

Figure 4-2. Applying the MVP approach. You can release earlier where the customer can use the value earlier and you can achieve an earlier ROI. Win-win for all!

A good way to think about MVP is to compare it to building a house. When you are a newly married couple with no kids, do you need to build a four-bedroom house for your small family? In most cases, you do not. Instead, you may build a smaller two-bedroom house with half the interior space, so that you can afford it, will be able to move in more quickly, and begin to enjoy the value of the house sooner. But if you did build a four-bedroom house, you would need to sustain parts of the house even if you won't use them. You would need to keep a few bedrooms clean, provide heat and air conditioning, and other maintenance for functionality (a.k.a. space) that you don't really need. However, if you build a two-bedroom house (the minimal viable product), you can always add functionality when you need it and when you will really value it.

Lack of identifying the MVP indicates a lack of customer engagement and validation. To prioritize requirements so that MVP can be identified, we need to engage with the customer continually. To be clear: Agile does not advocate arbitrary changes to requirements. Change must be strongly related to the priority that customers place on the value of what is being built. The Product Owner establishes this methodical prioritization process. This is especially delicate when the Product Owner interacts with multiple customers with different priorities.

Agile Pit Stop   Agile does not advocate an arbitrary change to requirements. Instead, change must be strongly related to the priority that customers place on the value of what is being built.

Although the MVP can be drafted on a speculative basis at the outset of a project, the subsequent Sprint Reviews need to be applied with continual customer participation to validate the need and adapt as appropriate.

You should be alert to the possibilities of adapting your MVP along the way. What would you do if a customer were to say during the middle of a project that if you could get them the functionality they just saw during the demonstration portion of the Sprint Reviews, they would buy your product? Because of the continuous engagement, you can deliver this value to them for a revenue increase on your end and a delivery of customer value on theirs. Even if you don't apply the MVP methods, you should at least apply basic customer priority techniques to ensure you build what the customer currently finds valuable.

Getting to Continuous Customer Engagement

The key is to understanding the elusive customer value is to know who your customers are and what they currently consider valuable. Identifying customers and segmenting them by target groups helps you get the right feedback for a particular feature. Yoking the concept of MVP with the concept of prioritization is foundational to understanding what customers consider most valuable. This knowledge enables you to provide the right value at the time customers need it.

Now that you have immersed yourself in the customer engagement material, I recommend a methodical approach to creating your vision for customer engagement. The reason I focus on a product level is that although the process of engaging the customer may be similar from product to product, the variety of customer groups will differ. To learn more about methodically creating a vision for customer engagement and validation, read Chapter 17.

Chapter 5 focuses on the benefits of empowering and engaging your employees and how it can contribute to gaining the benefits of Agile. If you focus on employees and provide them the space to make decisions and own their work, you can harness their vast brainpower and will begin to understand the value engaged employees can provide.

Importance of Employee Engagement

As a society we know the best way to organize people is freeing them to organize themselves. Why should it be any different in business?

—Thomas Petzinger Jr.

Employees are critical assets for an organization. It is difficult to calculate their value for a variety of reasons. When employees are disengaged, they take long lunch hours and leave at the stroke of 5, not staying a moment longer than they have to. More important, they will not fully engage their minds to solve problems effectively. They do not contribute to and can even impede their company's success. However, when they are engaged, they are crucial to the success of the company, bringing motivation, innovative ideas, and willingness to go the "extra mile" to get the work done. In this case, they can be a company's greatest assets.

"Our employees are our most valuable assets" has become a standard cliché, but few companies back it up. Yet studies prove that higher engagement scores are statistically correlated with increased corporate performance.[1]

---

[1]Brian E. Becker, Mark A. Huselid, and Dave Ulrich, *The HR Scorecard: Linking People, Strategy, and Performance* (Harvard Business Review Press, 2001).

One study found that of the forty best companies to work for, thirty-four included employee empowerment as part of their organizational strategy.[2] That study concluded that employee empowerment within the corporate culture is a "potential source for sustained superior financial performance." Employee empowerment can lead to tangible organizational performance and thus should be taken seriously.

Agile Pit Stop   Employee empowerment isn't just a warm-and-fuzzy benefit for the workers, but can lead to tangible performance and financial gain for an organization.

The goal for your company is to make people matter and introduce real action that will improve employees' engagement, ultimately leading to the financial benefit of the company.

Employee Empowerment

Everybody has heard the term *empowerment* in organizations—typically to hype up a new initiative so that employees will feel empowered. But it begs the question, "Shouldn't employees already feel empowered?" Empowerment should be a core value of an organization's strategy and not a trend that comes and goes. However, this is not the case for many organizations.

What exactly is employee empowerment? It is a framework that enables employees to control their own work and destiny. The brainpower and motivation of the talented folks who are hired are tremendous assets to a company. Jane Smith presents an employee empowerment model that includes three degrees of empowerment (Figure 5-1).[3] The first level encourages employees to play a more active role in their work. The second level asks employees to become more involved with improving the way things are done. The third level enables employees to make bigger and better decisions without having to engage upper management. The third level is key for an Agile culture.

---

[2]Darrol J. Stanley, "The Impact of Empowered Employees on Corporate Value": *Graziadio Business Review*, 8, no. 1 (2005).
[3]Jane Smith, *Empowering People* (Kogan Page, 2000).

Figure 5-1. Employee empowerment model with the goal of increasing empowerment

If management is earnest about applying a model like this, they can benefit in the following ways. They may see improvements in the quality of their product delivery, more innovation, increased productivity, and a gain in competitive edge.

Of course you want to empower your people. Yet somehow we have evolved into tribes and organizations where only management seems to know what is best. It is important to remember that management still has a role to play, and one of those roles is to get the most from their employees. This doesn't mean making them work longer hours, but gaining their input and allowing them to make the decisions they need to control the work at their level.

If you think about it, employees go home and make decisions in their daily lives and manage thousands of dollars in their own personal budgets. But when they go to work, many of them have little discretion over even $100 of decision making and are forced to seek approval for the smallest things.

Agile Pit Stop Why do employees who make decisions in their daily lives and manage thousands of dollars in their own personal budgets have so little discretion over the smallest things within their company?

An employee engagement practice allows teams to be empowered, self-organizing, and discretionary in making decisions at their level. Empowerment is enhanced when an adaptive framework like Agile is applied, which advocates a team-based model. If the team feels truly empowered and is allowed to self-organize, they will naturally increase their productivity because they own the work and the decisions to guide their work lives.

Self-Organizing Teams

So what does *self-organizing team* really mean? Diana Larsen writes:

> *When we say an Agile team is self-organizing, we mean that a group of peers has assembled for the purpose of bringing a software development project to completion using one or more of the Agile methodologies. The team members share a goal and a common belief that their work is interdependent and collaboration is the best way to accomplish their goal.*[4]

Attributes of self-organizing teams are that employees reduce their dependency on management and increase ownership of the work. This includes increasing team accountability and responsibility. A cultural shift involves pushing down the level of decisions to the lowest possible level—that is, reducing the need for numerous chains of approvals and decisions—can be a big change for most organizations. Changing the culture from a hierarchical command-and-control model to a more horizontal or team empowerment model (Figure 5-2) is unsettling.

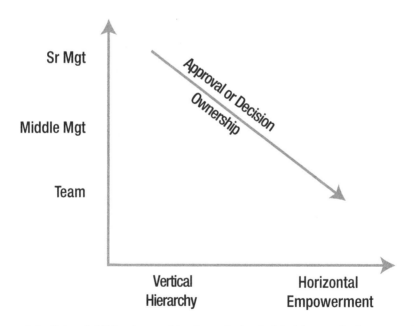

Figure 5-2. Cultural shift involves pushing down the level of decisions to the lowest possible level at which the most knowledge exists to make the best decision

---

[4]Diana Larsen and Industrial Logic, "Team Agility: Exploring Self-Organizing Software Development Teams," *Agile Times Newsletter* (2004).

The primary benefit of self-organizing teams is that employees feel they own the work, tend to have more passion in their work, and then are much more likely to invest more of their time and energy. The implication is that the company may gain the benefit of stronger employee commitment and performance, leading to potential superior financial performance.

Consider the example of renting an apartment versus owning a home. When you rent an apartment, you may respect the property, but you are probably unwilling to improve the apartment very much because you know you don't own it and thus have much less investment and attachment to the place. In other words, you are less likely to put your heart and soul into the apartment. It is just a temporary place to live. Now imagine that you own a home. You will not only respect the property, you will take much better care of it and are willing to invest time and money to improve it because you feel the pride of ownership. Not only are you more willing to invest in the home, you will be willing to protect and defend it. There may be passion in your drive to make the home as good as it can be. You are much more likely to place your heart and soul into maintaining and improving the home because of this sense of ownership.

This same premise holds true with our work life. If you don't feel that you own the work and the decisions therein, you do just the minimum. However, if you feel you have ownership, you are willing to invest more time and energy into the work. It is particularly important for senior management to understand the significance of this concept.

Evidence of Self-Organizing

What do self-organizing teams look like? The following are some demonstrable attributes of a self-organizing team.

- Decision making: Team members make their own decisions about their work. Who better to make decisions than those who have the details?

- Sizing work: Team members size or estimate their own work. Who better to size the work than the people who work on the product and know its complexity?

- Team spirit: Team members have a strong willingness to cooperate and know that unless all succeed in their part, none succeed in the whole.

- Common goals: Team members feel they are coming together to achieve a common purpose through release goals, sprint goals, and team goals.

- Trust: Team members value people relationships and share information (including bad news) without fear of retribution or of the information being used against them.

- Transparency: Team members willingly share information to help other members make progress and better decisions. There is similar transparency between management and team members.

- Communication: Team members willingly communicate the latest progress and challenges, gaining clarity and fostering teamwork.

- Collaboration: Team members realize that the ability to bounce ideas off each other leads to better solutions and efficiencies in work processes.

- Assertiveness: Team members feel ownership, are motivated, are willing to pull work for themselves, and do not wait idly for someone else to assign work.

- Iterative learning: Team members understand that there is a continuous acquisition of knowledge with opportunities to improve as the product is being built.

- Collective commitment: Team members make a conscious effort to mutually commit to the work in a time-boxed manner and then progressively work to achieve that commitment.

When applied with integrity, these attributes will make any team or organization effective. If you strive for these elements, then it is important for management to model this behavior as well if they wish their teams to do the same.

Ken Schwaber writes:

> For Scrum to work, the team has to deeply and viscerally understand collective commitment and self-organization. Scrum's theory, practices, and rules are easy to grasp intellectually. But until a group of individuals has made a collective commitment to deliver something tangible in a fixed amount of time, those individuals probably don't get Scrum.[5]

Another form of evidence of self-organizing from an agile perspective is reorganizing from functional groups into Agile Teams. For example, Scrum teams are designed so that they remove hierarchy, leading to a flatter organization, and are designed to gain collective commitment. To do this typically requires

---

[5]Ken Schwaber, *Agile Project Management with Scrum* (Microsoft Press, 2004).

a reorganization of resources. Figure 5-3 is an illustration of a reorganization from a hierarchical structure to a self-organized Agile Team structure.

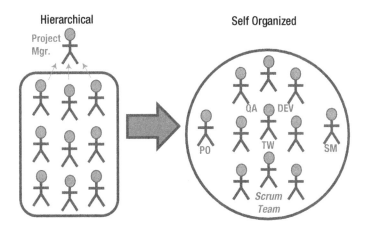

Figure 5-3. Moving from hierarchical to self-organized teams requires a reorganization

Notice how this involves moving away from a single point of leadership to a flat team model in which everyone is a leader when it is appropriate and no one person tells others what to do.

Stepping Up

Agile entails a radical change not just to the culture of management but also to the culture of those in engineering. There is a strong expectation that management will step back and allow the Agile Team to be self-organized. On the engineering side, there is an expectation that they need to step up, communicate more, and be more assertive. This can be challenging. Whereas there is a lot of focus on getting management to step back, there isn't enough focus on getting Agile Team members to step up.

Engineers tend to be introverts, so the notion of being assertive—let alone confrontational—can be uncomfortable. Often Scrum Masters end up doing a lot of the policing to ensure agile practices are being executed well. The Scrum Master may be seen "nagging" late arrivals to meetings and must push people to speak up. However, it is not just the Scrum Master's responsibility to be assertive; every team member must be willing. Remember, Agile is for everyone, and every team member should consider himself or herself a leader. Are you stepping up?

In a hierarchical world, projects are managed by directive. A hierarchy exists where decisions get made based not necessarily on full knowledge, experience, or information but on position. Often, decisions are made by a few folks and then shared with the team. Ultimately this establishes a culture in which people on the project team become timid, lack enthusiasm, and do not feel ownership in the work. If this culture has been embedded, it can take an even bigger effort to motivate more assertive and extroverted behavior.

Agile Pit Stop Though there is focus on getting management to step back, there isn't enough focus on getting team members to step up. Engineers tend to be introverts and may be used to getting instructions. Changing this culture may be more challenging than you think.

Then along comes Agile. When implemented correctly, the Agile mindset places a strong emphasis on a team's self-organizing capabilities. There is an expectation of limited command-and-control from management. The teams are trusted to make decisions because they are much closer to the details and have experience in that area. Team members feel invested in the work to come because they have a say in the direction of the product.

However, transitioning to an Agile culture does not immediately gain the advantages that you desire. There must be a recognition that managers and some overly directive people need to step back. However, when they do so, the team members must step forward to fill the leadership gap. If you want to feel invested in the work, you must be willing to take the responsibility of owning the decisions (see Figure 5-4). Otherwise, those people who stepped back—management—will have an habitual tendency to step forward again to fill the vacuum.

Figure 5-4. Agile Team members must step up to accountability of the work as the management are stepping back

This is where being assertive and proactive attributes become important. Some engineers may come from a culture where they are relegated to getting instructions. They are not expected to be leaders. With Agile, it is now their job to become self-organized and empowered, become leaders, and take assertive steps forward. For many engineers, this can be difficult because it takes them out of their comfort zone. However, when people move out of their comfort zone is when growth happens. Many managers' comfort zone is directing the work. We need them to step out and trust the team to direct the work, while the managers grow in their ability as coaches.

What does this mean in the Agile context? First, as you become part of an Agile project, you must truly internalize that employees are now equally part of the team and their thoughts, experience, and opinions matter. This does not happen overnight because the dynamics of getting to an Agile culture are challenging and take time. There will be those working against you, sabotaging the change to maintain the status quo. Make no mistake: it is up to you to step up and assertively empower yourself.

So the next time you don't think you are appropriately involved on the project or you think you need permission to speak up, stop for a moment. Change your mindset and be assertive, step up, get involved, become a leader, and start owning the decisions and work. Agile provides that opportunity. It is your opportunity to take advantage of it.

Understanding Value-Added Work

A concept that is important for employees to understand as they begin to own their work is what is considered valuable work to the customer. Part of the Agile mindset is to bring the business closer to the engineering team. One aspect of this is to understand what working software the customer finds valuable.

From a customer perspective, *value-added work* (VAW) is functionality that they find valuable at the time and place of their need. This includes the effort and "done" criteria steps (such as designed, developed, versioned, built, and tested increments) that are directly related to building the features to produce working software. Applying a minimal viable product (MVP) approach can provide you with a good framework for prioritizing and rank ordering the valuable work the customer needs.

Employees are typically aware of the *non–value-added work* (NVAW) they are asked to do. NVAW can be as simple as functionality the customer does not find valuable, or it can be unnecessary steps in the process of building working software. Examples of NVAW include:

- administrative-related tasks
- education and training
- all-hands and staff meetings
- writing status report
- defect correction introduced by poor quality
- refactoring tasks
- unnecessary steps or approvals

⬜ **Agile Pit Stop**   NVAW (a.k.a. waste or *muda*) are effort that do not directly add value as perceived by the customer and may include unneeded functionality or unnecessary steps in a process of building working software.

For a broader understanding of NVAW effort or waste, Mary and Tom Poppendieck provide a robust understanding from a lean software development perspective of the *Seven Wastes of Software Development*:[6]

- partially done work

- extra processes (or extra steps)

- extra (unwanted) features

- time involved with task switching

- time spent waiting

- tracking down information or needing approvals

- time spent correcting defects

In lean thinking, this is known as waste or *muda*. We have come to accept NVAW because we have done things for so long, we haven't reconsidered the value of the tasks and activities that we do and the process in which we work in quite some time. Although it may sound harsh and there is some internal value in this work at varying levels, the question becomes: where do you really want to spend your time, and is it a good idea to reduce the NVAW?

When applying an Agile and lean mindset, we need to consider the value of each task. Is the task being asked of the team considered value-added or non–value-added from a customer perspective? Sometimes folks have a hard time separating tasks into value and nonvalue because it highlights the nonvalued tasks. However, it really is important to understand your value-added and non–value-added breakdown so you can baseline the value level of the work and hopefully increase the value-added work over time (Figure 5-5).

---

[6]Mary Poppendieck and Tom Poppendieck, *Lean Software Development: An Agile Toolkit* (Addison-Wesley Professional, 2003).

Value of Work in a Sprint

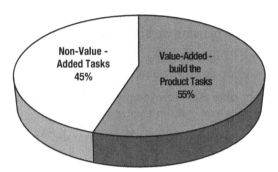

Figure 5-5. Baselining VAW and NVAW from a customer perspective

---

■ **Agile Pit Stop** It can be hard separating work into value-added and non–value-added because it can highlight the level of NVAW that is being done.

Another benefit of identifying VAW vs. NVAW is that when you are considering the velocity or productivity of teams in regard to building new functionality, the percentage of NVAW is a direct impediment to a team's ability to build new functionality. In other words, it is not uncommon for management to think that employees are using a majority of their work week building new functionality when the reality is that only 50 percent may be spent doing so.

Customers and Employees Matter: Are We There Yet?

When a company has a strong focus on the customer and the employee, there is a strong potential for financial rewards. The Agile Vision to Incentive Differentiator (AVID) model presented in Chapter 3 may work for you. If your company's business strategy includes objectives focusing on customer engagement and employee engagement, you can benefit from truly understanding what is most valuable to the customer and harness the brainpower of your employees. By adding the special ingredient of applying the Agile values and principles along with a continuous and adaptive framework (Scrum, XP, Kanban, etc.), there is the potential of incentives involving an increase in revenue for the company.

What were the perceived benefits obtained from implementing Agile? It is one thing to have certain reasons for moving to Agile, and quite another to see if the benefits are realized. Within the 2012 VersionOne survey on Agile, the results highlighted some benefits we are looking for.[7]

- 90 percent of those surveyed felt that "ability to manage changing priorities" "got better" within their company.

- 85 percent of those surveyed felt that "increased productivity" "got better" within their company.

- 84 percent surveyed felt that "team morale" "got better" within their company.

These results bode well for Agile. However, this does not accidentally occur. Companies must include this into their business strategy to highlight that they take the notions of customers, employees, and Agile seriously. Maybe the vision where "customers and employees really matter" makes sense after all. The question is: how important is it to delight your customers by building customer value and harnessing the brainpower of your employees? While it is easy to reflexively say "very!," the reality is that we get distracted by the day-to-day "administratium" of the company and forget our values. Ultimately your results will vary depending on the sincerity and commitment you have to customers, employees, and Agile.

---

[7]VersionOne, "7th Annual State of Agile Development Survey," November 2012, http://www.versionone.com/pdf/7th-Annual-State-of-Agile-Development-Survey.pdf.

Foundations of Agile

Agility is more attitude than process, more environment than methodology.

—Jim Highsmith

During one of my agile seminars, I ask people "What is Agile?" I bring up a list that includes, "Agile is a methodology," "Agile is a process," "Agile is a set of practices," and "Agile is a set of tools." I see a lot of heads nodding in the affirmative, believing that some or all of these are what Agile is. Then I cross them all out and bring up a single line that says, "Agile is a set of values and principles." Some have an aha! moment.

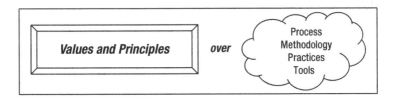

Figure 6-1. *Though there is value in the items on the right, we value the items on the left more*

I ask you to take a moment to understand this and learn more about the overarching values and principles of Agile.

Agile Is a Set of Values and Principles... Seriously!

The foundational building blocks of Agile are its values and principles. This is probably the most important point that is often misunderstood and needs to be recognized. Agile is not a process, methodology, practice, or tool but a set of values and principles. The implication is that Agile is more about a state of being: the Agile mindset. Processes and methodology can help you do Agile in the mechanical sense, but Agile is a culture shift that requires a willingness to adapt to the Agile mindset. Agile values and principles are components of the Agile mindset.

Agile Pit Stop   Agile is not a process, methodology, practice, or tool but rather a set of values and principles. The implication is that Agile is essentially a state of being: the Agile mindset.

It is important to not just read the Agile values and principles found in the Agile Manifesto, but embrace them. Why do you want to embrace these values and principles? Maybe it is because you believe in the importance of customer and employee engagement and that providing value to the customer is important to the success of your business. Maybe you realize that you need to be more adaptive because uncertainty exists and customer needs change. Reading Chapter 3 provides you a better understanding, but ultimately you own the answer to this question.

Manifesto of Agile Software Development

It is important to read and internalize the "Manifesto for Agile Software Development" (Agile Manifesto for short) if you are serious about understanding an agile state of mind and truly want to "be Agile." It is critical that personnel at all levels of the company understand and believe in the statements that represent the values and principles. Although many are aware of it or have seen it at one time or another, few remind themselves of what it implies to be Agile on a regular basis, particularly when they are buried in the mechanics of implementation.

Here is the Agile Manifesto—73 words signed by seventeen authors in 2001:[1]

---

[1]"Manifesto for Agile Software Development" at agilemanifesto.org

Manifesto for Agile Software Development

We are uncovering better ways of developing software by doing it and helping others do it. Through this work we have come to value:

Individuals and interactions over processes and tools
Working software over comprehensive documentation
Customer collaboration over contract negotiation
Responding to change over following a plan

*That is, while there is value in the items on the right,
we value the items on the left more.*

The last phrase helps us understand the authors' intentions. They are not saying there is no value in the items on the right, but instead that they have less value than the items on the left. Those who disregard the items on the right are either Cowboys or Bandwagon Jumpers who do not know better, or beginners who have not gained an appreciation of striking the right balance.

Agile Pit Stop   Because it is human nature to evolve over time, we should assume that the needs of customers will evolve.

A perspective that helped me understand the nexus of these values better was realizing that the items on the left can help drive the need and level of the items on the right. Here is a deeper look at the four polar pairs of agile values declared in the Agile Manifesto.

> *"**Individuals and interactions** over processes and tools."* Communication is the enabler for individuals to interact with their team members. The inspect-and-adapt model is an enabler for communication to occur throughout a project. The benefit is the continuous feedback. This helps us understand the process in which we work and how we may adapt it over time. This also ensures that a predefined process or tool set does not dictate how we interact.

> *"**Working software** over comprehensive documentation."* When you ask a customer what they value most—working software or comprehensive documentation—how do you think they will answer? Working software is the value that the company is delivering and the customer is buying. This helps us understand the business perspective of the product we are building. Working software also implies a certain level of quality, and it is only complete when it meets that level of quality. This helps us understand the engineering perspective of the product.

*"**Customer collaboration** over contract negotiation."* The team and stakeholders use collaboration as a method for establishing customer needs and allowing them to evolve over time through continued collaboration. While there will often be a need to execute a contract, the contract should not drive to a static list of exactly what will be built but allow collaboration to evolve the list. Remember, it is really in the customers' best interest to get a product that best meets their evolving needs instead of a product that is based on a list of requirements from the past—sometimes the distant past. Because it is human nature to evolve over time, we should assume that the needs of customers will evolve. A static list can get outdated fairly quickly. This is what makes customer collaboration so important.

*"**Responding to change** over following a plan."* To build working software that is considered valuable to the customer, we must be willing to respond to the changes in customer needs and market conditions. If you stick with the plan, make the schedule, and come within budget but miss delivering what the customer wants, are you successful? Though it is hard to have all happy customers, the inspect-and-adapt model seeks customer feedback from the incremental reviews of the working software. This allows us to incorporate customer feedback and more closely align with and deliver what the customer finds valuable.

Principles behind the Agile Manifesto

Supporting the Agile Manifesto are the "Twelve Principles of Agile Software." The Twelve Principles provide drivers for better understanding the values and are as follow:[2]

Principles behind the Agile Manifesto

We follow these principles:

Our highest priority is to satisfy the customer through early and continuous delivery of valuable software.

Welcome changing requirements, even late in development. Agile processes harness change for the customer's competitive advantage.

---

[2]"Principles behind the Agile Manifesto" agilemanifesto.org/principles.html

Deliver working software frequently, from a couple of weeks to a couple of months, with a preference to the shorter timescale.

Business people and developers must work together daily throughout the project.

Build projects around motivated individuals. Give them the environment and support they need, and trust them to get the job done.

The most efficient and effective method of conveying information to and within a development team is face-to-face conversation.

Working software is the primary measure of progress.

Agile processes promote sustainable development. The sponsors, developers, and users should be able to maintain a constant pace indefinitely.

Continuous attention to technical excellence and good design enhances agility.

Simplicity—the art of maximizing the amount of work not done—is essential.

The best architectures, requirements, and designs emerge from self-organizing teams.

At regular intervals, the team reflects on how to become more effective, then tunes and adjusts its behavior accordingly.

Take a moment now to reflect on these Principles. What are some of the attributes of the Principles that stand out? As you reflect on these, can you see if your product team or organization aligns with any of these Principles?

In Chapter 9, I dissect each of the Principles to better understand what it means to align it with the mindset that it represents. In Chapter 13, I provide an adaptable assessment mechanism that can be used to determine where your team or organization is in relation to being aligned with the Agile Principles and so having an agile state of mind. Remember, it is not enough to say I am mechanically "doing" Agile practices. Instead, to gain the business benefits of Agile, you need to "be Agile" and live these principles.

Introduction to Agile Processes and Methodologies

Now that we have discussed the Agile Manifesto and reflected on the values and principles within it, let us dive into the more commonly known agile processes and methods. Let us remind ourselves that there is nothing called the "agile process" or "agile methodology." Remember, Agile is a set of values and principles. The various agile processes and methods introduce a framework for approaching software development to ensure the customers gain more assurance that they get a solution that solves their business need.

▓ **Agile Pit Stop**　There is nothing called the "agile methodology." Remember, Agile is a set of values and principles.

With that in mind, there have been several frameworks, processes, methodologies, and practices established in an attempt to support and promote the agile values and principles. This section will focus on Scrum, XP, DSDM, and Kanban because they may be more commonly encountered. It will also discuss Lean and *Value, Flow, Quality* (VFQ). While they are not agile processes or methods, they can help us align with the agile values and principles. The purpose here is to understand them. Even though I am highlighting these, it does not imply that they are necessarily better than any of the others not discussed here. There is no one correct process or methodology to use. The best one is the one that suits your working environment and your type of work. Let us examine these in more detail.

Scrum

Scrum is an iterative and incremental framework used to build software. It follows an inspect-and-adapt process to support product development and consists of Scrum roles, events, artifacts, and rules. The *roles* inform and surround the Scrum Team; the *events* are planned team activities that are time-boxed within the concept of a sprint, typically 1 to 4 weeks; and the *artifacts* are the items used in Scrum that represent work in some manner and illustrate progress. *Rules* are applied to the roles, events, and artifacts.

Scrum is not an acronym, so it should not be in all capitals. The word derives from a team formation in rugby in which the team moves forward as an interlocking unit in a manner that each player has a specialty function yet all players are contributing equally and simultaneously to the team's forward progress toward a common goal. Scrum provides agile project and product management events or practices. Scrum is often used in tandem with XP, which provides many of the agile engineering practices.

▓ **Agile Pit Stop**　*Scrum* is a sports term borrowed from rugby. It is not an acronym, so do not capitalize the letters.

An important aspect of Scrum is that the customers can change their mind on their needs as necessary to ensure they are getting the product they want and need at the end. This approach recognizes that customer needs and market conditions change and does not try to stifle—and indeed welcomes—the change activity. Changes can be added to the Product Backlog at any time and reprioritized according to the customer needs. During the next Sprint

Planning session, any new changes can be considered for the new sprint. It is important to note that once a sprint is started, there should be no attempt by the customer or team to change the requirements. Instead, allow the team to focus on the prioritized requirements from the planning session. Although there are exceptions to this rule, it allows the team to focus in short bursts and produce working software that the customer can respond to.

The primary overarching role in Scrum is the *Scrum Team*. The Scrum Team is meant to be self-organizing so that members feel empowered to make the decisions and feel ownership of their work. The Scrum Team members are those committed to building the product and include the subroles of Scrum Master, Product Owner, and Development Team.

- *The Scrum Master* acts as a motivator for Scrum. This role acts as coach to the team to ensure that the Scrum roles, events, artifacts, and rules are understood and implemented effectively. He or she is the primary facilitator of the team.

- *The Product Owner* (PO) represents the customers, is the customer liaison, and is primarily responsible for understanding what is considered valuable from the customers' perspective. The PO is the primary owner of the product backlog, where value is expressed.

- The *Development Team* is a cross-functional group of engineers who build the functionality. They are made up of personnel with cross-functional skills so that they have the capabilities to build the product without having to rely on others outside of the team.

Scrum events are meant to provide an imbricated pattern for the work. Each event relies on the other and provides input to the next event. When one or more of the events are missing, this reduces the effectiveness and ability to inspect and adapt. The Scrum events include:[3]

- *Sprint Planning* is held in the beginning of each sprint and focuses on understanding the user stories that will be worked on in the sprint. The goal is for all Scrum Team members to plan this work. The list of work that can fit into a sprint is known as the *sprint backlog*.

- The *Daily Scrum* is a daily event time-boxed to no more than 15 minutes in which the Development Team communicates progress among themselves and introduces any encountered roadblocks.

---

[3]Ken Schwaber and Jeff Sutherland. *The Scrum Guide* (2013). www.scrum.org/Portals/0/Documents/Scrum%20Guides/2013/Scrum-Guide.pdf#zoom=100

- The *Sprint Review* is held at the end of a sprint. The Development Team presents the working software to the PO and customers to gain valuable feedback. This is part of the inspect-and-adapt process that allows the team to adapt to the needs of the customer.

- The *Sprint Retrospective* is the last event at the end of a sprint used to identify what went well in the sprint and what can be improved. It is an opportunity for the Scrum Team to reflect on the past sprint's activities, including team dynamics, processes, tools, and culture.

Extreme Programming (XP)

Extreme Programming—commonly known by its acronym, *XP*—is an agile process that revolves around a set of practices that emphasize teamwork and customer satisfaction. From the customer perspective, XP believes that requirement changes are a natural part of the software development process and introduces a rigorous set of engineering practices to support these changes. XP is often used in tandem with Scrum, which provides many of the Agile-minded project and product management practices.

In XP, the team is typically twelve or fewer members and meant to be committed, empowered, and self-organized so they can make the best decisions to move forward because they are closest to the challenges and work to be accomplished. The two primary roles in XP are the Customer and the Developer.

The *Customer* is the primary driver of the project and represents the end user. The Customer provides business knowledge and should set goals for the project. The Customer is the contributor of the requirements and may change them as they understand their needs more fully.

The *Developer* represents the cross-functional engineering team that is needed to design, code, build, and test the product and focus on the daily work of understanding the stories and converting them into functional working software. The team focuses on building the product from day one while continuously engaging the customer to meet their needs.

The other, less formal roles include the *Tracker* who focuses on the schedule, throughput of work, and risks of the project, and the *Coach*, who will help the team understand and execute XP practices.

Agile Pit Stop   The primary roles in XP are the Customer and Developer. Other, less formal roles are the Tracker and Coach.

XP provides practices and rules that revolve around planning, designing, coding, and testing. Some include:[4]

- *User Stories* are scenarios written by the customer for things they need within the product.

- *Release Planning* is applied at the beginning of a project and used to lay out the release plan and schedule.

- *Iteration Planning* is the process by which the customer determines the user stories for an iteration that fit the estimate of effort as established by the team velocity.

- *Sustainable Pace* determines the amount of designing, coding, testing, integration, and product-ready work a team can do within an iteration.

- *Project Velocity* focuses on measuring the progress on an XP project by adding up the estimates of the user stories that are finished during an iteration.

- *Stand Up* is a short daily meeting in which members of the team stand up and communicate their progress.

- *Retrospective* is applied at the end of an iteration and focuses on fixing XP or the way it is being applied when things are not running well.

- *Simplicity* is a design practice that has the team focus on the simplest thing that will work first.

- *Refactoring* focuses the programmers on continuously streamlining the code by removing unused functionality, reducing redundancy, correcting poorly written code, and improving on existing design.

- *Spike Solutions* are a special focus meant to solve a challenging technical, architectural, or design problem.

- *Pair Programming* is a coding practice in which two programmers work together at the same computer while programming a user story or task.

- *Customer Availability* asks the customer to always be available to and become part of the development team.

- *Collective Ownership* refers to everyone owning the code and tests.

---

[4]Don Wells. *Rules of Extreme Programming* (1999). www.extremeprogramming.org/rules.html

- *Continuous Integration* advocates that programmers merge their code into the code baseline whenever they have a clean build that has passed the unit tests.

- *Unit Test* focuses on testing the code changes at the development unit level prior to merging it into the project branch. Otherwise the code change cannot be considered complete.

- *Acceptance Testing* focuses on establishing specific acceptance tests for each user story.

Dynamic Systems Development Method

The Dynamic Systems Development Method (DSDM) is an iterative and incremental agile project management and delivery framework. DSDM is based on *Rapid Application Development* (RAD) and focuses on continuous user involvement. Prototyping is a key component of DSDM and is found throughout the activities within the project life cycle. DSDM is periodically updated with guidance from the DSDM Consortium.[5] DSDM follows eight principles to guide the mindset for adoption:

- Focus on the business need

- Deliver on time

- Collaborate

- Never compromise quality

- Build incrementally from firm foundations

- Develop iteratively

- Communicate continuously and clearly

- Demonstrate control

Unlike other agile methods that focus on just the project lifecycle, DSDM utilizes three phases focusing on the *pre-project, project*, and *post-project*. The pre-project phase focuses on commitment and budget. The project phase focuses on the activities within a project life cycle. The post-project phase focuses on maintenance, bug fixes, and enhancements. In DSDM, you may iterate through an activity several times before moving to the next.

The project life cycle phase starts with "study" activities focusing on a feasibility study to ensure that DSDM will work for the project and is accepted by management and then a business study to ensure the project is worth doing.

---

[5]http://www.dsdm.org/

This is a bit unusual since most agile methods do not specifically have a step to verify if the method will be suitable and instead assume it will just work. However, ensuring that the methodology is aligned with the work and having management support are critical to the success of the project.

This is one of several DSDM's success factors. DSDM specifically calls out the need to ensure management agrees to use the method and looks for a commitment moving forward. The other success factors are having customer involvement, an empowered project team, and a strong relationship between the customer and vendor. DSDM views the full picture of software development as areas to focus on because it is understood that any one piece that goes awry can lead to problems. It should be noted that DSDM may be combined with other methods and techniques like PRINCE2, XP, and Scrum.

Kanban

Kanban is a continuous flow method for managing the development and delivery of products. *Kanban* is a Japanese term that translates roughly to "signboard" or "story card." This is because Kanban is primarily focused on making the workflow visible and highlighting the constraints to that flow. The origins of Kanban can be traced back to Taiichi Onho and the Toyota Production System. In its more modern form, David Anderson identified five core principles that support a successful implementation of Kanban.[6] They are:

- Visualize your work so that you can see the work and in context with other work.

- Limit the *work in progress* (WIP) using a *pull system* so there isn't an overflow of work at any step along the way and so pace is understood.

- Manage the flow of work, applying measures so the team knows how much work to commit.

- Make the process policies explicit so that improvements can be made to acknowledged baselines.

- Improve collaboratively so there is the opportunity to improve the working process and workflow.

Whereas in Scrum you would use a sprint to develop a batch of work, in Kanban there is a continuous pull of single pieces of work.

---

[6]David J. Anderson. *Kanban. Successful Evolutionary Change for Your Technology Business*. Blue Hole Press, 2010.

Agile Pit Stop   I have found that Kanban is effective when the work is more interruption-prone and when priorities can change from day to day.

One of the advantages of implementing Kanban over Scrum is that Kanban can be implemented successfully in traditional and command-and-control cultures. While Scrum provides a set of practices or events, it does align with the Agile Principles, which lead to an Agile mindset, implying a change to the traditional culture. With that being said, Kanban will not get you to the Agile mindset if you are only interested in the Kanban principles and practices so it may not be as agile as many believe. However, if you approach Kanban under the auspices of the Agile Manifesto, then you may achieve the Agile mindset.

Lean Software Development

Lean is an approach that focuses on building value by defining what is needed, building it with the minimum amount of effort, and delivering it when it is needed. The origins of Lean can be traced back to Taiichi Onho and the Toyota Production System. I include Lean not because it is directly an agile process but because it focuses on customer value, which is aligned with the agile values and principles.

Often when Lean is discussed, there tends to be a strong focus on eliminating waste—and rightly so. However the real focus of Lean is the identification of value to the customer: delivering what they want, when they want it, and with the minimum amount of effort. To be sure, what is considered valuable also becomes a driver for what is considered wasteful.

Mary and Tom Poppendieck advanced Lean thinking into software development. Their "Lean software development" approach presents the traditional Lean principles in terms that relate to software development.[7] They established seven Lean development principles:

- Eliminate waste: Continuously focus on eliminating waste. This can be in the form of unneeded customer features, unnecessary process steps, and more.

- Learn constantly: Use iterations, use continuous feedback, and speak to the people with knowledge, all to support continuous learning.

---

[7]Mary Poppendieck and Tom Poppendieck. *Lean Software Development: An Agile Toolkit.* Addison-Wesley Professional, 2003.

- Deliver fast: Make software available via a steady flow of customer value in smaller batches on a just-in-time basis.

- Engage everyone: Allow the team to own their decisions, apply their own brainpower, respect each other, and have opportunities for excellence.

- Build quality in: Apply the nonfunctional qualities into each feature as well as a quality level of "done" criteria to ensure the working software has high quality.

- Optimize the whole: Focus on the entire value stream, not the short-term profits. Ensure the details are managed at the right level and you provide a working solution, not just software.

- Keep getting better: Always look for opportunities to improve. Failures are learning opportunities. The key is to develop your people.

Agile Pit Stop   Often Lean is discussed in terms of eliminating waste. However, the real focus of Lean is to identify value to the customer: deliver what they want, when they want it, and with the minimum amount of effort.

It will be important to adapt these principles into your working process.

Value, Flow, Quality

VFQ is an educational framework that helps you achieve results in ensuring you are delivering customer value, establishing optimal flow, and achieving high-quality working solutions. VFQ applies a work-based learning program based on Agile and Lean and focuses on the importance of applying the attributes of value, flow, and quality when it comes to building product.[8] The intent is for the practitioner to use these attributes to help an organization identify the best approach for them to achieve the business results they are looking for. VFQ does this through the belief of applying skills in practice. I include VFQ not because it is directly an agile process but because it focuses on customer value, which is aligned with the agile values and principles.

---

[8]www.valueflowquality.com

VFQ education applies a number of learning pathways based on roles designed to select the most appropriate core of knowledge required by each role. However, because agile methods rely on cross-functional skills, the best option continues to be to take a team approach and study the course as a whole. The full course covers a wide variety of topics and emphasizes end-to-end organizational flow. The VFQ approach is intended for all levels, from a newly qualified developer to senior executives, and encourages those whose departments who are strongly affected by what occurs in IT, perhaps marketing and operations to participate.

Back to Values and Principles

I started this chapter by underscoring that Agile is *not* a set of processes, methodologies, practice, and tools. Rather, Agile is a set of values and principles. I took you on a tour through some of the many Agile-based processes, methods, and frameworks: Scrum, XP, DSDM, Kanban, Lean, and VFQ. However interesting and useful you may find any of these frameworks, never forget the key proposition that Agile is that set of values and principles that drives an agile approach regardless of the framework you select.

Agile is essentially a state of mind—being Agile—that is bound up with a change to your culture. The agile state of mind understands the importance of customer engagement to value and of employee engagement to self-organization and ownership. Ultimately, it doesn't matter what processes, methodologies, and practices you apply. What is important is that you shape your implementation around the agile values and principles with the goal of gaining an Agile mindset and achieving business results.

Ready, Implement, Coach, and Hone (RICH) Deployment Model

Before anything else, preparation is the key to success.

—Alexander Graham Bell

During my journey in helping teams adopt Agile and transforming them to an Agile mindset, the deployment approach I have found most successful is applying a Ready, Implement, Coach, and Hone (RICH) framework. This framework provides not only a methodical approach to mechanically applying agile methods but a strong focus on realizing an Agile mindset to achieve a successful agile transformation.

So what is the difference between agile adoption and agile transformation? When I think of *adoption*, I think of a team or organization that is applying a new set of practices, tools, and techniques. I call this gaining the ability to "do Agile." When I think of *transformation*, I think of a team that understands why they are applying the new elements and has changed their behavior so that a new culture emerges that aligns with the Agile values and principles. They have effectively crossed the agile chasm and have the ability to "be Agile."

The RICH framework specifically focuses on readiness activities that help you prepare not only to adopt the mechanical aspects of agile processes, methods, and practices but also for a transformation of behavior toward an Agile mindset. The framework does this by providing a focus on readiness, implementation, and continuous honing, surrounded by effective coaching (Figure 7-1).

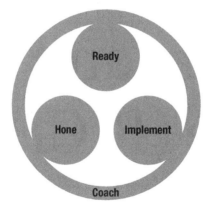

Figure 7-1. RICH deployment framework

When initiating the journey to Agile, I have found that it is important to begin the process of conditioning the mind toward the Agile mindset. *Readiness* is the beginning of the process of conditioning, and it includes making decisions on the elements for your implementation. While it is important to lead with readiness, this framework may be used iteratively depending on whether you plan for a more holistic deployment or iterative deployment of certain elements. With that in mind, I strongly encourage activities focused on readiness to begin your goal of agile transformation.

Readiness Activities for Agile Transformation

To be a successful farmer, one must first know the nature of the soil.

—Xenophon, *Oeconomicus*

Readiness starts the moment someone asks the question, "Is Agile right for me?" The goal is to work through this question, understand your context, and figure out how Agile might be deployed. Readiness can start weeks and even months before you really get serious about moving down the agile path. However, it can also be worked through quickly if you are ready to commit. Readiness shouldn't be taken lightly. It is important to understand the *what* and the *why* prior to discussing the *how* and the *when*.

Once you believe Agile is a direction you would like to take, then aspects of readiness activities are akin to conditioning the soil prior to growing the seeds. It is good to take a hard look at the conditions of the fields, equipment, and people. Strengthening the soil helps improve the physical qualities of the soil, especially in its ability to provide nutrition for plants. You can make poor soil more usable and rebuild soil that has been damaged by improper management.

Agile Pit Stop   Readiness activities are akin to conditioning the ground prior to planting the seeds. Conditioning the mind with an understanding of Agile principles improves the ability to adopt Agile in a way leads to being Agile.

This is exactly what readiness activities can do. It is good to examine the condition of the environment where Agile is being considered. You must begin the process of conditioning the mind with an understanding of Agile's values and principles and the business benefits that can be gained. This can improve the ability to adopt Agile in a way that the participants begin to understand the drive of being Agile. By conditioning the organization toward the Agile principles, we can begin the process of understanding value and empowering people.

I have found it important to understand the context in which Agile is being introduced. For example, it is imperative to gauge the buy-in of executives and stakeholders and willingness and capability of teams. Within an organization, due to improper management, the employees are often reluctant to speak up because of the lack of empowerment allowed and command-and-control behaviors exhibited (explicitly or implicitly). Understanding this context provides valuable insight on ways to adapt and move forward.

Readiness provides us with an opportunity to assess the current environment; lay the groundwork of Agile values and principles; discuss the agile business benefits and the various agile processes, practices, and educational elements; gauge the willingness; and then shape the agile implementation according to the context of an organization.

Any of a variety of readiness activities that may be undertaken to understand the conditions and help you prepare for more than just an Agile adoption— to get the team and organization to transform to the Agile mindset. Please understand that you do not need to complete these activities to begin implementing, but I have learned that if you begin implementing Agile, you quickly realize that you will need to address these areas in some manner, so it is better to be proactive. With this in mind, an iterative approach may be used. Here are high-level readiness activities that you may consider. As always, feel free to adapt this list of activities if it benefits you.

- Establish a common understanding of Agile.

- Understand the drivers for organizational change.

- Provide Agile mindset education on the agile values and principles and drivers for why we are changing.

- Add "Customers and Employees really matter" to the company vision and "customer engagement" and "employee engagement" to employee objectives.

- Understand levels of executive and stakeholder buy-in.

- Establish an overall strategy and backlog for the agile transformation (including mitigation of risks).

- Understand the current state of engineering and Agile.

- Determine team willingness and capability.

- Determine suitability of product.

- Identify subject matter experts (SMEs) and resources.

- Evaluate and adapt IT governance.

- Identify and establish agile roles and organization.

- Determine education needs.

- Establish agile frameworks and practices that may be used. (This should not be prescriptive model but a flexible framework, because each team is different.)

- Establish done criteria, user story framework, and sizing techniques.

- Craft measures of success and general metrics.
- Identify agile tool and infrastructure needs.

A benefit of readiness activities is that you can adapt the implementation approach based on what you learn. Another advantage is that if you find that there are challenges in an area, you can address and improve the situation. For example, you may find that there is not a clear driver for moving to Agile. This can initiate discussions on business benefits of Agile, motivational factors behind the move, and what it really takes to be Agile.

When you are ready to embark on readiness activities, consider treating them as agile tasks with an iterative approach, adding them to a RICH backlog as the first sprint of activities. Conduct iteration planning and initiate the readiness activities with the goal of producing deliverables that align with the activities and help you establish your direction. Finally, I recommend that once you embark on these activities, you initiate periodic stand-ups to gauge progress, mitigate roadblocks (such as risks and issues), and adapt along the way. Chapter 11 discusses the importance of managing your transformation as a project while using agile process and practices as your framework.

Implementation Activities for Agile Transformation

Implementation activities focus on the application of agile elements within a team or organization. With proper conditioning during readiness activities, the participants will understand why they are applying Agile. I have found that it is best to align implementation activities with the beginning of the lifecycle of a project that is first applying Agile. This allows for a just-in-time learning and work-based approach as the participants begin adopting and adapting to the new processes, methods, practices, tools, and mindset.

The key to an effective implementation is ensuring that the readiness activities have been performed. As mentioned, if you begin implementing Agile on a team or into an organization without considering the readiness factors, you will quickly realize that you need to address these areas in some manner during the implementation.

Another key to effective implementation is to be aware that an agile implementation for each product team will be different based on what you have learned from the readiness activities. As you implement the agile framework, there are many adaptions that may be implemented, depending on the team's situation—experience, distribution, type of work, and so forth. Implementation begins the cycle of the team or organization getting Agile working on the ground. Here are implementation activities that you may consider. As always, feel free to adapt this list of activities to benefit your implementation.

- Provide agile education—just-in-time and work-based.
- Provide an Agile Team foundation workshop.
- Provide a Product Owner workshop.
- Provide a Scrum Master workshop.
- Provide agile education for executives and management.
- Initiate periodic Agile Q&A sessions.
- Establish an agile online community (resource website, social website, etc.).
- Apply the agile framework and practices.
- Apply agile tools.

During the implementation, consider adding these activities to the RICH backlog as the next sprint of activities. I recommend that once you embark on these activities you continue periodic stand-ups to gauge progress and adapt along the way. Also, as you are implementing, expect some roadblocks. An effective implementation of Agile will affect those across the organization. Be ready to resolve, mitigate, or improve these challenges. This is where coaching and honing activities come into play.

Coaching Activities for Agile Transformation

Coaching accompanies the readiness, implementation, and honing activities. Coaching activities focus on helping the team and organization adapt to the new culture and align with the new way of being. Coaching also helps teams understand the details of activities to achieve to a more successful agile transformation and helps remove the roadblocks along the way. It is highly recommended to use the services of a Agile Coach who has the following qualifications:

- Experienced in deploying Agile
- Veteran in organizational change
- Versed in the notions of business value and customer engagement
- Practiced at setting up self-organized teams and employee engagement

Coaching activities come in several forms. Some coach from an agile perspective, some from a culture change perspective, and others from a sponsorship perspective. Although an experienced Agile Coach may be responsible for deploying Agile, coaching is not just limited to that person. Scrum Masters, Agile Team members, Product Owners, executives, senior management, and middle management all have coaching roles to play. Everyone should share responsibility in the success and help each other along to get there.

Agile Pit Stop   Coaching activities are not just limited to an Agile Coach. Executives, management, and team members all have roles to play.

Coaches are responsible for facilitating, leading, coaching, and mentoring in the ways of Agile during the readiness, implementation, and honing activities, but they stop at owning any of these activities. This is because as part of the move to Agile, the team or organization must feel they can make decisions and own the work so that Agile becomes part of them. This leads to an increase in buy-in and pride, which increases the chances of a successful adoption. This eventually leads to a transformational change in behavior and culture that is needed to achieve an Agile mindset.

The key to coaching activities is getting the team or organization ready for Agile, helping them through the implementation activities, and then helping them hone their processes, methods, practices, and mindset. At a high level, here are coaching activities (or responsibilities) that may be undertaken to help achieve the transformation to Agile. Feel free to adapt this list of activities if it benefits coaching opportunities.

- Lead and facilitate agile deployment during the readiness, implementation, and honing activities.

- Gauge attitudes, mindset, patterns of behavior, and overall health of the team during the deployment.

- Provide continued support and mentoring as issues and challenges are raised by teams.

- Identify issues that affect customer value, workflow, and quality of the product being built.

- Lead periodic check-in meetings to monitor direction and challenges.

- Provide in-session coaching to apply Agile and validate the implementation of Agile and adapt as appropriate.

- Initiate assessments to determine adoption level of the practices and transformation level of the behavior and culture, sharing results only with the team.

- Groom Scrum Masters, Product Owners, Agile Team members, executives, managers, and any local Agile Champions.

Because coaching occurs throughout the RICH framework and is not as discrete as the readiness and implementation activities, you do not need to explicitly add these activities to the RICH backlog unless you feel it is appropriate.

Agile Pit Stop   The goal of a coach is to educate enough people and groom enough leaders that they coach themselves out of a job.

Honing Activities for Agile Transformation

A key part of the Agile mindset is the Twelfth Principle behind the Agile Manifesto: "At regular intervals, the team reflects on how to become more effective, then tunes and adjusts its behavior accordingly." This aligns with the notion of *kaizen*—the Japanese word for "improvement." Agile embraces kaizen and enhances it to ensure continuous improvement by applying a reflect-and-adapt approach. Within the context of the RICH framework, once you have implemented the agile processes, methods, practices, tools, and mindset, it is not time to relax. Instead, it is time for the team to continuously look for opportunities for improvement within their work environment.

Even as early as the readiness activities, you will see issues, challenges, and roadblocks both locally and across the organization. Be ready to resolve or mitigate these challenges immediately. In particular, you will find challenges and room for improvement during implementation. Be flexible in whatever you decide and be ready to learn and adapt it over time to fit the team's situation. What you thought would work well for a team initially may need to be changed. There may need to be additional education in certain areas. You may find that several of the practices need to be adjusted to better fit the team's situation. You may find that you have to revisit the Agile values and principles.

Here are several suggested honing activities that can be applied. As usual, feel free to adapt this list of activities if it benefits the honing activities.

- Make use of periodic team retrospectives for improvement.

- Initiate periodic assessments to gauge adoption level and alignment with Agile values and principles.

- Hone implementation elements (framework, practices, education, tools, etc.) to fine-tune the adoption and team performance.

- Discuss consideration for automation and other factors with the objective of improving velocity.

Once you have reached the honing activities in the RICH framework, the team retrospectives will be a key driver for continuous improvement at the product team level. Honing activities at the organization level may be facilitated by the coach using assessment and survey mechanisms. However, I strongly encourage only showing the results of any assessment to the level of participants who contributed to it. Those outside this circle may use the results in a negative way and will not be aware of the full context of the results. For example, if a product team participated in an agile assessment, the results would only go to the product team members.

Are You Ready?

A vast quantity of material is readily available that focuses on how to implement Agile from a "doing" perspective. Yet there is a scarcity of material that focuses on how to achieve the Agile mindset. The goal of *readiness* is to condition the mind toward the Agile mindset and then incorporate this mindset into the decision-making process for your proposed implementation. With that goal in mind, I focus most of the rest of this book on readiness activities. Let the readiness games begin!

Motivations for Moving to an Agile Culture

Motivation is the fuel necessary to keep the human engine running.

—Zig Ziglar

When moving to something as all-encompassing as Agile, it is important to state clearly the objectives and equally important to explain the motivations behind the need to change. This is one aspect of conditioning the environment toward Agile. Stating the objectives helps folks understand what you are intending to do, and explaining the motivations brings clarity to why you are trying to achieve those objectives.

In Chapters 4 and 5, I introduced two important objectives that should be considered when initiating an agile effort: customer engagement and employee engagement. Or, to turn these objectives into exhortations: "Engage customers!" and "Engage employees!" This chapter explores the benefits of communicating the motivations behind these objectives, the various types of resistance, the importance of adapting rewards, the various motivations for moving to Agile, the benefits of establishing a common definition of Agile, and the importance of storytelling to help achieve the culture you are seeking.

Communicating Motivations

On an annual basis, companies typically communicate objectives for the upcoming year. Communicating "why we are moving in this direction" gives employees a sense that the objectives have been carefully thought out. More important, discussing the motivations with your employees can help you adapt the motivations and gain buy-in for the objectives. Although getting employee input may be risky, it can help you understand how realistic the objectives are. Also, employees feel valued when you ask for their feedback. It can help get the most out of people.

If your motivations are compelling and honest and benefit employees, this can lead to employees being willing to participate in the change. A clear role in achieving the objective further enhances an employee's willingness to participate in the change. The more meaningful the "why" behind the motivation, the more willing the employee will become to support the objective.

If you find that you haven't established objectives and accompanying motivations behind your agile initiative, now is the time to do so. Consider discussing the objectives and motivations of your agile initiative with key employees to communicate direction and gain feedback as to what can help motivate them toward the change. This helps you understand the work you need to do for readiness as part of the RICH model. Ultimately this helps answer the question, "Are you starting in the right direction?"

Adapting Rewards

The objective and motivation should be accompanied by an aligned benefit to the employee. The benefit or reward could be in many forms and does not always have to be monetary. For example, the reward can be self-organized teams. "What's in it for me?" is a common question about change. For employees, the benefit can be true empowerment. This is why it is critical to understand what drives your workers and weave these drivers into your objectives and motivations. When the change involves a shift in the culture, this typically means that the organizational reward system must be adapted to support the change.

Agile Pit Stop Employees will notice what actions gain reward. Objectives that do not have aligned rewards for the employee can doom the change effort.

The need to adapt the reward system is particularly relevant when moving to an agile culture. If the "hero" continues to be better rewarded (instead of the team) or if management continues to get rewarded for command-and-control attributes (instead of leading their team), this will become quickly evident to the employees and can effectively doom the change.

The reality is that employees notice the actions that gain rewards (and rightly so) and will adapt and "follow the money trail." Any objective that is out of sync with the actual reward for the employee cannot be sustained and will ultimately fail. When you add the compelling reward of self-organized teams, employee empowerment, and some monetary incentives to support the objective of engaging employees, you will increase the chances for employees to become self-motivated behind the "what" (objectives) and "why" (motivations).

Managing Resistance

Resistance is a common reaction to a change initiative. As organizations attempt to grow, it is difficult to avoid change. Change can occur for many reasons. When moving to an organization that is embracing Agile, there is often a need for a significant culture change. Agile brings about a change in objectives, which affects both employees and customers. Changes can create new opportunities, but they will also meet with opposition. Many scenarios engender resistance:

- *"Here we go again!"* It is comforting when things remain the same. Employees have seen change efforts come and go without any true commitment and may attempt to wait the new ones out. Commitment to change must be visible with clear motivations and rewards.

- *Lack of communication.* Employees need to know what is occurring to them. As information trickles down from the top, the message can be lost. This is why a plan for continuous communications at all levels is important.

- *Change in employee roles.* Some employees like to retain the status quo and do not want to see their roles changed. When roles are vague, some don't know where they fit in the new culture, making them feel excluded. When they have no say in their new roles, they can feel alienated. Discussing with employees the changes in their roles and adapting as appropriate are key.

- *Competing initiatives.* Introducing an agile initiative when there are already multiple initiatives occurring can lead to employees feeling overwhelmed, causing them to resist. Hardly an auspicious start to the agile initiative! It is important for management to prioritize initiatives and focus on the higher priority initiatives.

- *Regime change.* New leaders often feel they must show they are action-oriented. They may reason that the change that worked in their previous company should work here. Some know their term is short, so they are not interested in long-term change. Some are unaware of what it takes to affect culture. Employees who are used to this power-game scenario may resist.

Common Motivations for Moving to Agile

There are various motivations behind moving to Agile. Some are proactive and some are reactive (Figure 8-1). Proactive motivations tend to be accompanied by a greater understanding of the business benefits of Agile and the culture change it implies. However, this is not always the case. The reasons behind the motivation can determine your chances to achieve a real Agile transformation. Let's take a look at some motivations for moving to Agile and what you can do to enhance your chances of gaining the business benefits of Agile.

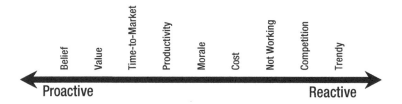

Figure 8-1. Proactive and reactive reasons for moving to Agile

- "It's the trendy thing to do." Agile is popular, so we should do it. This is reactive and not a strong motivator for change. When another trend comes along, Agile may be abandoned. Agile may be seen as a hollow initiative and some may wait it out to see if it will go away. It will be important to investigate the benefits of Agile to see if it is right for you. Then determine if real commitment can be gained.

- *"The competition is doing it."* Others are doing it, so we better do it. This is reactive. Although it may provide a driver for change, it does not provide clarity on why Agile was chosen. Some will question why what a competitor does is good for us. What happens when they do something else? It will be important to investigate the benefits of Agile to see if it is right for you.

- *"What we have isn't working."* We've been using another process to deliver software and it isn't effective. This is a reactive reason with little understanding of Agile, but it may provide an initial motivation for change. However, blindly moving to Agile without understanding what it takes may lead to a failed deployment. It is best to understand the root cause for the failures in the past, because this can affect your change to Agile.

- *"We need an agile tool."* This is a proactive but insufficient reason. It sees Agile only as a tool to manage the work without realizing that it requires a change in culture. This is a very limited view of Agile and will not lead to its business benefits.

- *"We need to reduce costs."* This is a reactive and insufficient reason whereby Agile is seen as a tool to cut costs and maybe the workforce. This will not lead to the business benefits of moving to Agile. Although it may be an outcome, other benefits of Agile may be gained if you are willing to adapt the culture.

- *"We hope to increase employee morale."* This is a proactive reason based on an understanding of the importance of employee engagement and empowerment to improve morale. Validate that there is real commitment to empowering employees and self-organizing teams.

- *"We hope to improve productivity."* This is a proactive reason when the goal is to empower employees and help them improve productivity. The danger is that management may believe that Agile is something someone else must do to increase productivity or the real intent is to make employees work harder. The other challenge is that productivity may come at the expense of sacrificing quality. It will be important to investigate all of the benefits of Agile, not just productivity.

- *"We aim to decrease time to market."* This is a proactive reason in which Agile is seen as a way to shorten release cycles. If there is an understanding that this implies a change across the organization to get from market idea to release and it is meant to satisfy the customer, then this is a good starting point. It is still important to discuss the benefits of Agile to see if it is right for you.

- *"We want to deliver customer value."* This is a proactive and genuine reason if Agile is seen as a way to engage the customer and understand value. Validate whether there is a real commitment to delivering value and an understanding of the need to change organizational behaviors and processes to get there.

- *"We believe in the Agile Values and Principles."* This is a proactive and genuine reason where Agile may be seen as a positive change in company vision and behavior. Validate a drive toward continuous customer engagement and employee engagement that can help gain the business benefits that Agile can bring.

In all of these cases, you need to validate commitment to the values and principles and the culture change it entails. Once the initial motivation is understood, you can work to adapt it with the goal of better gaining the business benefits of going Agile.

Benefit of Establishing a Common Understanding of Agile

Establishing a common definition of Agile provides the organization with a singular understanding. Even if there is unanimity on the objective of moving to Agile, lack of consensus as to what Agile is will impede movement. Don't assume that everyone has a common understanding. There are a wide range of thoughts on what Agile is, and often those are laden with misconceptions. As discussed in Chapter 6, many believe that Agile is a methodology, a process, or a set of practices and tools. But Agile is really a set of values and principles. This is a good place to start.

First, I try to find out what Agile means to the team or organization. Depending on the answer, I begin some education to ensure they understand the Agile mindset and in particular the Agile Values and Principles found within the Manifesto of Agile Software Development (see Chapter 6). This ensures that everyone has a common understanding of Agile after any misconceptions are discussed and discarded. Also, much of the "what is Agile?" discussion is an attempt to normalize the team on agile values, principles, business benefits, methods, techniques, and more.

Once a common definition of Agile is established, it is beneficial to enhance this with common terminology. I often get asked for a glossary when I am helping teams adopt Agile. This gives folks one way to learn and get introduced to new terminology. Terminology may be collected from the Agile Manifesto and various processes, methods, books, and articles. It is important to discuss the terminology with associates who will be initially working with Agile. You may adapt terminology to suit the organization if this is beneficial. For example, if the word *sprint* is more acceptable then using the term *iteration* to describe a time-boxed period, then use the term sprint. Through deploying agile processes, training, seminars, and workshops, the terminology can spread.

Agile Pit Stop   When introducing Agile, avoid referring to any agile methods, tools, or techniques. Instead, initially discuss only the Agile Values and Principles.

Aligning Storytelling with the Culture You Want

Stories are the creative conversion of life itself into a more powerful, clearer, more meaningful experience. They are the currency of human contact

—Robert McKee

Storytelling is a technique that is used to convey a message. Stories can be used as the delivery system to reinforce the culture you are looking for. Stories are often much easier to remember than objectives and facts, which is why stories are very powerful. Stories also reveal what people are really thinking, which can motivate or demotivate people. There is the story that is told and the story that people walk away with. This is why it is important to align your stories with the culture you hope to achieve. There has been an increasing amount of focus of conveying information in the form of stories. Stories can either align with and strengthen a culture or reveal a misalignment and weaken the cultural message. Let's look at several examples.

> A manager thinks it is important for everyone to be on time to the staff meetings. He explains that it is a token of respect for people's time and this benefits the team in terms of their productivity. Although everyone comes to the next meeting on time, the manager was late and provided a flippant excuse, saying, "I was just wrapping up an important meeting."

What story does the staff walk away with in this case? The manager had discussed the importance of respecting people's time, and then his actions indicated to the team that the manager didn't respect their time. This left the employees resentful and unhappy. Let's look at another story.

This company established a new objective called "employee equality." This sounded great to everyone involved. As part of that objective, the senior team decided to hold a full-company meeting each month to share their thoughts. The first session in which the topic of employee equality was discussed went well. For the second session, one of the executives kicked it off by discussing his yachting trip. In the third session, another executive, not to be outdone, told of the magnificent house he was building at the beach. After this, employees started finding reasons to miss these sessions.

What story do the employees walk away with in this example? Although the "objective" was to create a company culture of equality, the senior management team discussed things that highlighted that they weren't equal at all, instead of things the average employee could afford. How many of those in the company could afford to go yachting? How many could afford to build a large house at the beach? This is an example of where storytelling can send the opposite message. The employees felt like they were being put in their place and stopped believing in the equality objective. Now let's look at another case.

A company was trying to introduce Agile into their culture. They promoted the principles of collaboration, trust, self-organizing teams, and sustainable pace. It was initially led by an Agile Coach who built a self-organizing team made up of Agile Champions (internal employees) from across the company to promote buy-in. They applied a collaborative approach to build the agile framework. It became quite successful, and many teams began adopting Agile. Several senior managers saw the accomplishments and wanted to make the agile program their own. They disbanded the champions' team and used their own functional team to lead the agile effort, even though they were not experienced in Agile and hadn't received any training on it. This new management shared the story that they would provide more structure to Agile. They said they all learned Agile by reading a book. They also said they would assign a project manager to the projects to help the teams estimate correctly.

What story are the teams walking away with? The story employees walked away with was that Agile was no longer being taken seriously. It was clear that management was now only giving lip service to Agile, really didn't believe in the Agile Principles, and didn't really trust their employees. In addition, the story about how this management believed that reading a book on Agile made them knowledgeable became a common joke among the employees.

What type of stories are being told in your organization? Are senior managers telling stories that align with the objectives of Agile? Are middle managers sharing stories that align with the needs of their team? Are team members repeating the stories that strengthen the new culture or stories that are demoralizing? Leaders must keep in mind that when they are speaking to the people, they are effectively telling a story. Ensure that the messages in the stories align with the objectives and principles that you would like to see in your teams and new culture.

Building the Agile Culture You Want

Adapting an organization's culture is effectively an effort in change management. For most organizations, moving to an Agile culture is a significant change management activity. Changing a culture is hard. People underestimate the difficulties of a culture change within their organization. I have seen large efforts get started with poorly stated objectives and motivations, a lack of employee involvement, and a lack of thinking through the effort. Also, most people are not educated in change management or how to achieve a cultural change. I have seen companies assign a member of senior management as the change agent, yet that person has neither education nor experience in change management. A better approach may be to hire an Agile Coach with change management experience.

Creating or adapting a culture is not done by accident. It must be considered a change initiative and thought through. As part of readiness within the RICH deployment model, start the process of adapting to an Agile mindset and the culture you are looking for. What are some activities that will help you move to an Agile culture? They include:

- Recognize that moving to Agile is a cultural change.

- Share the Agile Values and Principles (often).

- Establish and share objectives and motivations.

- Gain feedback from employees along the way.

- Adapt the reward system to align with the new culture.

- Identify techniques to help gracefully mitigate resistance.

- Evaluate management and lead employees to see if they have the personality that aligns with an Agile culture.

- Start living the values and principles that help you get to the culture you are looking for.

- Provide messaging or storytelling that aligns with the culture you are looking for.

- Identify and apply the agile processes, methods, practices, and tools that align with your objectives.

- Apply an inspect-and-adapt approach to gauge progress.

Achieving an Agile Mindset

It is not the strongest of the species that survives, nor the most intelligent that survives. It is the one that is the most adaptable to change.

—Charles Darwin

We humans like to control our own lives and destinies. This is the natural order of things. Great pioneers determined their own paths. We learn and adapt as conditions change. This was true a thousand years ago and is true today. There are often barriers that prevent us from what we would like to do, but when we have the ability to control our own destiny, great innovation can occur.

It is ironic that in this new millennium whose watchword is *innovation*, many software-related companies have chosen a path of rigidity, with prescribed processes leaving little room for adaption or a sense of ownership. Companies are surprised that they are not getting the customer and employee engagement that fosters innovation and leads to valued products. More control and more processes are not the solution. Agile, which cultivates a mindset of values and principles, brings back the vital evolutionary interplay between the constraints of nature and the flexibility of cultural adaptation.

Agile Pit Stop An Agile mindset moves away from the pretense of predicting what the customer wants a year in advance.

Agile principles steer software developers away from the delusion that they can predict what customers want a year in advance. Instead, it shapes them to build and adapt according to continuous customer feedback. Agile principles oppose thinking of employees as cogs to be moved or replaced and instead views workers as self-organized owners of their work who use their brainpower to build value.

What words come to mind when you think of Agile? How about *value, principles, working software, transparent, adapt, self-organizing, disciplined, empirical, collaborative, iterative, incremental*? This vocabulary is a first step in moving toward agile culture.

Agile thinkers bring a different frame of mind to their work. In traditional and waterfall approaches, the work is well planned with very specific milestones, and changes are often frowned on or discouraged. You don't have to think about why you are doing something or your behavior. Agile, on the other hand, inculcates the principles and "why" of being Agile and recognizes that behavior is an important element of the Agile mindset. The agile world is fluid, and dynamic change is the norm. Agile promotes learning in response to change in the direction of value.

Agile Pit Stop   Agile promotes adaptation not in a whimsical and carefree manner but in a methodical, empirical, and disciplined manner.

Agile is essentially a risk-management system that helps you avoid building something the customer doesn't want and helps you make the best use of employee energies.

As discussed in Chapter 6, education on agile values and principles underpins the Agile mindset and initiates the behavioral changes that are needed to align with Agile. An essential educational step is to dissect the principles behind Agile.

Dissecting the Agile Principles

Acquisition of an Agile mindset first requires awareness of the cognitive patterns of the old ways of thinking, such as the common belief that big up-front requirements are the correct way to approach delivering product—despite overwhelming evidence to the contrary. Some believe that aligning with the project plan is more important than adapting to customer value. Anytime you try to move from one culture to another, you'll find cognitive patterns that do not align with the new culture. This baggage inhibits movement in the new direction. The goal is to eliminate the old thinking patterns and adapt to the new patterns that Agile provides by application of its values and principles.

When I ponder the elements of the Agile mindset, I review the Manifesto for Agile Software Development (Agile Manifesto, for short). Then I refer to the important Principles behind the Agile Manifesto to realize what the mindset represents. To better understand the new cognitive patterns needed for the Agile Principles, I dissect the Principles to better understand the intentions behind them and what behaviors they entail.

Agile Pit Stop　The key to understanding an Agile mindset is to read and understand the Principles behind the Agile Manifesto.

In the next section I expand on each Principle and model how to marshal supporting evidence that a culture change may be occurring. Other descriptions, actions, and evidence will occur to you and should be applied freely and continuously. The key is that you should take a hard look at the Principles, define what they mean to you, and evaluate the evidence for culture change in light of whether you are aligning with the Principles. Internalizing an inspect-and-adapt criterion for evaluating proofs of agile change becomes the embodiment of achieving the agile culture.

Satisfy Customer with Valuable Software

Our highest priority is to satisfy the customer through early and continuous delivery of valuable software. Satisfying the customer means delivering valuable software in a timely manner (that is, in the market window) for a reasonable cost. Continually striving to meet elusive customer value is important. Ultimately, the key measure of value for customers is an increase in sales and the continued loyalty of existing customers.

How do you know that you are moving in the right direction of building value? It starts with understanding your customers: who they are and what motivates them. Their profiles include such information as their challenges, their vision for your product, and their buying trends.

Delivering value continues with an effective Sprint Review process where the customer gains an opportunity to review and provide feedback on working software. If customers can sense that their input is valued during the demos, their satisfaction can increase. This is particularly true if the customers see that their feedback from the last demo has been incorporated in the working software of the current version.

In addition, it is beneficial to use the Product Owner (PO) as the delegated voice of the customer to solicit acceptance criteria on what the customer would expect when they see a particular requirement or feature in action. You may also conduct periodic customer surveys to gauge their level of satisfaction with the product or solution.

What actions exhibit "satisfying customer with valuable software"?

- The PO works to understand customer value, constantly prioritizes and grooms the backlog, and discusses customer needs with the team.

- The PO creates customer profiles to recognize motivations.

- The backlog is your single source of requirements (aka value).

- The *Customer* role reflects how you wish to engage your customers.

- Strategy focuses on delighting the customer.

- Customers are invited to Sprint Reviews to provide feedback and validate what they feel is valuable.

- Acceptance criteria are been captured and met for each user story.

- Customer satisfaction surveys are periodically conducted.

- Criteria are applied to ensure the software is built with quality.

- Customer revenue metrics are captured and reviewed.

What is the level of belief?

- Do you believe in continuous customer engagement, adapting requirements, and validation as a means of building valuable software to satisfy the customer?

Welcoming Change to Requirements

Welcome changing requirements, even late in development. Agile processes harness change for the customer's competitive advantage. From an agile perspective, you embrace change to increase the chances of delivering value to the customer. You understand that change is necessary because you understand that customer needs, market conditions, and general demand change over time.

Welcoming change implies several things. The first is that there is a positive attitude toward change from the team and management. The second is that there is a process that allows change to flow without obstruction. This doesn't mean that all changes are accepted but that changes are prioritized along with existing requirements in the product backlog and methodically discussed.

What actions exhibit "welcoming change to requirements?"

- The PO continually engages with the customer to identify new requirements or changes to requirements.

- No person or process restricts change.

- The backlog is continually groomed and reprioritized.

- Sprint Planning is applied to introduce the newly prioritized requirements.

- Continuous customer engagement via customer visits and Sprint Reviews are applied.

What is the level of belief?

- Do you have a positive attitude toward change even late in the development cycle?

Frequent/Continuous Delivery

Deliver working software frequently, from a couple of weeks to a couple of months, with a preference to the shorter timescale. "Continuous delivery" refers to the capability of frequently releasing software to the customer when they want it. This ensures that when customers believe there is value from what was built and they want it, it can be delivered instantly. Because timing is critical, the key phrase is "when a customer wants it." Identifying the elusive customer value means you can release when the customer wants it. If it is delivered too early, the customer may not be ready for it; if it is too late, the market opportunity is missed.

Agile thinking includes a world that is fluid, where changes are continuous and welcome, and teams have the capability of releasing frequently, which applies to the delivery of software. This ability to frequently release highlights the importance of infrastructure that can help with continuous integration, building, and testing. This ability assumes a level of automation that needs to be in place. Automated testing increases the possibility of testing as much of the functionality as is reasonable, including the capability of performing nonfunctional testing such as performance testing, load testing, and more.

What actions exhibit continuous delivery?

- A release capability to incrementally and rapidly deploy software

- Iterative framework with Sprint Reviews

- Continuous integration supported by merging process and configuration management system

- A continuous build process supported by an automated build management system

- Test automation infrastructure that can support continuous testing

What is the level of belief?

- Do you believe in continuous integration, building, and frequent delivery?

Business and Development Work Together

Business people and developers must work together daily throughout the project. Agile attempts to bring an understanding of business value to the development team. To do this, it attempts to integrate business and development as one team. In traditional methods, there is often little interaction between the business (e.g., product management, sales, and marketing) and development (aka cross-functional team). On the business side, Scrum introduces the PO role and XP introduces the Customer role as the bridge between the customer and the development team. These roles allow for a closer embodiment of the business and development team spirit and avoids fiefdoms and throwing work "over the wall" from one group to another with little interaction.

The intent is to make a sincere effort to build a collaborative, amicable relationship between business and development. Development benefits from a better understanding of what the customer finds valuable. The business side benefits because development will ask for details that business may not have thought about it. In both cases, the result is a product that more closely aligns with what the customer finds valuable.

What actions exhibit business and development working together?

- A dedicated business contact (namely, the PO) who works continuously with the Development team.

- Development comprises a cross-functional team with developers, testers, technical writers, designers, and so on.

- The PO and Development Team work together during Sprint Planning to build a mutual understanding of the requirements.

- The PO and Development Team work together during the demo of the working software and gain customer feedback.

- The Development Team can reach out to the PO as needed throughout the project life cycle.

What is the level of belief?

- Do you believe that business and development should work continuously together as a team?

Trust Motivated Individuals

Build projects around motivated individuals. Give them the environment and support they need, and trust them to get the job done. Motivated individuals make for a more engaging and productive workforce with good morale. There are strategies to get employees engaged, continually educated, and building on their strengths. Management values employee opinions, appreciates them, and trusts that they can get the work done. Motivated individuals are empowered, feel ownership of their work, and size their own work.

As part of getting work done, there need to be clear release, sprint, and organizational goals provided by the right people who can energize employees and encourage them to invest more effort in building a better product. Vague goals can reduce commitment and motivation. Increased transparency between management and teams increases communication and promote trust.

What actions exhibit trust of motivated individuals?

- Teams have the ability to make decisions, such as sizing their own work.

- Management trusts team decisions and minimizes command and control.

- Teams are kept whole and members are treated like people, not fungible resources.

- Management provides transparency in decision making.

- Management provides organizational goals such as employee engagement.

- The PO provides release and sprint goals.

- Team members demonstrate their working software during sprint reviews.

- The Scrum Master provides a servant–leader approach.

What is the level of belief?

- Do you believe in motivating employees and trusting them to get the job done?

Promote Face-to-Face Communication

The most efficient and effective method of conveying information to and within a team is face-to-face conversation. Agile puts a premium on face-to-face communication. Because of the nonverbal cues built into communication, there is a benefit of harvesting visual cues during interpersonal interactions. Face-to-face discussion improves the overall communication experience and understanding. From an Agile perspective, a Scrum team (about seven people) should be as collocated as reasonable or should use technology to emulate face-to-face interaction as much as possible.

With communication comes the importance of listening. Listening means hearing and understanding what the other is saying and what they are not saying (hence the importance of nonverbal cues). Determining if silence is because of a lack of understanding, simply not being engaged, or a variety of other reasons should be probed. Another aspect of collaboration is being assertive. Quietly listening often does not lead to building ideas. Therefore, communication is a balance of being a collaborative speaker and a respectful listener.

What actions exhibit promoting face-to-face communication?

- Ideally, individual teams are colocated.
- Teams are kept small (about seven members)
- Rooms are available for face-to-face discussion and communication in teams.
- Technologies are used to emulate face-to-face discussion whenever colocation is not possible.
- Listening skills are emphasized.

What is the level of belief?

- Do you believe in the importance of colocation and face-to-face communication?

Working Software as Measure of Progress

Working software is the primary measure of progress. From an agile perspective, working software is the best measure of progress. Working software must be produced at the end of each time-boxed period (sprint). You may use other measures to help gauge progress, such as Sprint Burndown, but they should be minor in relation to the criterion of working software.

The reason for this new thinking on measures is that when you follow waterfall, you may be 50 percent through the project schedule and have no working software. From a customer perspective you haven't accomplished anything. Although there may be internal benefit to gathering requirements, preparing a plan, and doing design and development work, an external paying customer only values the actual working software. You don't get credit for in-progress stuff, only the working software.

This is why, at the end of each time-boxed period, working software is delivered and validated with the customer during the demo. In addition, working software must meet done criteria to ensure that it is of high quality.

What actions exhibit working software as a measure of progress?

- Progress is measured by working software.

- Sprint Burndown tracks work done and work remaining.

- Done criteria are established that reflect engineering standards that are applied to user stories.

- Sprint Reviews are conducted to demonstrate the working software and gain customer feedback.

What is the level of belief?

- Do you believe that working software can be produced incrementally and is a measure of progress?

Sustainable Pace

Agile processes promote sustainable development. The sponsors, developers, and users should be able to maintain a constant pace indefinitely. The concept of sustainable pace has been quantified by Kent Beck, who recommends working no more than 40 hours a week and never working overtime for more than one week at a time (not consecutively).[1] When you maintain a reasonable pace, you can sustain a constant pace indefinitely. Studies have shown that when you consistently work more than 40 hours in a week, the overtime produces lower-quality software and a reduction in productivity.[2]

A team establishes *velocity* based on a 40-hour work week to determine how much work they can do in a sprint.[3] Using velocity allows the team to empirically determine the amount of work they can build into working software in a given iteration. More important, does management trust the team's velocity, or do they disregard it and force them to do more?

---

[1] Kent Beck. *Extreme Programming Explained*. Addison-Wesley, 2005.
[2] Lonnie Golden. *The Effects of Working Time on Productivity and Firm Performance: A Research Synthesis Paper*. International Labour Office, Geneva, 2011.
[3] *Velocity* is the number of units of work (aka *story points*) that a team can complete in an iteration or sprint.

Another driver for sustainable pace is the concept of social responsibility: the obligation to benefit the people as a whole and maintain a work/life balance. With this in mind, a key to a strong Agile team is the notion that no one succeeds unless everyone succeeds. This promotes team spirit, whereby members collaborate and help each other out so that no one or two people are burdened with extra work while others have free time. To do this, each team member should gain secondary skills so they can ramp up quickly should there be a bottleneck. A side effect of sustainable pace is that it often leads to improved team morale. Folks do not feel burned out and come to work with fresh minds, which can lead to innovative ideas.

What actions exhibit sustainable pace?

- Each member of the team works only 40 hours a week.

- Velocity is used as a measure to define the number of story points a team can complete in an iteration or sprint.

- Management trusts the team velocity.

- Management does not force the team to work longer hours or initiate death marches.

- All team members have secondary skill sets and pitch in when needed.

What is the level of belief?

- Do you believe in sustainable pace where working approximately 40 hours a week is a healthy norm?

Technical Excellence

Continuous attention to technical excellence and good design enhances agility. To strive for technical excellence, you need team members who have knowledge and experience to produce sound architecture, good design, and quality software. It is important to have the capability of making the best technical decisions balancing design, usability, and maintainability. Such capability requires a seasoned and professional team. In Agile, employees should want to do the work in the context of career learning and growth.

To strive for technical excellence, effective done criteria should be established that include engineering standards in design, UX, development, technical writing, configuration management, building, and testing. To achieve quality, it may include implementing various XP practices, such as continuous integration and build, coding standards, pair programming, refactoring, simple design, and test driven development that are applied to improve the technical excellence of a product. In addition, the use of retrospectives help the team reflect on opportunities to build their skills and further achieve technical excellence.

What actions exhibit technical excellence?

- Team members motivate each other toward technical excellence, including sharing technical practices and actively participating in code reviews.

- Team members may apply continuous integration and build, coding standards, pair programming, simple design, refactoring, code reviews, and test-driven development.

- Team members apply done criteria that include engineering disciplines' need to deliver a quality product.

- Team members employ learning plans that include a focus on technical excellence that are actively managed.

What is the level of belief?

- Do you believe in applying technical practices that promote technical excellence and provide technical educational opportunities for employees?

Simplicity

Simplicity—the art of maximizing the amount of work not done—is essential. Striving for eliminating unnecessary work is the goal. This should include identifying the minimum amount of features for a customer release (MVP) for it to be successful. It should include reducing non-value-added work that team members are asked to do. It may involve reducing unnecessary steps of a process to deploy a release.

To simplify, you need to proactively remove the seven wastes in software development as defined by Mary and Tom Poppendiek and discussed in Chapter 6: eliminating partially done work, extra features, the need to relearn, hand-offs, task switching, delays, and bugs.

Agile thinking focuses on short iterations and small increments. This way you can fail fast, learn, eliminate waste, and then succeed more quickly. You may also right-size your documentation with a focus on documenting decisions and why you made them.

What does this look like in action?

- There is continuous focus on staying lean and removing waste via retrospectives.

- During demonstrations, customers are asked not only what they need but what they don't need.

- The PO applies continuous prioritization via the backlog with a focus on *minimum viable product* (MVP).

- Documentation is right-sized and includes key decisions and their rationales.

What is the level of belief?

- Do you believe in simplicity, removing waste, and continuously prioritizing requirements based on customer value?

Self-Organizing Teams

The best architectures, requirements, and designs emerge from self-organizing teams. Self-organizing teams have a combination of greater ownership and responsibility to achieve a common goal of building valuable software and reducing dependency on management. The team has the authority to be self-organizing and make decisions regarding architecture, requirements, and design as they evolve the product. The team needs to be cross-functional so that they have the skills and talent to make the decisions to develop the product.

A self-organized team moves away from the command-and-control hierarchy in which one person assigns the work. Instead, a self-organizing structure is one in which everyone participates in decision making and volunteering for work from the backlog. This is easier said than done. Therefore, prior to considering Agile, an assessment of the openness of the culture is helpful for gauging the starting point.

Having self-organizing teams also means thinking beyond the individual, since this can constrain collaboration and the team mindset. The focus should be on instilling team spirit: "You only succeed if the team succeeds." Rewards should be team-based to drive the notion home.

The team notion also means hierarchy—such as title, levels, grades, heroes, and egos—needs to be removed as barriers to team success. Instead, promote equality among roles. Treating everyone on the team as equals leads to more engaged members. Nonetheless, team members should respect the fact that some people have more experience in certain areas and others can gain from this experience.

What actions exhibit self-organizing teams?

- The team makes the decisions about its work, specifically regarding architecture, requirements, design, and sizing or estimating.

- Cross-functional teams include the right mix of skills among developers, testers, technical writers, UX designers, the PO, and the Scrum Master.

- There is no hierarchy on the team, although levels of skills and experience are respected.

- Rewards are given at the team level.

- Team members pull work from the backlog at their own initiative, rather than being assigned to it by their functional manager.

- Management reduces command and control and provides boundaries of authority.

- Management articulates goals to help the team focus their work and make their own decisions.

What is the level of belief?

- Do you believe in self-organizing teams who have authority to make their own decisions, manage their own work, and are rewarded as a team?

Reflection for Improvement

At regular intervals, the team reflects on how to become more effective, then tunes and adjusts its behavior accordingly. The reflection for improvement is critical to the adaptive framework and the Agile mindset. Although what has occurred cannot be undone, reflecting on it can lead to action that will prevent the issue from recurring. With this in mind, the team should apply a periodic retrospective to reflect on the previous time-box of activity and become more effective in the future.

Remember, the team is self-organizing, so they own the practices, techniques, rituals, and particularly the behaviors. A key to real improvement is that team members are willing to let their guards down and be open and honest with each other. Otherwise, only the more superficial areas are discussed. Also, retrospectives should be private and closed sessions so "dirty laundry" can be discussed. The Scrum Master may act as the facilitator so that it is kept professional with the goal of identifying actions for improvement. Another key is that the team commits to support continuous improvement.

It may be important for teams to use root-cause analysis techniques such as Ishikawa (fishbone) diagrams to identify the cause of specific issues. In addition, Agile applies an empirical approach whereby data can be used to identify areas for improvement and help in decision making based on observation and experimentation. However, it is for the team to make the commitment to adapt and improve.

What actions exhibit reflection for improvement?

- A private team retrospective is used to identify and prioritize areas for improvement.

- The team is open and honest so that real improvement can be made.

- Retrospectives are conducted periodically.

- The team commits to implementing improvement actions.

- Retrospective actions are tracked, and progress is discussed in the retrospective session.

What is the level of belief?

- Do you believe in reflection activities and empowering the team to make the improvements?

A Group Exercise on the Principles

This chapter has examined the Agile Principles to gain a deeper appreciation of the behaviors and beliefs that are needed to align with the Agile mindset. This chapter is not meant to be comprehensive, but a starting point. As an exercise, walk through each Principle with the team and ask them what each one means to them.

This exercise has two benefits. The first is that the team will learn the Principles in a manner in which they have to think about what the Principles mean. This will help condition their minds toward a deeper understanding of Agile. The second benefit is that as they become aware of what it takes to achieve an Agile mindset, they may understand that their old way of thinking needs to be adapted to "be Agile."

Evaluating Executive Support and Team Willingness

The first and most important step is to get senior management backing. Without support from the very top, it is generally impossible to make significant changes.

—Watts Humphrey

Two important criteria for a successful agile implementation are support from your top executive and willingness to apply Agile by the team. By "executive," I mean your most senior manager within the scope of deployment. If you are looking to initiate an agile enterprise change, then you need top-level executive sponsorship and management support for the transformation. Because moving to an agile culture represents a significant change for the teams, it is important to have team members willing to make the changes for an effective transition.

As a company approaches Agile, executive support and team willingness should be evaluated so that you understand your starting point. At the executive and management levels, a good way to determine support is to understand what support is needed, evaluate the level of support, and identify ways to increase support. At the team level, a good way to determine willingness is to evaluate the level of willingness and identify ways to improve it.

■ **Agile Pit Stop**   It is important to evaluate executive support and team willingness to understand your starting point and what you need to do to improve each.

Gaining the full business benefits of Agile requires an enterprise-level initiative with executive support. Agile implementation occurs at many levels: top-down, grassroots, and from the middle in both directions. It is essential when scouting the possibility of an agile implementation to canvass and gauge the level of support from the stakeholders at the highest level of your organization that is in scope.

A good place to start is to understand the organizational scope of the change you are planning. Are you targeting the enterprise, a portion of the enterprise, a solution area made up of several products, or a single product team? This determination constrains the highest level of management support you will need and which teams you need to gain willingness from.

In general, all stakeholders should be evaluated so that you understand their levels of engagement, attitudes toward Agile, and what they may need to gain the Agile mindset. As a starting point, it is important to understand the agile personality types that you may encounter within an organization.

Agile Personality Types

In the agile world, people tend to work from different motivations. This differentiation helps you understand who you are dealing with. There are essentially seven types of people who can affect your agile transformation. They are the Innovator, Champion, Workhorse, Bandwagon Jumper, Cowboy, Deceiver, and Denier. Figure 10-1 places the seven personality types into quadrants based on level of experience with Agile on the horizontal axis and attitude toward Agile on the vertical axis.

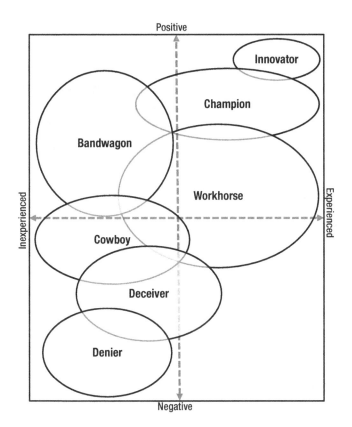

Figure 10-1. The seven agile personality types based on their agile experience and attitude toward Agile

I discuss each of the personality types in turn, highlighting their experience levels in Agile, their attitudes toward Agile, the common roles that may fit into a type, and thoughts on their motivations. As you consider your stakeholders and team members, identify which personality types they may fall into. These insights can help you understand who will help you positively drive Agile and whom you need to work with to build their knowledge and alignment.

Innovator

Innovators make up a small population of folks who are very experienced and very positive about Agile. The signatories of the Agile Manifesto certainly fall in this camp, as do seasoned Agile Coaches, writers, presenters, and authors. They are motivated to help organizations adopt Agile and extend its capabilities into all areas of software product development.

Champion

A Champion tends to know Agile well and is willing to advocate for it in a very positive way across an organization. There are even some Champions who may not be well versed in the practices of Agile but have seen the benefits of implementing and using agile methods. Key Champions may include your executives and senior management as well as Agile Coaches, Scrum Masters, Product Owners, and leaders in engineering. They are motivated by the business and organizational benefits of Agile.

Workhorse

The Workhorse has learned about Agile by implementing it within a team context. Workhorses are mostly positive about Agile, have worked or are working in the trenches as Agile Team members, and will be fairly honest about what works and what does not. Workhorses commonly use Agile on a daily basis. They bring a pragmatic approach and are often the first to experience the agile culture colliding with current company culture. They are motivated to improve the agile deployment so their lives are better. A lot can be learned from this group.

Bandwagon Jumper

The Bandwagon Jumper sees benefits in the move to Agile. If Agile is perceived to be "hot" within their company, they will jump on the bandwagon. This crowd tends to be inexperienced with Agile but generally positive until it is out of fashion. They are motivated by improving their own image. Bandwagon Jumpers may include middle and senior management and engineers who believe they can get ahead by aligning with the hot new trend. Some Bandwagon Jumpers will see the value of Agile and may become Workhorses or Champions.

Cowboy

The Cowboy sees Agile as an opportunity to abandon discipline and process so that they can enjoy the "Wild West" life. Cowboys are not necessarily negative about Agile. Their motivation is that they know that they get away with pretending to be Agile because those in the Bandwagon Jumper crowd really have no idea what it is. Ultimately, these pretenders can give Agile a black eye in the organization, since others will believe from a Cowboy's actions that Agile means no discipline or process.

Deceiver

The Deceiver will agree to applying Agile but will either silently attempt to sabotage the change or continue doing things the waterfall way. A Deceiver is negative about Agile. Deceivers behave this way either because they resent having been forced into using Agile or because they feel threatened by the change but do not want to lose credibility by bad-mouthing the new direction. They may have had some agile experience that was thrust on them. Deceivers are the most dangerous because they undermine and obstruct the potential success that Agile can bring to an organization.

■ **Agile Pit Stop**   It is actually better to have Deniers than Deceivers, because with the former you know where they stand.

Denier

The Denier will deny outright the benefits of moving to Agile. They are typically set against Agile from the beginning because they see that it will interfere with what they perceive to be their currently successful role. They may be motivated by incentives, expecting that Agile will affect their reward structure in a negative way. Deniers typically do not have much agile experience. Many times, it can be beneficial to listen to reasons Deniers give for dismissing Agile. Their input may help you look for a way to overcome their reasons, therefore strengthening the perception of Agile within the organization.

Executive/Senior Management Support

For Agile to truly succeed in an organization, everyone has to be dedicated to the initiative—especially the executive team.

—Robert Holler

It would be great if everyone were an Agile Champion, but this is seldom the case. At a high level, you can start with the rhetorical question of what personality types are the executives, senior management, and other key stakeholders. Though we want them all to be champions, usually we have to build them up to become a catalyst for change. We should consider the level of support we need. Then we should discreetly evaluate the level of support currently conveyed, followed by activities to increase support.

Agile Pit Stop Gauging the level of executive support is an ongoing activity that includes understanding what type of support you need, discreetly evaluating support levels you are actually receiving, and working to increase support levels.

Once you have identified the scope of change you are looking for, then you should identify the top management and key internal stakeholders who are important to the success of an agile implementation effort. Internal stakeholders may include the highest level of management within the level, product management involved in the product and requirements direction, middle management who have resource responsibilities of their team members, and IT governance, HR, and finance personnel.

Early on, we may not really know the level of agile support from executives, senior management, and key stakeholders. This is why it is important to periodically gauge the level of support with the goal of increasing the level of support and creating Agile Champions within your organization.

Support Needed from Executives

As you consider the support you need to achieve an effective agile deployment, you want the most senior executive or manager within the organizational scope you are working with to become the sponsor and rallying point as a catalyst for change. You need this person to accept the sponsor role and acknowledge the responsibilities involved.

Some examples follow of the types of responsibilities involved in the sponsor role. A sponsor does not have to implement all of these areas but must advocate for and support them.

- *Obtain funding and resources for the implementation.* This sponsor responsibility may include hiring Agile Coaches, procuring training, acquiring tools, and allowing time to adapt to Agile.

- *Align leadership around Agile.* This responsibility may be in the form of establishing an Agile Deployment Team or steering committee led by an organizational-level Agile Coach or change agent and internal people who are or striving toward becoming an Agile Champion.

- *Provide ongoing communications.* Keeping the organization informed is important to the success of Agile. This sponsor responsibility initially includes communicating about the agile initiative and why it is good and continues with messaging of progress and successes. Prepare a communication plan and share with the executive as discussed in Chapter 11.

- *Build middle management support.* This responsibility may include working directly with management to ensure they are becoming educated and aligned with Agile. Middle management is often where change falters because they represent the glue between executives and senior management and team members.

- *Manage resistance.* This responsibility involves mitigating signs of resistance from senior and middle management and indirectly helping mitigate resistance across the teams. Mitigation may come in the form of Q&A sessions, education, coaching, and so forth.

- *Adapt budget language toward value and investment and away from schedule and cost.* This responsibility helps set the tone that value for the customer matters most. If you hit the schedule and cost targets but few customers find the deliverables valuable, then you have not succeeded.

- *Educate executives around agile values and principles.* This responsibility includes promoting agile education for the executive's management staff and key stakeholders. Begin with sharing Chapters 6 and 9 of this book.

- *Provide education at all levels.* Agile is a fundamentally different way of doing and being. It requires continuous education in the early stages to move the company in the right direction. This responsibility includes instructor-led training, in-session coaching, webinars, seminars, Q&A sessions, and so on. (Learn more about agile education in Chapter 16.)

- *Promote objectives for Agile at all levels.* This includes aligning organizational and team objectives toward Agile and advocating for team-based goals instead of individual goals. Add "Customers and employees really matter" to the company vision and "customer engagement" and "employee engagement" to management and employee objectives, as discussed in Chapters 4 and 5.

- *Support an organizational realignment toward building effective Agile Teams.* Adapt resource management along the lines of Agile Teams. This responsibility comes in the form of establishing Agile Teams whose primary responsibility is driven from the backlog and not from the functional manager. This means bringing together the business side (such as Product Owners) with the engineering side.

This is not a comprehensive list. You need to articulate the type of support that you need for your agile transformation.

■ **Agile Pit Stop**   It is very important to assure the executive that you, acting as Agile Champion, will support their sponsorship activities and keep them informed of the latest progress so they appear knowledgeable regarding the agile initiative.

Once you have drafted this list of the type of support you want, it is important to share it with your senior executive within the organizational scope of your agile implementation. The list begins the discussion that helps you understand their level of support. You should initially ask if the executive can become the sponsor of the initiative. Ensure that the executive understands that you will support them in their sponsorship activities and will keep them informed of the latest progress regarding the deployment of Agile so they appear both knowledgeable and confident.

Evaluate and Increase Executive Support

Evaluating executive support is an aspect of the inspect-and-adapt model of Agile. The person who is the acting Agile Champion and lead of the agile deployment should discreetly evaluate the executive's position of support. The relationship between the lead and the sponsor should be one of trust and support. To know what to adapt, this person should inspect (or in this case evaluate) the level of support. Then in the discussion with the executive, you can understand what can be done to help increase support.

The evaluation should be done discreetly and privately. Although you may share the list of support needs with the executive, you do not share your evaluation. It is only meant for you to understand the level of support so you can adapt along the way with the goal of increasing support. More important, the evaluation becomes a risk indicator of whether you are receiving the level of support you think you need for a successful transformation to Agile.

The purpose of the evaluation is to identify actions for the sponsor. The lead and the sponsor can work together to determine the best means to implement the actions. Assuming the actions will be carried out, this continues the notion of the inspect-and-adapt model to the benefit of the overall agile deployment.

You may also wish to evaluate the support of all key stakeholders who are within the organizational scope of the agile initiative. Any one of them can be a roadblock to the success of an agile transformation. Likewise, any one of them can become a strong Agile Champion.

Team Willingness

Willingness may be defined as a disposition to be accommodating and even enthusiastic. It implies that the willing person is doing something out of choice rather than under compulsion. When people are willing to do something, it means they are open-minded and receptive. In the context of being Agile, willingness means embracing the change toward Agile. It is important when you begin educating a team toward agile adoption that you gauge their level of willingness. Gauging their willingness can mean the difference between a successful or failed adoption.

The goal is to cultivate team members toward becoming Agile Champions and Workhorses. The good news is that many on an Agile Team are willing to move to Agile for multiple reasons. One reason is that they look at Agile as something new and exciting. Others realize that Agile provides business benefits to their personal growth and an increase in employment opportunities. Having Agile on the résumé is a benefit because many companies include it as one of the skill sets they are looking for.

Agile Pit Stop Agile Team members are willing to move to Agile for both singular and aggregate reasons. Some realize the benefit to their personal growth and an increase in employment opportunities.

Some of the Agile Team members may be Deniers and Deceivers. Some will take a wait-and-see position because they do not have a basis to form an opinion. This is why it is important to begin the education process to build team knowledge of Agile and then introduce the retrospective. The retrospective provides a platform for team members to speak honestly about challenges and seek opportunities for improvement.

Willingness Needed

As you consider willingness in relation to Agile, you need to direct the energy of the willing toward building knowledge and gaining experience in Agile. Though you cannot expect all of the team members to become Agile Champions, you would like them to at least become Workhorses. Some examples of the types of activities in which the Agile Deployment Lead or Agile Coach may observe willingness and building agile knowledge include the following:

- *Agile educational activities.* There is a willingness to take training and attend sessions to ramp up the teams toward the processes and practices they will be applying. As time goes on, education may include agile Q&A sessions and agile sharing sessions.

- *Agile process and practices deployment.* If using Scrum, there is a willingness to actively apply the Scrum events such as Sprint Planning, Daily Scrum, Sprint Review, and Sprint Retrospective.

- *Agile values and principles behavior.* Team members exhibit the behaviors that bring the principles to life, such as self-organizing teams, simplicity, reflection, technical excellence, and collaboration.

- *Team collaboration.* An Agile mindset means that no one succeeds unless everyone succeeds. Each team member willingly learns a secondary skill that can help the team complete a task or story. This may include a developer learning to run tests or tester participating in code reviews.

Although this is not a comprehensive list, the key is for you to articulate what areas can help you evaluate the levels of willingness needed for your agile transformation. For example, you may add individual Agile Principles to the list to determine willingness toward each. Once you have drafted this list, it is important that you share it with the teams within the organizational scope of your agile implementation. This evaluation of willingness begins the discussion that helps you understand their level of willingness.

Evaluate and Increase Team Willingness

Evaluating team willingness is a subset of the inspect-and-adapt model. To know what to adapt, conduct an inspection, or in this case evaluate team willingness. Then you know where you are and have a better understanding of how to improve.

Instead of a formal evaluation, it may be better to use a combination of observation techniques and discussion with team members as you introduce Agile. For example, as an Agile Deployment Lead, Agile Coach, or Scrum Master, observe an Agile Team when they take training and when they participate in the agile events. Such evaluation should be done discreetly and privately. It is only meant to gain an understanding of willingness so you can adapt along the way with the goal of improving willingness. More important, this evaluation becomes a risk indicator of whether there is willingness for a successful agile transformation.

You should consider each person on the team according to his or her willingness. The key is to find those who are more positive about Agile (Champions, Workhorses, Bandwagon Jumpers) and those who are more negative (Cowboys, Deceivers, and Deniers). This distinction can help you determine the best course of action to improve willingness.

On the positive side, provide those whom you recognize as Agile Champions the opportunity to gain more experience. They are already on your side, so make them your strong ally to help you improve willingness among other team members. Some approach Agile as Bandwagon Jumpers. They know enough to align with the trend within the company, but may know very little about Agile. Help them understand the benefits of Agile and provide them with working experience. The Workhorses already have a bit of agile experience. Give them more ownership opportunities. See if they would like to be groomed as Scrum Master or Agile Coach. The ownership opportunities will give them some leadership responsibilities within an agile context.

On the negative side, ask those whom you recognize as Cowboys if they are willing to get more serious about Agile. If so, provide them the opportunities to participate more fully. For Deniers, it can be beneficial to listen to the reasons they dismiss Agile. That input can help you work with them (if they are willing) to gain experience to at least become a Workhorse. Deceivers may be hard to identify because they may be initially exhibiting the characteristics of a Workhorse or Bandwagon Jumper. Continue to keep your eyes open. Over time, they may expose themselves. Keep in mind that even with your efforts, you may not be able to influence these latter three types into becoming willing members of the team.

In some cases, a team member might be willing to apply Agile Principles but unclear about what they are supposed to do. You may need to proceed with further education.

Breakfast of Champions

As a company approaches Agile, executive support and team willingness should be evaluated. The evaluation provides a platform for determining and initiating actions to increase support and improve willingness. Having support from executives and willingness from team members can be the difference between a successful or failed agile deployment. Whether it is an executive or team member, ultimately the goal is to create Agile Champions who are willing to support the agile deployment.

Treating Agile as a Transformation Project

If you do not manage culture, it manages you, and you may not even be aware of the extent to which this is happening.

—Edgar Schein

Moving to Agile is a move to a new culture, and cultural changes are difficult for a team or organization. To transform your organization to Agile, organizational values and individual behaviors need to change. Because of this I strongly recommend that a change toward Agile must be thought of as a transformation or change initiative, treated as a project, and actively managed. True to the spirit of Agile, using an inspect-and-adapt model can help you manage the change and adapt along the way based on the feedback you gain from those involved.

As a starting point for the transformation, those within the organizational scope want to know the *what* and *why* of the change. Chip and Dan Heath write: "If you want people to change, you must provide crystal clear direction [because what] looks like resistance is often a lack of clarity."[1] Start with establishing a vision or objectives about why you are implementing Agile. The objectives may center around customer and employee engagement (Chapter 4 and 5) or around wanting to work by the Agile Principles (Chapters 6 and 9). Along with objectives, add the organizational motivations for change to Agile (Chapter 8). The objectives and motivations begin the path toward clarity.

Agile Pit Stop   As you establish your agile direction, it is important to share objectives and motivations. Whether you call it a *project*, *program*, or *initiative*, the objectives and motivations help foster clarity around the effort.

Within the project context, there are other elements that you should apply that will help you manage the transformation. As illustrated in Figure 11-1, the rest of this chapter focuses on the element of treating Agile as a transformation project. This treatment includes writing objectives and motivations, understanding the scope of the effort, establishing a deployment team to help lead the effort, crafting a communication plan to convey progress, identifying suitable work, ordering the work in a deployment backlog, and then applying an inspect-and-adapt process to deploy Agile into the organizational scope.

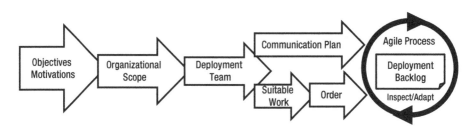

Figure 11-1. Project elements that help in an agile transformation effort

Scope of Agile Deployment

In planning an agile deployment, you need to define the organizational scope. Are you targeting the enterprise, part of the enterprise, a solution area made up of several products, or a single product team? Your target scope becomes the cornerstone for the project. The scope helps you understand the breadth of the effort and those with whom you will be working.

---

[1]Chip Heath and Dan Heath, *Switch: How to Change Things When Things Are Hard*, Crown Business, 2010

The less favored scenario is to apply Agile to just one project with the idea of abandoning it afterward. Although this may be beneficial for exercising agile processes and getting the release out, you may not receive the business benefits of Agile because you need behavior change at a much broader level. It is also a bit of an effort for the employees to adapt to a new approach only to abandon it. However, if the results are good, it can launch you into a more consistent use of Agile for the product.

A more favored scenario is applying Agile to a product line or product team. A product team represents a consistent group of people whose goal is to provide long-term business, development, and support for a product. This aligns with the notion that the longer you work as a team, the better your chances of forming strong working bonds and manifesting the attributes of teamwork. Also, when a person is aligned with a product for a long period of time, there is a tendency to have a greater sense of ownership and to be more invested in the success of the product. Alignment to the Agile Principles is more likely because it often takes time to align. Implementing at the product level allows Agile to be applied consistently and gain inspect-and-adapt benefits where feedback is used to build business value.

Agile Pit Stop   I have found it useful to deploy Agile within the context of a product team. A product is represented by a consistent team whose goal is to build and support the product, and they tend to have a greater sense of ownership and are invested into the long-term success of the product.

The enterprise level is where you may gain the most business benefits from Agile. Because Agile requires a culture change, aligning the whole enterprise to Agile values and principles helps everyone understand the need to adapt to gain the business benefits. To achieve an enterprise-level transformation to Agile, it is advantageous to combine the activities identified in the RICH model for deployment (Chapter 7) and add organizational-level aspects (Chapter 23). At the enterprise level, you can also leverage economies of scale and mini-mize similar efforts across multiple teams using a common deployment model, tools, and training across teams.

Agile Deployment Team

If Agile is to be taken seriously, it is good to form a team made up of the agile sponsor and Agile Champions within the organizational scope where you are looking to deploy Agile. The objective is to include a combination of agile experienced and committed personnel to help guide the organization and product teams. More important, it will help those adopting Agile to remove roadblocks.

If the agile adoption is focused on the whole organization or a large part of it, then the most senior-level executive within that scope should form a deployment team of Agile Coaches who have experience in enterprise-level agile deployments and Agile Champions within whose purview fall the products that are flagged for agile adoption. Even if the agile deployment is occurring on just one product team, at the very least, the Product Owner, Scrum Master, and the most senior manager within the scope of the product should become the Agile Deployment Team that focuses on the progress of the adoption.

Agile Deployment Backlog

As part of the project in which Agile will be deployed, it is important to establish a list of tasks that help the organization and product team deploy Agile. Creating a backlog helps the team understand the work involved and ensures key activities are performed to effect an Agile transformation. The activities for the backlog are found in Chapter 7, where the RICH deployment model is discussed and divided into *Readiness* tasks, *Implement* tasks, *Coach* tasks, and *Hone* tasks. These tasks can form the basis for your backlog. However, you do need to brainstorm and add other tasks that will help you adapt to Agile within your organizational scope. If there are multiple product teams adopting Agile, consider the backlog as a reusable element for each product team's needs.

Agile Process for Agile Deployment

In the spirit of Agile, I recommend that you apply an inspect-and-adapt approach in deploying Agile within your organization. Establish a deployment backlog with tasks discussed in Chapter 7. Consider a Scrum approach in your deployment. Starting with Sprint Planning, prioritize the tasks and extract a Sprint Backlog derived from the overall backlog. You then hold Daily Scrums (or at least twice a week) to gauge progress and learn and mitigate the risks. At the end of each sprint, you can review what tasks were completed and those not finished and why, as well as review any measures focused on moving to Agile. This is followed by a retrospective of what was learned and can be improved on. Applying a Scrum approach will help you deploy Agile, adapt to organizational needs, and learn one of Agile's processes along the way. It is also important to identify measures that can help you determine if you are being Agile and moving in the right direction. More details on measures can be found in Chapter 14.

Agile Communication Plan

When embarking on an agile journey, it is essential to strategize how to communicate about the deployment to those within the organizational scope you are targeting. It is equally important for senior management and executives to periodically provide public support for Agile. Once a communication plan is formulated, portions of this can be executed over time to keep employees aware of the progress and accomplishments of the deployment.

When preparing your communication plan, you will find that it is not a one-size-fits-all approach. It is important to identify the various elements of communication and then craft a communication plan for the organization's needs. The primary elements of a communication plan (with examples) include:

- Message types (objectives, motivations, milestones, opportunity, successes, reinforcement, tips)

- Audiences that will receive the communication (everyone, senior management, product teams)

- Types of communications (newsletters, briefings, presentations, focus groups)

- Types of communication channels (email, social media, face-to-face, internal TV, webinar, blog)

- Frequency of communications (daily, weekly, monthly, ad hoc)

Ultimately, the communication plan should include your strategy for communicating the various messages being encapsulated into certain communication types, in what communication channels, shared with what audience, and with what frequency. This keeps everyone informed and aware of the continued support for Agile.

Considering Work Suitable for Agile

I am often asked, "What type of work is best suited for Agile?" The short answer is: "Any work where you have uncertainty. The more uncertainty, the greater the need for Agile." This adage typically applies to new and unique products. Agile's inspect-and-adapt model helps identify the complexities of the idea while providing the team with an iterative opportunity to learn more quickly and adapt both their processes and the product direction.

Agile may also be applied to legacy products for which management has decided to reenergize the functionality. A good example is an older on-premise product to which management wants to have a cloud version or wishes to add mobile-enabled functionality. The challenge in applying Agile to legacy product teams is that there is inertia to continue as is. It will be challenging to change the attitudes of the team members who are Cowboys, Deceivers, or Deniers posing barriers to change. However, these challenges can be overcome if the benefits of Agile are compelling.

For teams that are focused on sustaining engineering and support work on an existing product, Kanban may be appropriate. If the work is interruption-driven and focused on defects, then applying a planned approach such as Scrum may not be possible. I have also seen Agile applied to products that are in great trouble and others that have great urgency.

Deciding Which Teams Go First

As you are working through the readiness tasks, there should be discussions around which teams will move to Agile and in what order. When embarking on the deployment of Agile, it is best to set up early successes. Early success can have a positive effect on the transformation to Agile. The positive messaging and local Agile Champions that are created will help influence others who want to move to Agile.

■ **Agile Pit Stop**   Identifying candidate product teams that align with the agile sweet-spot characteristics is a good place to start your deployment and give you experience.

It is best to target the candidate product teams where Agile has the highest rate of success. The information that follows highlights the team characteristics that represent the agile sweet spot. Keep in mind that you can be successful with Agile even though you do not align with the sweet-spot characteristics.

- *Agile team is willing.* This makes it easier to advocate for changes needed to use Agile effectively. It is critical that your first deployment of Agile occurs on a team that is very willing to adopt it. Having the Product Owner, Scrum Master, stakeholders, and Team willing to commit to Agile will make it easier to deploy. You learned how to gauge the team willingness to move to Agile in the Chapter 10.

- *Product team is small.* Most agile processes tend to favor smaller teams—typically no more than ten members. This way team members get to know each other and what they are working on well, which increases communication and team collaboration.

- *Team is colocated.* Project work benefits from face-to-face communication. Agile is no different. This allows for continuous and synchronous communication between team members and reduces the time of communication hand-offs.

- *Customer is readily available.* Customer availability and access ensures that the team has direct access to the customer, who continuously provides feedback on the functionality, leading to a product with strong business value to the customer.

- *Product Owner/Customer Representative is committed, readily available, and colocated with the team.* A committed and accessible PO ensures that the team can readily and interactively ask questions throughout the project regarding the requirements of the work at hand.

- *Application is interactive.* New products that are interactive and customer-facing can gain more advantages from Agile's inspect-and-adapt approach.

Aligning the Agile Deployment around Product Release Schedules

Although the Readiness activities can occur outside of a product release cycle, I have found that it is best to align Implementation activities with the beginning of a project or release life cycle for those product teams that are first applying Agile. This allows a just-in-time learning and implementation approach as teams begin adopting and adapting to the new processes, methods, practices, tools, and mindset.

You definitely want to avoid an agile implementation in the middle of a project's life cycle if you can help it because of the disruption that the change will bring. If the project is in crisis with some months to go prior to release, however, there may be a strong benefit in moving to Agile.

Project Framework to Transform

With Agile, you have the ability to educate, inspire, motivate, and transform. But this does not happen by accident. It should be a managed change with a starting point and a direction. It is beneficial to employees to treat a deployment of Agile as a project. It provides visibility and highlights the importance of Agile within the organization. Adding objectives and motivations behind them adds clarity to the deployment of Agile. Having an Agile Deployment Team of Agile Champions provides guidance as you work through the deployment backlog. A communication plan that is effectively executed keeps employees aware of the progress and accomplishments of the deployment. Applying an iterative approach to deployment activities shows a commitment to Agile.

The question is: How much focus and clarity do you need to provide your employees to transform your organization to Agile? If you do not manage the deployment of Agile, it will manage you, and you may not gain the business results you are looking for. Treating your Agile deployment as a transformation project can help you get there.

Adapting to Agile Roles and Responsibilities

Culture does not change because we desire to change it. Culture changes when the organization is transformed; the culture reflects the realities of people working together every day.

—Frances Hesselbein

When moving to an Agile world, there is a significant shift in roles and responsibilities. In a more traditional project, decisions are typically made in a hierarchical manner, and roles are specifically established to support this structure. If you are serious about moving to Agile and gaining an Agile mindset, then maintaining traditional roles will get in the way of this change. In the Agile world, there is a purposeful focus away from hierarchy and a strong focus on getting people to work together every day.

To get to a fully robust agile organization, it is important for everyone to play a role. Although managing a successful project from an Agile perspective requires three core roles, there are many others in the organization who must play a role to ensure success. Everyone from customers, executives, and management to sales, marketing, finance, and HR must understand the Agile mindset. It takes an organization to get to an agile culture.

Figure 12-1. Core roles and beyond—it takes an organization to get to an agile culture

Because it is takes a very concerted effort to adapt to an Agile culture and move away from a hierarchical culture, adapting to new roles that are not easily recognizable offers awareness that change is occurring and provides everyone with an opportunity to ask, "What is the change in the role and responsibilities?" As part of the RICH deployment model, gaining an understanding of Agile roles and then beginning the steps of implementing those roles is a good starting point. I have provided details on the Agile core roles and beyond. As you read this section, consider what your organization's product teams may look like.

Core Agile Roles

The core roles within Agile represent the group of people who are focused on directly building the product. Because Scrum is the primary Agile process that is used within many organizations, I align the Agile roles with Scrum. If you plan to follow a specific agile method, consider following the roles specified by that process.

Scrum Team

The Scrum Team is the group of professionals on a project who work together to build the customer value they have collectively committed to complete within a sprint. The Scrum Team is a self-organizing group with enough cross-functional skills and experience to build working software independently. The Scrum Team includes the roles of Scrum Master, Product Owner, and Development Team.

- The members are committed full-time team members, focused on completing the work for the product release.

- They are equally accountable and empowered to make decisions, determine sizes for stories, contribute in identifying risks, and articulate roadblocks.

- The team size is seven (± two) members with a healthy balance of development and test skills.

There will be other skills needed on the team focused on architecture, user experience, documentation, and configuration management. Though it would be good for these roles to be full-time, often there is not enough work involved for them to be continuously engaged.

Scrum Master

The Scrum Master acts as a facilitator and *servant leader* for the team and an enabler for Scrum, ensuring that it is understood and followed. This role may act as Coach to ensure that the Scrum roles, events, artifacts, and rules are understood and implemented effectively on the Scrum Team. The attributes of servant leadership include listening, empathy, healing, awareness, persuasion, and foresight.[1] It is important for a soon-to-be Scrum Master to read more on what is expected of a servant leader.

Agile Pit Stop A Scrum Master should have the attributes of a servant leader, which include listening, empathy, healing, awareness, persuasion, and foresight.

A Scrum Master facilitates the Scrum events. This does not mean that they direct the activities but that they ensure the events are occurring along with the behaviors of an Agile mindset. In addition, the Scrum Master removes roadblocks or finds the right people to remove roadblocks to ensure team progress. The Scrum Master also does the following:

- Helps the Product Owner enact effective backlog grooming techniques.

- Establishes and produces the Sprint Burndown, velocity, and other metrics that help the team improve.

---

[1]Larry C. Spears and Michele Lawrence (eds.). *Practicing Servant-Leadership: Succeeding through Trust, Bravery, and Forgiveness.* Jossey-Bass, 2004.

- Facilitates Sprint Planning, the Daily Scrum, and the Sprint Retrospective.

- Facilitates the Sprint Review with the Product Owner.

- Manages risks, issues, and dependencies for the team.

- Gauges the health and well-being of the teams, ensuring they are following a sustainable pace.

- Builds a trusting environment where problems can be raised without blame with emphasis on healing and problem solving.

- Liaises with architecture and operations when there are dependencies to systems and infrastructure.

- Acts as a shepherd for the team, moving them down the general path instead of telling them what to do.

- Coaches and trains the team on the agile behaviors and Scrum events, including how to self-organize.

Anyone who is desires to be a Scrum Master should take the *Certified Scrum Master* (CSM) training. This will help them understand their role, events, rules, and artifacts and gain understanding of the servant leader role they will be playing. The CSM training does not make you a seasoned and experienced Scrum Master. It is the first step in a lifetime of truly understanding what the role of the Scrum Master is really about.

Who Best Plays the Scrum Master Role

As teams consider adopting Agile, one of the most important decisions is who can make a good Scrum Master. Because the Scrum Master is the promoter of Agile values and principles, it is critical that this role be filled with someone who is dedicated to implementing the Agile mindset.

So who makes the best Scrum Master? The short answer is that anyone can become a Scrum Master if they believe in the Agile values and principles and can act as a servant leader. Some will ask if there is a traditional role that plays the Scrum Master the best. Here are some options.

Project Manager as Scrum Master

The traditional role that seems the obvious choice to play a Scrum Master is that of project manager. On the positive side, a project manager has experience in being part of a team and so may already have a trusting relationship with the team. Some project managers have gained facilitative skills to lead work in a nondirective yet influential manner. Many already have the skills and the insight into an organization to appropriately remove roadblocks. On the negative side, some project managers had success using command-and-control attributes and the more traditional project management practices, which will not work well in an Agile environment. It can also be hard for some project managers to eliminate their traditional mindset of detailed project planning and control.

Functional Manager as Scrum Master

Quite possibly the most problematic role to play the Scrum Master is a functional manager (aka *line manager* or *technical manager*). Anyone who has played a role in which they have successfully directed people must make a major concerted effort to remove their command-and-control behavior. On the positive side, they may have skills and insight into appropriately navigating the organization and the ability to remove roadblocks. On the negative side, because they have been a manager of a team, they may have issues with the team trusting them as a peer because they are used to being judged by managers. A functional manager may have been successfully using command-and-control attributes. These will not work well in an Agile environment. They must strive to remove their directive attributes and instead build facilitative skills.

Technical Lead as Scrum Master

One of the better traditional roles to play the Scrum Master is a technical lead (aka *QA lead* or *development lead*). By *lead*, I do not mean a manager who has direct reports, but someone who is considered a lead by his or her peers and has no interest in directing people. Such people have a balance of leadership skills while wanting to get the work done. On the positive side, they have technical experience in the product and their specific field (development, QA, technical writing, etc.) and so can appropriately aid the work by providing meaningful insight without direction or coercion. They have experience at being part of the team, and thus may already have a trusting relationship with their peers. On the negative side, they may have to build their facilitative skills to lead work in a nondirective yet influential manner. Also, they may not yet have the skills or insight into an organization to appropriately remove externally facing roadblocks.

The best answer to the question of what role best plays the Scrum Master is not a role at all. Instead, it is which person best exemplifies the Agile values and principles, possesses the attributes of servant leadership, has a good grasp of navigating his or her organization, and can help remove roadblocks.

Product Owner

The *Product Owner* (PO) represents the voice of the customer. He or she is the customer liaison and is responsible for understanding what is considered valuable from the multiple customers who may need or are using a product. The PO must straddle the responsibilities of being continuously available to customers to identify value while being continuously available to the Development Team to communicate customer value to them. Most POs I have worked with find this both challenging and quite rewarding when implemented well.

The PO is the owner of the Product Backlog, where value is initially expressed (e.g., as requirements). A PO must digest the various customer needs and stakeholder demands and establish a meaningful list of user stories into the backlog for the development team to work from. A key skill that the PO needs to acquire is the ability to decompose large requirements or epics into stories that can be built within the time-boxed period of the sprint.

The most challenging role of the PO is to rank the Product Backlog items according to value. As depicted in Figure 12-2, a PO talks with multiple existing customers, potential customers, sales, marketing, management, and more, all of whom are attempting to get their need highest in the ranking. A PO is beholden to many but is the final arbiter, and everyone must respect the PO decisions. This can be quite challenging in cultures where a more hierarchical and command-and-control approach rules. The PO also does the following:

- Parses customer problems and needs into meaningful requirements that highlight business value.

- Grooms, prioritizes, and ranks the Product Backlog items.

- Removes roadblocks and rules on issues where disagreements arise.

- Coordinates the Sprint Review, invites customers and stakeholders, solicits customer feedback, and updates the backlog with feedback provided by the customers.

- Attends Sprint Planning and provides details, answers, and clarification to the Development Team.

- Adapts requirements when customer needs and market conditions change, to ensure that what is built and delivered aligns with customer needs.

- Works with sales and marketing to get their requirements into the backlog.

Figure 12-2. Product Owner beholden to many

Who Best Plays the Product Owner Role?

The PO role is very important to a successfully running Agile team. In fact, when a team considers adopting Agile, deciding who will be the PO is critical to gaining the benefits of Agile, owing to the importance of the customer value and validation activities to ensuring that the team is building something the customer actually wants. So the question arises: is there a traditional role that plays the PO the best?

Business Analyst as Product Owner

What does a traditional *business analyst* (BA) do? A BA is someone who analyzes business needs, works with stakeholders to understand their needs, and recommends solutions that meet these needs. At a deeper level, a BA focuses on eliciting, documenting, and managing requirements. The BA act as a liaison between business and technical groups. It is because of the work a BA already does and in particular the focus on requirements and the liaison role between the business and technical groups that this role a good candidate to be the Product Owner. However, a traditional BA may not have the experience in working in an agile manner. He or she may not have experienced the continuous requirements elicitation process (per the sprint cadence) and Sprint Reviews to gain feedback, so skills and experience in these areas would have to be earned. The BA would need training in the agile process used and the PO role.

Product Manager as Product Owner

What does a traditional *product manager* do? A product manager examines the market, the competition, and customer needs and then establishes the product direction that is considered valuable to the market and the customers. A good product manager focuses on the financial considerations including the *return on investment*. In addition, the product manager is involved in the requirements gathering and management process. Because of their work focused on what is valuable to the customer, a product manager makes a good candidate for the PO role. However, a traditional product manager may have little experience in the Agile space. Skills and experience in the continuous requirements elicitation process and Sprint Review areas may have to be built. A product manager may need training in the PO role and agile process used.

Project Manager as Product Owner

What does a traditional *project manager* do? A project manager is responsible for planning and managing a project from the beginning to closure. He or she focuses on project costs, schedule, and scope. A project manager may also help build the project objectives, help manage the requirements management process, and manage project risks, issues, and dependencies. Because there is little customer involvement within the project manager role, this person may not be a good fit for the PO role. Although there are some abilities a project manager brings that can help in the PO role, there is very little direct customer focus, which is a big part of being the PO.

Those who have played either a traditional BA or product manager effectively may have the best chance of becoming an effective PO. In general, anyone who has played a role in which they work with customers to collect needs and then work with teams to build products or solutions that meet those needs can became an effective PO. I suggest that anyone who is interested in becoming a PO should consider taking training, reading related books and articles, and gaining guidance in this area with an Agile Coach to help them better understand this role and the activities they will need to perform to play this role effectively.

Development Team

The Development Team is a cross-functional group of engineers who build the product functionality. The team should be made up of personnel with different skill sets. This means that the team has the capabilities to build the product without having to rely on others outside of the team. In Scrum, the team size is typically seven, plus or minus two members. If you have too few, you may not have all of the cross-functional skills you need on a team. If the team becomes too large, it becomes too hard to self-organize.

The skills within the Development Team include but are not limited to analysis, design, programming, configuration management, testing, and technical writing. Because this team will be working closely together, the various members must learn to collaborate and cooperate well. To build this collaboration,

Development Team members must respect each other's values and opinions. They do this by breaking user stories into tasks together during Sprint Planning, crafting and honing done criteria, and establishing acceptance criteria together as a team.

Agile Pit Stop   The development team must learn how to decompose stories into tasks, which they can build into working software within a sprint. They must respect each other's values and opinions to become a collaborative self-organizing team.

Members of the Development Team must be committed to the work as well as empowered and self-organized so they can make the best decisions to move forward because they are the closest to the challenges and work to be accomplished. I prefer to call this team the "engineering" team because "Development" Team seems to imply that it is only development-focused, whereas it is really a cross-functional team.

A key skill that Development Team members need to acquire is the ability to decompose stories into tasks. This can be difficult when you are used to working with large requirements and never having to break them down. Team members must also have the ability to build working software within a time-boxed period aligned with a sprint. This can be hard for some team members who have previously had the luxury of having months to build software.

Those with a testing focus must have the ability to help the PO in crafting acceptance criteria. The testers on the team may identify techniques such as *test-driven development* and initially have the ability to rapidly build test cases for the user stories at the same time that developers are building functionality from the user stories. Often, I see too much focus put on development and too little on user experience, testing, configuration management, and technical writing. There will be a realization that all capabilities in good measure are needed to complete working software within a sprint. Development Team members also do the following:

- Participate in the Daily Scrum, communicating progress and roadblocks.

- Engage in Sprint Planning, gaining clarification, decomposing stories into tasks, and sizing the stories.

- Assist in the Sprint Review, demoing working software on behalf of the Product Owner.

- Contribute to the Sprint Retrospective, identifying what went well and what could have gone better, and committing to actions for improvement.

- Focus on the daily work of converting stories into functional working software.

- Maintain a sustainable pace of work to avoid burnout.

- Apply the quality criteria known as "definition of done" as they build their working software .

It is strongly recommended that each Development Team member has both primary and secondary skills to volunteer on any task that needs to be completed (realizing the true meaning of *team*). The goal is for the team to think of themselves in a more holistic way to optimize throughput and continually increase their velocity.

Agile Roles beyond Core

Gaining the business benefits of Agile implies that everyone within an organization plays a role. In addition to the core roles, other roles can significantly contribute to success within an agile context.

Customer

The customer is the primary driver of business value. The customer role represents buyers and users of the product. This role represents the business interests who are paying for the product. The customer provides business knowledge, input, and feedback to the Product Owner to help determine priority and rank order of the stories and goal setting for a release.

The most important responsibilities the customer enacts are contributing requirements and attending the Sprint Review to provide the feedback that helps the PO adapt the product toward the direction of value. The customer also contributes in establishing acceptance criteria.

There are several customer target groups. There are *current customers* and *potential customers*. Current customers are buyers of your product, must be treated well, and are your highest priority. Within the potential customer group, there are the potential buyers and the browsers. As you identify customer value, knowing what the current customer wants, you will keep them satisfied and loyal. Knowing what potential customers want helps you increase revenue and grow your business. (Learn more about customer target groups in Chapter 17.)

■ **Agile Pit Stop**   Customers are the drivers defining business value. As you build products, you must consider value from current customers and potential customers.

It may be challenging to get the customer fully engaged on a continuous basis. Most customers have been used to providing requirements up front and not revisiting the product until the user acceptance period at the end. Agile asks for continuous interaction. Finally, if no customer or customer representatives are available, then you are really not performing Agile. How can you adapt to customer needs when customers are not available?

Executives/Senior Management

Executives and senior management have key roles to play if they want to transform the organization to Agile. The key role for the most senior-level executive within the scope is to become the sponsor of the Agile initiative. They must buy in to the Agile values and principles and understand the behavioral changes that are needed for an effective transition to Agile.

They should know that those within their organization will only take Agile seriously based on the executive level of visible support. They should periodically provide public support for Agile. Once a communication plan is formulated, portions can be executed over time to keep employees aware of the progress and accomplishments of the deployment. Further discussion on communication planning and the sponsor role is found in Chapter 11.

Part of the executive or senior management role as sponsor is to get introduced to the Agile values and principles and educated in the business benefits Agile can bring, including more revenue for the company. They should understand the language that Agile brings and be conversant in agile values and principles. Executives should look at their own behavior and align it with the Agile mindset.

A key responsibility is ensuring their staff, middle management, and leads understand that the organization is moving away from command-and-control and toward a self-organizing team model. Executives should act as mentors to their staff as they help management adapt to Agile. It is strongly recommended for executives to bring in Agile Coaches to help teams not only move to Agile but also help their staff shift to the behaviors that exemplify an Agile mindset. Executives may also need to be involved with making adjustments to staff members who cannot make the switch away from command-and-control. This can be hard to do, but if they don't, then those around them will not take the change seriously.

An executive should learn how to read agile metrics and measures of success. Gaining an understanding of Sprint Burndowns, release burnups, value capture, release frequency, Agile Mindset, Values, and Principles (MVP) Advisor, and other Agile-related metrics can help ensure the organization is moving in the right direction. Further discussion of agile metrics can be found in Chapters 13 and 14.

Executive should also initiate an effort to adapt the employee compensation model toward agile behaviors being sought and away from rewarding command-and-control attributes. To change behavior, they should recognize the behavior they want to change, evaluate the reward system, and adapt it to the behavior that is needed for Agile. Without aligning the reward system to Agile, you will not get to behavior you want.

Agile Pit Stop   Remember, if you don't align the reward system toward agile behaviors, you will only get the behavior you reward, not the behavior you want.

The executive should form an Agile Deployment Team of Agile Coaches who have experience in the scope of the deployment that is needed and Agile Champions within that scope of the organization that is committed to adopting Agile. More information on an Agile Deployment Team follows.

Executives should also be invited to attend the Sprint Reviews of their top products within their organizational scope. They will gain a genuine sense of progress and see actual working functionality of their products.

Middle Management

Middle management are critical to the success of an effective Agile deployment because they are the lynchpin between the executive's vision for Agile and middle management's willingness to allow Agile to thrive on a team. If they are engaged and buy into Agile, then the change may succeed. Even when executives and senior management buy in, if middle management does not do likewise, they can block a team's ability to succeed with Agile.

Middle management is often made up of direct managers of many of those on Agile teams. Many are functional managers who are used to directing and assigning the work to their team members. If they don't understand their role in the new order or feel threatened by the change, they may become Deceivers or Deniers. Because of this, it is critical that middle managers are educated on Agile at the same time their teams are.

Middle management must learn to gently back away from their functional leadership and act more as servant leaders who trust their teams, help them remove roadblocks, and support the agile practices. Their direct reports are now on Agile teams, so they cannot assign them any work. They may attend the Sprint Review to see the working functionality, which is better than a status report in gaining a sense of progress.

Often middle management have less to do in an Agile world. The good news is that they may consider options such as changing their role to resource management, where they manage more people but do not own an organizational functional area. They may consider a Product Owner role if they have been engaged in collecting requirements and interacting with customers. Although this role should no longer be managerial, a PO helps shape the product by collecting and grooming the requirements.

A big adjustment and learning opportunity for middle management is to help Agile teams become self-organizing. This requires a change in behavior. Middle management must also learn how to establish the concept of bounded authority where teams can make their own decisions, organize, and commit to their own work. It does not mean that teams can do whatever they want. The balance is that managers keep limited responsibilities to provide a vision and support their staff, while allowing teams the ownership of their work.

Agile Pit Stop   Management have bounded authority whereby they provide their teams a vision and the ability to be self-organizing, so that communication and trust can thrive.

Management needs to allow the employees to feel that they own the team decision making and can make their own commitments to the work they do at the team level. Management must also be willing to be transparent about what is going on in the organization and be willing to communicate this information to the team.

Agile Project Manager

If a project is made up of more than one Agile team, then there may be a need for an *Agile Project Manager* (APM). An APM does not play the tradition project manager role within an agile framework. There is little need to create a large project plan because planning occurs every sprint, when a Sprint Backlog is used as the artifact to identify and manage the work.

An APM can help the multiple Agile teams associated with one project in three ways. First, the APM can help manage risks and dependencies across teams and help teams remove roadblocks. This can be in the form of a project Scrum of Scrums. Although there are various forms of Scrum of Scrums, the basic version is a periodic meeting among Scrum Masters and Product Owners to discuss project progress and dependencies across the teams, resolve issues, and mitigate risks. The APM can be used to help provide support for Scrum of Scrum sessions.

Second, an APM can provide project-level reporting that may be required by management. This may involve providing a release burnup from the teams. The challenge an APM may have is that Agile teams work very lean from a reporting perspective, whereas those on the outside of the project will expect more traditional project-reporting detail. The APM must educate those outside of the Agile team toward understanding metrics geared toward Agile.

Third, the APM can be the touch point between the product team and the IT governance within the organization. When an organization has a governance process that approves projects, the APM can help the Scrum Masters and Product Owners pull the necessary vision information together for discussion within the governance sessions.

Agile Coach

The key attributes of an effective Agile Coach include experience in deploying Agile, in organizational change, in playing agile roles on a team, and in working with the business benefits of Agile.

If you don't know what an agile culture and effectively running agile practices look like, then how do you learn to recognize it? This is one of the key values of having an Agile Coach to help you. A Coach possesses deep agile deployment knowledge to ensure the product teams are implementing Agile effectively. This includes helping teams both mechanically *do Agile* and behaviorally *be Agile*.

Another benefit of an Agile Coach is that they help sustain the adoption of Agile practices and mindset. Agile training provides initial knowledge for teams. However, team members can easily revert back to traditional habits. An Agile Coach reinforces agile values and principles and ensures that the team continues both the expected practices and behaviors.

An Agile Coach can provide consistency when multiple teams are adopting Agile at the same time. The Agile Coach also understands both the short-term and long-term pitfalls that can occur when a hierarchical organization is moving to Agile. They can help mitigate the challenges ahead of time.

■ **Non-Agile Pit Stop** A coach can help an organization avoid the following situations: "We don't need to document anything because we are Agile"; "We don't need any management support because we are self-organized"; and "We can't tell you what we're building until the end of the project because we are using Agile."

A special quality of a great Agile Coach is the ability to enable a team to achieve Agile while being "behind the curtain." Although the coach will motivate and influence the team, he or she wants the team to feel the ownership of the change to Agile. Other talents that a coach should bring to an Agile team are the ability to be a mentor, a facilitator, teacher, problem solver, conflict navigator, and collaboration conductor.[2]

Agile Deployment Team

If Agile is being adopted across all or a large part of an organization, it may make sense to form an Agile Deployment Team to help guide the desired transformation to Agile. This team may also be called the Agile Leadership Team or Agile Transformation Team.

This team should be made up of the sponsor, who is typically the top executive within that organization scope; an Agile Coach, who has experience in enterprise-level deployments; and local Agile Champions within the organizational scope where you are looking to deploy Agile. The Agile Coach may act as the Agile Deployment Team lead. The objective is to include a combination of Agile-experienced, enthusiastic, and committed folks to help guide the organization and product teams toward Agile and remove roadblocks.

When you find yourself in the situation where there are some in your company wanting to adopt Agile, or if it is already happening in an ad hoc manner, an Agile Deployment Team can help lead the organizational change. Michael Spayd recommends that an "effective change team" be established.[3] The combination of Agile Coaches with local Agile leadership can provide the framework for Agile adoption but still allows for adaptability and decision points so teams feel ownership of their working process.

What are some of the benefits of the Agile Deployment Team? This team can help you establish and manage the following:

- Agile deployment roadmap: design activities to help a product team deploy Agile based on the Ready, Implement, Coach, and Hone (RICH) Deployment Model (discussed in Chapter 7) with emphasis on readiness.

- Agile framework and practices: collaboratively establish an adaptable set of agile methods and practices with the rest of the organization.

---

[2]Lyssa Adkins. *Coaching Agile Teams*. Addison-Wesley Professional, 2010.
[3]Michael Spayd, "Evolving Agile in the Enterprise: Implementing XP on a Grand Scale," Agile Development Conference, 2003.

- Agile training: establish a common set of Agile training aimed at various levels of the organization, which can reduce the cost of using multiple vendors.

- Agile communities: establish an enterprise agile website with links to resources and Agile communities.

- Agile coaching: provide coaching to product teams across the enterprise that need it most. Coaching can significantly increase Agile adoption success and ensure teams do not regress into traditional habits.

- Agile measure of success: establish a common set of agile success measures to see what progress is being made in the Agile adoption within the company.

- Agile challenges *point of contact* (PoC): establish a PoC to manage internal challenges via the website, email, and Agile FAQ allowing for mitigation and awareness.

- Agile vendor liaison PoC: use a PoC for managing relationships with the Agile vendors to ensure the organization gains leverage from negotiations for volume discounts of Agile-related materials and tools.

Finally, when a team is ready to go Agile, it can be comforting to know there is ready support for their deployment. Conversely, it is problematic when the employees are seeing wide variations of "agile" being deployed, with little support surrounding it. It can be a benefit to have an Agile Deployment Team with Agile Coaches and local Agile Champions available to help you navigate to a successful adoption of Agile.

More Roles

Within an enterprise perspective, peripheral roles like sales and marketing, finance, and human resources should be brought into the agile fold. Although they do not need to work in an agile manner, they should embrace the same concepts of leadership, self-organizing teams, collaboration, and eliminating waste.

Sales and marketing are actively involved with bringing a product to market. They can work with the Product Owner by contributing requirements and gaining clarification to ensure you are building something the customer needs. They need to understand that the Product Backlog and prioritization are owned the Product Owner. Also, they need to learn that requirements should be funneled to the Product Owner and avoid making commitments without the Product Owner's agreement. Those in sales and marketing of should consider attending the Sprint Review to gain an understanding of what the new functionality does as well as the progress being made.

Within a company going Agile, the finance organization must enable the level of agility and flexibility that is asked from the people and the agile processes. Finance should be flexible in understanding that while they can still manage to cost, the scope is the important variable for delivering customer value.

If performance objectives are part of the organization's processes, then it is important for HR to establish a performance review process that supports team goals. This helps support the principle of self-organizing teams. You will learn more about adapting performance reviews for Agile teams in Chapter 23.

Product Team and Organizational Restructuring

It is best to apply Agile at the product level. The effort to move a team to Agile may not be cost-effective on a single project because a project typically has a short life and once it is done, the practices and disciplines gained may be lost. However, if you make the commitment of moving to Agile at a product level, then each project can get the benefit of Agile and subsequent projects can become more effective at using Agile over time. It takes time to fully grasp the concepts of Agile and apply them effectively. When a team gets a chance to learn Agile together and then hone it over time, their productivity and accuracy in sizing improves, particularly as retrospectives are implemented and the resulting improvement ideas are put into action.

Bringing the Agile mindset to organization hierarchy often requires a restructuring of the organization toward a flatter organization. The effect on a traditional organization is twofold. First, there is a reorganization to Agile teams. Agile motivates a move from functional groups into Agile teams as illustrated in Figure 5-3. For example, Scrum Teams are designed to remove hierarchy and gain collective commitment, leading to flatter organizations.

Second, because of the agile principle of self-organizing teams, there tends to be less of a need for management who typically direct the team. The move to Agile teams involves moving away from a single point of leadership, often a functional manager, to a flat team model in which everyone is a leader when it is appropriate and no single person tells others what to do. The group that is affected the most is middle management. But as already mentioned, there are options for middle managers who may be affected depending on the skills and experience they may have.

Although some of the structural change is driven by self-organizing teams, other change is driven by who prioritizes the work. In an agile framework, the person who prioritizes the work moves from functional management role to the Product Owner, who is the key contributor in making Agile successful. The Product Owner contributes insight from the marketplace, customers, product roadmap, financial implications, current negotiations, and other details.

This broader view and additional information ensures that the product teams build the right product.

What Does Your Team Look Like?

Everyone within the organization should be focused on understanding and delivering customer value every step of the way. Getting to that value-oriented mindset is critical to the success of Agile. It takes teamwork to get there, and adapting roles and responsibilities toward Agile helps in making this shift. If an organization is serious, then the top executive within the organizational scope should become the sponsor. Having an Agile Coach and Agile Deployment Team can help you adapt product teams and involve management. The question to you is who will become the Product Owner, who will be trained to become the Scrum Masters, and how will you balance your teams to ensure they have a healthy balance of cross-functional skills? Understanding agile roles and responsibilities and the change in behavior that it brings will move you in the right direction.

Evaluating Agile, Engineering, and Team Capability

Sometimes it is good to know the situation you are getting yourself into.

—Mario Moreira

When starting an Agile deployment effort, it is advantageous to know your starting point. Otherwise, it will be hard to measure how far you have come. This is why I am a fan of baselining the current situation. By this, I mean evaluating the current level of agility, engineering, and team capability. As part of the RICH readiness and deployment model, this allows you to know your starting point, information on where you are strong and where you can improve, and input to prepare an adaptive roadmap for achieving your Agile transformation goal. Important questions that help you gauge your agility are those that help you understand your level of *doing Agile* and *being Agile*, with the latter being much more important. Here are two such questions:

- *How do you know you have adopted agile processes and practices? This question asks if teams are mechanically "doing Agile" (e.g., applying Scrum). The answer captures whether the mechanical elements of Agile are being applied.*

- *How do you know you are Agile?* This question asks if teams are "being Agile" (if their behavior and culture align with Agile values and principles). The answer captures whether the values and principles of Agile are being applied.

There are two more questions whose answers will help you understand your starting point:

- *What is the current state of your engineering practices?* This question asks how effectively the team is currently applying engineering practices. If current practices are poor, it can affect your ability to do Agile. The answer helps you know if you have hurdles to overcome.

- *What is the current level of Agile experience and interest?* This question asks how experienced the team is in applying Agile. The level of experience helps you adapt training and other elements of a deployment.

Now let's delve more deeply into these questions and what such a survey would look like to help you gain answers and establish your baseline.

Agile Practices Adoption

The Agile Practices Adoption survey helps you answer the question, *"How do you know you have adopted the agile processes and practices?"* This survey tool provides visibility into a team's adoption level of the agile process and practices that they are applying. These data can be collected via self-survey from team members or through observation by an Agile Coach. The benefit of collecting data around Agile adoption is that you can understand how well your team is "doing Agile." The results are only for the team to gauge their progress and identify actions for improvement.

To construct a survey, identify the agile practices you want the team to adopt. Then build a set of statements that each team member rates that help you know if the practices are being adopted. Collect the responses and tally for results. Figure 13-1 provides an example of the results from a Sprint Planning adoption survey.

Sprint Planning	Individual Team Member Ratings (1 - 5)									Averages	Action
Sprint goal(s) established	5	4	4	4	5	4	5	4	4	4.3	
All Team members attended	3	4	3	3	4	3	4	4	3	3.4	Get India resource to particpate
Team Velocity used for planning	2	3	4	2	2	3	3	2	3	2.7	Prepare educate on velocity
PO identifies stories for sprint	4	4	5	5	4	5	4	5	4	4.4	
PO ranks stories by business value	4	4	4	3	4	5	4	4	4	4.0	
PO prepares acceptance criteria	2	2	2	3	2	3	2	2	2	2.2	Educate PO and add to grooming
Team scrub stories for details	4	5	5	4	4	5	4	4	5	4.4	
Team sizes each story	4	4	4	5	5	5	4	4	4	4.3	
Team commits to work	4	4	5	5	5	5	5	5	4	4.7	
Averages	3.6	3.8	4.0	3.8	3.9	4.2	3.9	3.8	3.7	3.6	

Figure 13-1. Sprint Planning adoption survey to determine what the team thinks their level of adoption is in applying elements of Sprint Planning

In this example, "Team commits to work" is the most highly rated, and "PO prepares acceptance criteria" is the lowest rated. From these results, the team may initiate actions for improvement. A survey like this can be periodically conducted to help the team understand if they are moving in the right direction. From these same data, a trend metric on Sprint Planning adoption over time may be created. See Figure 13-2 for an example.

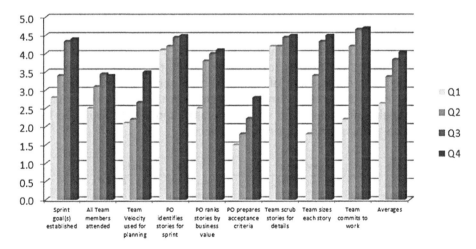

Figure 13-2. Sprint Planning adoption trend to observe direction of adoption

Notice how "Team Velocity used for planning" was poorly rated in Q1, Q2, and Q3. However, in Q4, the rating increased because after the Q3 survey, the team initiated an improvement action to get educated on the usage of velocity. The periodic results can also be an input into a Sprint Retrospective.

Agile Mindset, Values, and Principles Advisor

The Agile Mindset, Values, and Principles (MVP) Advisor helps you answer the question, *"How do you know you are Agile?"* A similar question is, "How do I know if I or my team are 'being Agile'?" The results of this survey provide visibility into the behavioral transformation toward the Agile principles. To create this visibility, each team member self-rates the individual Agile Principles based on what they see in practice, what they personally believe, and what they think the organization believes. For organizational-level visibility, this survey should include input from all of stakeholders and team members to ensure broad coverage.

Agile Pit Stop If you can evaluate yourself on the principles, you can get an idea of whether you are aligned with the Agile Principles and thus the Agile mindset.

The Agile MVP Advisor survey comes in three parts: principle, evidence of principle in action, and rating area. As you prepare the survey, there should be a discussion of what evidence you would expect to see to bring more objectivity to the process. If you can evaluate your situation highly on the principles, this can give you an idea of whether you are aligned with the Agile Principles and thus whether you have the Agile mindset.

Figure 13-3 is an abbreviated example of the Agile MVP Advisor focusing on just four of the Agile Principles. It is recommended to administer this survey prior to starting a deployment of Agile and then periodically to gauge if you are moving toward the behaviors that align with the Agile principles. The results can help you understand where you align and where you need focus. It can also be an input into a Sprint Retrospective.

Principle	Evidence	Rating									
Satisfying the Customer	Customer profiles Customer surveys Sprint reviews Acceptance Criteria	In Practice	1	2	3	4	5	6	7	8	9	10
		Your Belief	1	2	3	4	5	6	7	8	9	10
		Org Belief	1	2	3	4	5	6	7	8	9	10
Business and Developers work Together	Cross-functional team Dedicated Product Owner Team/PO in Sprint Planning Team/PO in Sprint Review	In Practice	1	2	3	4	5	6	7	8	9	10
		Your Belief	1	2	3	4	5	6	7	8	9	10
		Org Belief	1	2	3	4	5	6	7	8	9	10
Technical Excellence	Learning Plans Engineering practices Done Criteria Technical sharing	In Practice	1	2	3	4	5	6	7	8	9	10
		Your Belief	1	2	3	4	5	6	7	8	9	10
		Org Belief	1	2	3	4	5	6	7	8	9	10
Self-organizing Teams	Cross-functional teams Iterative and incremental Assertive and willing Boundary of authority	In Practice	1	2	3	4	5	6	7	8	9	10
		Your Belief	1	2	3	4	5	6	7	8	9	10
		Org Belief	1	2	3	4	5	6	7	8	9	10

Figure 13-3. Abreviated version of the Agile Mindset Values and Principles (Agile MVP) Advisor, a survey to gain an understanding of how Agile you are

Revisit Chapters 6 and 9 to refresh your insight into all of the values and principles to establish a full survey framework to determine whether your team
or organization is being Agile.

Having implemented various Agile survey mechanisms in the past, I am a strong
proponent of sharing only the aggregate results and sharing them only with
those who have taken the survey. No individual results should be shared. If a
product team takes the survey, then the aggregate results go only to the team.

If an organization takes the survey, then the whole organization may review
the aggregate results. To gain the business benefits of Agile, the whole organization should align with the values and principles. With this in mind, it is
beneficial for the whole organization to take this survey. An Agile-minded
product team that exists in a hierarchical organization will suffer from this
external partnership with the rest of the organization. In other words, if
those outside the product team still operate in a hierarchical and big-upfront
manner, it can affect the team's ability to align with the Agile values and
principles. You may also wish to periodically take this survey to form a trend
metric, which will help you understand if the product team or organization
is moving toward the direction of transforming their behavior toward Agile
values and principles.

Engineering Practices

The engineering practices survey helps you answer the question, "*What is the
current state of your engineering practices?*" Although applying agile practices
is important, the level of engineering practices applied is equally important.
When you are considering a transition to Agile, you may find that the current
engineering practices are problematic. This is why I recommend that prior to
implementing Agile, you learn what is working well and what can be improved
within the context of engineering practices.

This knowledge has two benefits. The first benefit is that you will better understand
the engineering challenges on the team prior to moving to Agile. This baseline
determination prevents the Agile deployment from being blamed for an existing
engineering problem, and it allows you to more clearly understand these
challenges so that they can be addressed as part of the agile transition. The second
benefit is that if you find that you have poor practices in engineering areas, you
may want to address them before moving to or in parallel with Agile.

To construct a survey, identify engineering practices that you deem important
to technical excellence. Then build a set of statements that are self-rated by
team members to help you verify if the engineering practices are being
followed. Collect the responses and tally for results.

Figure 13-4 provides an example of the results of a state-of-engineering survey. In this example, the team applies version control, architecture, coding standards, and refactoring practices effectively. However, there is significant opportunity for improvement in applying code reviews, unit tests, and regression testing. From these results, the team may initiate actions for improvement.

Engineering Practices	Individual Team Member Ratings (1 -5)									Averages	Action
Design elements are established and applied (e.g., call to action, breadcrumbs applied, etc)	3	4	4	4	3	3	4	4	4	3.7	
Architecture practices defined and applied (frameworks, processes, non-functional, etc)	3	4	5	4	4	5	3	4	4	4.0	
Version Control used to version code and checked in nightly	5	5	5	5	5	5	4	5	4	4.8	
Effective branching and merging strategy is applied.	3	4	4	3	4	3	4	4	3	3.6	
Effective code review practices are applied	2	3	3	2	2	2	3	2	3	2.4	Implement code review practice
Coding standards exist and applied	4	4	5	5	4	5	4	5	4	4.4	
Refactoring work is part of development	4	5	5	4	4	5	4	4	5	4.4	
Unit tests are written an applied	3	2	2	3	2	2	2	2	2	2.2	Establish unit test strategy
Regression tests are prepared and automated	2	1	1	2	1	2	1	2	1	1.4	Identify test automation framework
Averages	3.2	3.6	3.8	3.6	3.2	3.6	3.2	3.6	3.3	3.2	

Figure 13-4. Engineering practices survey to determine what is the current state of your engineering practices

Agile Team Capability

The Agile Team capability survey helps you answer the question, "*What is the current level of Agile experience and interest?*" Most people are not in a position to hand-select Agile-minded people for their product team. Instead, an existing product team is asked to adopt Agile. This survey can help you understand team members' levels of training, knowledge, experience, and interest.

To construct a survey, identify areas that help you understand the team's experience and interest. Within the context of this survey, you are looking for objective data. Build a set of statements that are answered by team members. Collect the responses and tally for results. Some questions you may ask are:

- Have you had formal training in Agile?
    - If so, specify the name and length of the training.
    - Do you think you would benefit from Agile training?
- Have you read any books or articles on Agile within the past year?

- • If so, specify recently read items.
- • Would you be interested in reading Agile books or articles in the future?
- • Have you used Agile on any recent projects?
  - • If so, specify what agile process was used.
- • What are the biggest challenges of applying Agile?
- • What are the biggest benefits of applying Agile?

Notice that this survey is short and asks for objective details. It helps you understand the level of knowledge and interest a person has. It also provides insights into what they think are benefits and challenges to Agile. This gives you insight into their experience (both good and bad) with Agile. If you are looking to understand a person's beliefs in the Agile values and principles, then you may use the Agile MVP Advisor described in the second section of this chapter. The Agile Team capability surveys received from team members can be converted into a matrix, as in Figure 13-5.

Team Survey	Scrum Team Member A	Scrum Team Member B	Scrum Team Member C	Scrum Team Member D
Formal training in Agile?	No	Yes	No	Yes
If so, training name and length of course	No	Scrum Overview -1/2 day	No	Certified Scrum Master -2 days
Could you benefit from Agile training ?	Yes	Yes	Yes	No
Read any books/articles on Agile last year?	Yes	Yes	Yes	No
If so, list recently read books/articles	Scrum Guide	Scrum Guide	Article on Linkedin	n/a
Interested in reading Agile books/articles ?	Yes	Yes	Yes	No
Used Agile on any recent projects?	No	Yes	Yes	Yes
If so, what Agile process was used.	n/a	Scrum	Kanban	Scrum hybrid
How long did you use Agile ?	n/a	1.5 years	6 months	1 year
Biggest challenges of applying Agile?	Org commitment & command-and-control	QA involvement & command-and-control	Some command-and-control	Not enough structure
Biggest benefits of applying Agile?	Building product earlier	Team owned sizing	Was able to pull work	Lots of data

Figure 13-5. Team matrix to identify experience, interest, training, challenges, and benefits

The matrix is a summary allowing for a single-view evaluation. This information should only be used at the team level and should not be shared with others. From this matrix, you can see that training is important to at least three of the team members. Notice how Scrum Team members A, B, and C express concern with command-and-control. This is good insight and can help the

Agile Coach and/or Agile Deployment Team to be aware and help mitigate this challenge. You may also notice that Scrum Team member D may be problematic. Although this person has been trained, he or she indicates no interest in reading about Agile. This could be someone who wanted the Scrum Master certification but is not really invested in Agile. The information in this matrix can help you understand knowledge levels, risks to be aware of, and if there are any particular areas to focus for training.

Baseline and Improve

The primary purpose of this chapter is to provide you with survey mechanisms that can help you determine your baseline and then improve. The surveys are designed to answer the four questions stated at the beginning of this chapter help you evaluate your overall agility, but, more important, they allow you to know the starting point. You may periodically evaluate how far you have come in the transition.

Baselining provides you visibility into your situation and then information to help you adapt as you move forward. You can consider "baseline and improve" as another form of "inspect and adapt." Bear in mind that the Agile adoption practices and Agile MVP Advisor survey results can become part of your agile success measures, discussed in the next chapter.

Establishing Agile Measures of Success

Customer-based measures are important, but they must be translated into measures of what the company must do internally to meet its customers' expectations.

—David P. Norton and Robert S. Kaplan

Getting to "be Agile" is a journey. As part of that journey, how do you know you are gaining the business benefits of moving toward agility? The answer depends on the question you ask and the goal it implies. This is why it is important to ask the right question. The most important question is:

- *How do you know if Agile is having a business impact?* This question asks if you are receiving business benefits from being Agile. If the goal is understanding business results, then capture measures regarding revenue.

Establishing agile measures of success involves a framework focusing on metrics for the organizational level, product team level, and Scrum Team level. This helps frame the metrics toward those that gain the most benefit.

▓ **Agile Pit Stop**   A measure is a numerical value at a point in time. A metric is a mathematical calculation of measures over time that may represent a trend. "Number of defects collected today" is an example of a measure. "Defect average per day over a month" is an example of a metric.

Establishing a framework will require capturing project, product, revenue, and survey data. Presented in metric form, the data should help you make decisions and adapt toward the goal of increasing revenue.

This chapter is not intended to be an end-all for agile measures of success. It is meant to provide you with enough information to get started in building your measures of success framework and use it to determine if you are achieving your goals of being Agile and receiving business benefits. Later in this chapter, I share the "Agility Path"—a framework developed by Ken Schwaber and Scrum.org to help organizations establish measures of success and guide them toward an agile transformation. As part of readiness within the Ready, *Implement, Coach, and Hone* (RICH) deployment model, you should craft a measures *for success* framework and identify metrics that can lead you toward Agile.

Lagging-to-Leading Metric Path

Ultimately success is measured by an increase in revenue. Having a customer revenue metric helps you understand whether company products are increasing revenue. Capturing revenue is a good starting point. However, it is a *lagging* indicator and resulting outcome. To supplement lagging measures, you need *leading* measures that provide you with visibility into what is currently occurring within the organization. This visibility is important because it provides input for making decisions as you move forward. Making the right decision leads to improved results. As you consider measures, think about how they help you gain visibility and input to decisions.

▓ **Agile Pit Stop**   A revenue measure is the ultimate agile metric because Agile is about improving the business. However, revenue is a lagging measure, so you need to establish leading measures that provide timely visibility into what is occurring to help you make decisions that lead to an increase in revenue.

Although customer revenue is an important metric to collect, the question is, what metrics can we put in place to ensure we are moving in the right direction? For every lagging metric, you need to establish at least one leading metric that provides visibility and information for current decision making to ensure you are moving in the direction you want that is represented by a positive lagging metric (e.g., increase in revenue). I call this the *lagging-to-leading metric path* (see Figure 14-1). Examples include:

- *Customers attending Sprint Reviews:* a leading metric involving the Sprint Reviews, where you capture how many customers are actually attending the review and how much feedback you are receiving from them.

- *Customer satisfaction from Sprint Review:* a leading metric with which you capture customer satisfaction from the functionality they viewed within the Sprint Review.

- *Customer satisfaction of product usage:* a lagging metric involving the satisfaction of the customer in the usage of the current product, including comments.

- *Customer revenue:* a lagging metric involving the revenue coming from customers.

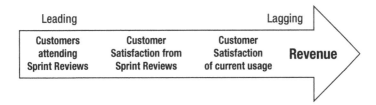

Figure 14-1. Lagging-to-leading metric path, using leading metrics to ensure you are moving in the direction of a positive lagging metric

Another example is that to get to the goal of "employees matter" within an agile context, you may start with first training employees about Agile (and a metric on numbers trained in Agile), then focus on implementing Scrum (and a metric on Scrum adoption), and then focus on self-organized teams (and a metric on aligning with Agile values and principles).

In Agile, although the results that matter most are often represented by lagging metrics, you will need leading indicators to ensure you are moving in the right direction, to provide visibility, and to help you with decision making.

Value of a Metric

You may observe that although many metrics are created and shared, only a few of them are actually being used for decision making. You have to continually ask what measures can help a team or organization move in the right direction. Before we discuss suggested metrics, it is worth having a discussion of the relative value of a metric.

The value of a metric is defined as its usefulness divided by the effort it takes to collect it. The dividend implies that the metric serves a useful purpose, such as decision making. The divisor implies the metric costs energy in collecting data and generating the metric. If the value of the metric is outweighed by the energy to generate it, then it may not be worth preparing the metric.

Non-Agile Pit Stop   The metrics you exhibit will affect behavior. If you collect defects and reward people on identifying defects, then you may get a behavior focused on identifying and possibly creating defects to reap a larger reward.

Some metrics may have a short life cycle, being valuable for only a certain time based on the usefulness it provides. As an example, if a training program commences, it may be of value to collect number of people trained. This provides visibility into ensuring the actual number of employees being trained is increasing as desired. However, once we have trained 90% of the target audience, it may no longer be useful to collect this data and keep creating this metric.

Because the relative value of a metric changes over time, it is beneficial to periodically assess the value being generated. If a current metric no longer provides value, it may be time to retire it. If a new one is of value, it may be included if the value outweighs the energy to generate it.

Organizational and Product Team Metrics

The agile measurement framework that I recommend is divided into three clusters. The first cluster is product team metrics, which provide visibility into how the team is progressing through its work, how well they are adopting agile processes, and how aligned with the Agile values and principles they are. The second cluster is organizational metrics, which provide visibility into the effect of Agile on the business and focuses on how aligned the organization is to Agile values and principles. The third cluster is the individual Scrum Team metrics. These are metrics that help a Scrum Team operate and improve. Scrum Team metrics are discussed in Chapter 19; product team and organizational metrics are discussed in this chapter.

Product Team Metrics

Product team metrics help a team understand value and where they are in respect to a release, and they help ensure that the team is adapting to customer needs. To add to the product team metrics, consider supplementing with the Agile Practices Adoption survey discussed in Chapter 13. A trend metric can be created to ensure that your adoption levels indicate a positive movement toward successful adoption of agile practices.

Value Capture

The *value capture* metric creates visibility for the percentage of value-added work you are doing compared to the non-value-added work. This measure captures how much value is being built and delivered within a Sprint and from Sprint to Sprint compared to the non-value-added work. When adapting toward Agile, there is often a lack of awareness of the amount of non-value-added work that is occurring. Value-added work is functionality requested by customers to produce working software. Non-value-added work does not directly add value as perceived by the customer. (To gain a deeper understanding of value-added and non-value-added work, consider reviewing Chapter 5.) The benefit of this metric is it brings focus on the non-value-added work, so that you can then reduce it and increase the level of value-added work for the customer.

To calculate this measure, identify all value-added and non-value added work within your Sprint (see Figure 14-2). You may decide to categorize the non-value-added work further (defects, status reports, etc.) and assign a priority rating to it (defect = NVA-1, status reports = NVA-4). This can give you an overall understanding of where the most waste is occurring and begin the process of reducing or eliminating this waste.

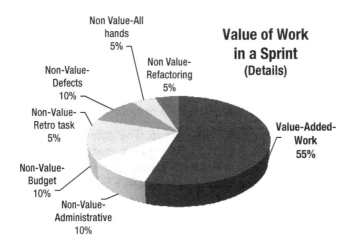

Figure 14-2. Value of work per Sprint at a detailed level

You can track this on a sprint basis, accumulate it over a release basis, or trend it over time from Sprint to Sprint (as in Figure 14-3) with the goal of seeing an upward trend of value-added work.

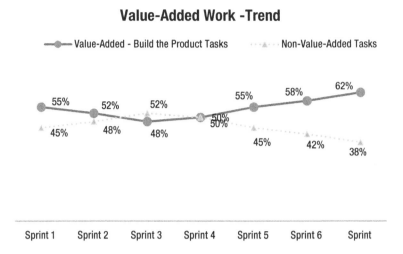

Figure 14-3. Value of work from Sprint to Sprint (trend line)

The big advantage of this metric is that it helps you (1) be aware of the value and non-value-related work that your team is doing, and (2) it allows you to make adjustments if you want to increase your value-added stream of work. Your goal is to remove non-valued-added work that is unnecessary and reduce non-value added work that is necessary for the system to function. Although this may force you to make tough decisions (i.e., identifying what is value-added and what is not), it will help you get your team more productive and focused on building customer value.

Release Burnup

A *release burnup* is a graphical metric that indicates how much work has been completed. The benefit is that it is used to enable a team to predict the scope level they may be able to accomplish for a project.

At the release level, I recommend a burnup. The difference between a burn-down and burnup is that instead of tracking how much work is left, a burnup tracks how much work a team has completed, so the line goes up, not down (see Figure 14-4). The other difference is that in a Sprint, we know the target velocity so we can burn down from it. However, at the release level, because we purposefully avoid big up-front scoping of the work so we can adapt to change, we do not know our release scope or our velocity for the entire release. Nevertheless, the burnup gives a team the ability to gauge how much scope they may eventually build over time to help you anticipate when the minimum viable product (MVP) scope level will be reached and predict a potential release date.

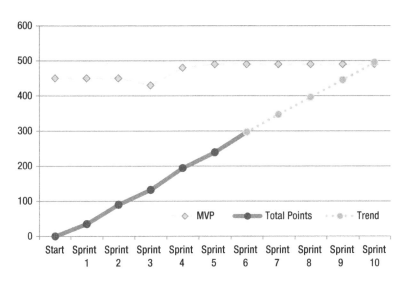

Figure 14-4. Release burnup

Figure 14-4 indicates that as of Sprint 6, the team has built 297 points of working software. Because their MVP is estimated at 490, following the trend line based on the average velocity, it will take the team until Sprint 10 to build the remaining functionality.

Customers Attending Sprint Reviews

This metric provides visibility into whether customers are attending Sprint Reviews. To continuously adapt to customer needs, customers are invited to Sprint Reviews to gain their valuable feedback. The benefit of this metric is that it objectively reveals whether customers are actually attending. It is also considered a leading indicator of customer revenue so it can give you insight into whether you are moving into the right direction. I often hear people say that they hold Sprint Reviews and then learn that no customers attend. How can you adapt to customer needs if you are not including customers in Sprint Reviews and adapting to their needs?

Two variations of this metric are measuring how much feedback is being received and how much of the feedback is leading to a change in the product. Another is including the number of internal stakeholders attending, which may include management, sales, marketing, and others who have a stake in the product. This metric can reveal who internally is committed to understanding the progress and the details of the functionality being built.

To construct this metric for each Sprint Review (Figure 14-5), collect such measurements as number of customers invited, number who attended, number of internal stakeholders, amount of feedback received, and amount of feedback used to adapt the product.

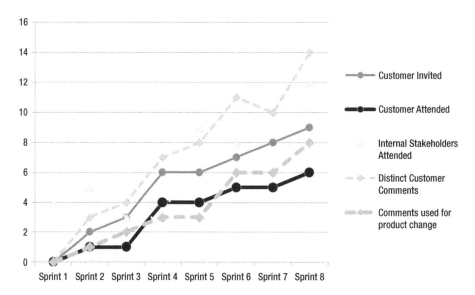

Figure 14-5. Customer attending Sprint Reviews

Organizational Metrics

Organizational metrics indicate if the organization and teams therein are aligning with the Agile values and principles and if a positive business effect from the adoption of Agile is being seen. To add to the organizational metrics, consider supplementing them with data from the Agile Mindset, Values, and Principles (MVP) Advisor survey (Chapter 13). A trend metric can be created to ensure that behavioral levels indicate a positive movement toward the Agile mindset at the organizational level. It can also be used at the product level.

Employee Satisfaction

Employee satisfaction is a way to gauge employees' feeling of contentment within a workplace. Employee feedback allows you to engage in meaningful improvement opportunities based on their feedback. The benefit of conducting employee satisfaction surveys is that it lets employees know that you care. Poor satisfaction can lead to higher than normal attrition rates and low productivity. Satisfied employees can lead to loyalty and higher productivity. By giving your employees a voice, they can express their interests and concerns.

Employee satisfaction surveys can energize and empower employees provided their results and improvement opportunities are taken seriously.

When commencing an agile program, it is important to gauge satisfaction. It can help you understand how satisfaction levels change. Keep in mind that during an agile change, although many become more satisfied, some may find their positions of control being reduced and become less satisfied. Because there are many forms of employee satisfaction metrics, consider researching the various forms and identify what is right for you.

Customer Satisfaction

Customer satisfaction is a way to gauge if a company's products and services meet or surpass customer expectations. The benefit of customer satisfaction is twofold. First, it is considered a leading indicator of customer revenue, so it can give you insight into whether you are moving in the right direction. Second, it can focus employees on the importance of fulfilling customers' expectations. Although customer satisfaction is measured at the individual level, it is often reported at a cumulative level. It may be measured along various dimensions: the usefulness of a product, the relationship with the company, and responsiveness to problems.

Customer satisfaction surveys should be conducted periodically—say, on a quarterly basis—to provide a continual gauge of the customers' view of the company's products and identify actions for improvement. Postpurchase surveys can reflect the satisfaction of the individual customer at the time of product or service delivery. Because there are many forms of customer satisfaction metrics, consider researching the various forms and identify what is right for you.

Customer Revenue

Revenue is a complex term that can be interpreted in many ways. I am referring to net revenue, which is the amount of money a company receives from sales of products and services less negative revenue items like returned items, refunds, and discounts. Although revenue is a lagging indicator, the benefit of revenue metrics is that they are the ultimate indicator of whether customers find value in the products you are building.

Revenue metrics can be generated at product, product line, business unit, or organizational levels. Start at the product level, so you can understand if there is value coming from a product. When you gain revenue, it is beneficial to initiate a customer satisfaction survey to understand what specific value the customer found. Because revenue is a lagging metric, ensure you create a *lagging-to-leading metric path* so that you have leading indicators to help you gauge your path to an increase in revenue. There are many forms of revenue metrics, so consider researching the various forms and identify what is right for you.

Release Frequency

A release frequency metric provides visibility into the rate in which you are delivering customer value into production. The benefit of this metric is that it can help you fine-tune your release cycle toward the need of the customer and the revenue you want to gain. Although you do not have to technically release your product, knowing you have the ability to do so can help you be ready when a customer says that they would like the functionality now and you can then gain revenue. The ability of a customer to use the new release is directly related to the customer value of the release and the customer's ability to absorb the release.

If you have an on-premises product that takes two weeks to install into a customer environment, another two weeks to integrate with other customer products with verified functionality, and another two weeks to train users in the new functionality, then reducing release frequency may not be reasonable. However, if you have customers demanding more functionality on a regular basis and you can reduce installation times, understanding your release frequency can help you baseline where you are and what you want to achieve. If you have a SaaS product, the release frequency is dependent on your internal processes and customer demand.

You can use release frequency as an indicator for revenue. By having both metrics available, you can have visibility into what happens to a product's revenue when you increase the frequency of release. Because release frequency may take many forms, select the metric that is right for you. It may also be combined with your revenue metric.

Agility Path

The *Agility Path* is a framework developed by Scrum.org that links current enterprise activities and their metrics with a process for continuous improvement. The first step is gathering and analyzing the business and process data needed to assess the current state of a company in each of its critical function areas. The next step is using these data to identify where improvements to business practices are most needed to have a positive effect on the company's performance.

The Agility Path is broken down into *enterprise metrics,* which reflect the business value a company generates, and *foundational metrics,* which measure organizational agility and flexibility in creating this value.

The enterprise metrics include:

- Revenue per employee
- Cost/revenue ratio of relevant domains
- Stakeholder satisfaction
- Investment in agility

The foundation metrics include:

- Release frequency
- Release stabilization
- Usage index (unused code)
- Innovation budget

The *Agility Index* is used by Scrum.org to quantify the gains achieved by those businesses engaged in the Agility Path. It is a blended metric that is designed to measure the improvement in business outcomes. Its premise is simple: organizations that are changing the way they do business to achieve agility will derive benefits shown in their business value metrics. A metrics snapshot is taken at the initial phase of the Agility Path and then measured again at regular intervals so that progress can be tracked across time.

It is beneficial for a company to assess its product value practices with help from the Agility Path. A snapshot is created that represents a point-in-time profile of your development organization's performance and capabilities. A series of snapshots reveals trends that help manage the investments and optimize future capabilities.

What Are Your Measures of Success?

It is important to consider your agile measures of success framework. The material in this chapter can give you a jump start in establishing metrics that give you visibility into aligning with Agile and its benefits. Make sure to consider lagging and leading metrics and metrics that provide visibility at the organization and product team levels. It is advantageous to gain an understanding of your alignment to Agile prior to starting, so that you understand your baseline and how far you need to go. Measures of success can provide you with a dashboard to indicate if you are moving in the right direction, tools to help you make decisions, and insights into adapting or staying the course.

Constructing a Scalable Agile Framework

A total commitment is paramount to reaching the ultimate in performance.

—Tom Flores

When introducing agile processes, there is a tendency to focus at the team level. Processes like Scrum, Extreme Programming, and Kanban work well for small to mid-size teams. However, to gain the full business benefits of Agile, you will need to scale your implementation to embrace the organization. To do this you may need to scale teams, contend with geographical distribution, align roles within the organizational scope to Agile, and enhance project structures with Scrum of Scrums. In addition, it is important to scale the process for larger and more complex projects, which may include incorporating a Sprint 0, Agile Release Planning, and automation.

The goal of this chapter is to provide insight on how to scale your agile framework to an organization or to a large product team. It is not meant to be exhaustive and will conclude with scaling agile resources that can help you along. The key is as you scale, ensure that you are continuing to promote the spirit of the Agile values and principles.

It Takes a Village

Although Agile tends to occur on a product team, you will gain the most business benefits when it occurs at the level of the organization. Some areas that will help you scale your teams and organizations toward an agile culture include a focus on team size, roles, Scrum of Scrums, and geographical distribution. Two other areas that will help you scale at the organizational level are adapting IT governance and performance reviews toward an Agile mindset, discussed in Chapter 23.

Team Size and Geographical Distribution

What do you do when faced with a large and distributed team? The larger the team, the more challenging it is to keep it moving forward with cohesion and productivity, whether you are doing Agile or a variant of waterfall. The question is: How do you configure teams to keep sizes manageable, have the skills that are needed, and be as colocated as possible, while aligning with the Agile mindset in team configuration?

The first step is to promote small yet appropriately skilled teams. The team should be large enough to have the right skills and experience in design, development, and testing to build the product—but small enough to self-organize and maintain high productivity. When teams get too large, they are harder to self-organize and this negatively affects productivity. For example, for a project team size of 35, it is best to divide the team into five Scrum teams of seven, with each team having the skills and experience to thrive.

Agile Pit Stop   Three attributes of Agile teams that align with the Agile mindset are small yet skilled teams, ownership of a functional piece of the product, and colocation.

The second step is to promote ownership of a functional piece of the product. When a team feels ownership of a piece, they will begin to take pride in their work and become more productive over time as they become more familiar with their component. This requires that the product be designed in such a manner that functional components are clear and Scrum Teams can align with those areas. For example, the product may be made up of 12 components or functional areas and the first Scrum Team owns the order entry and billing functionalities.

The third step is to promote colocation. Because it is not uncommon to have distributed product teams, you attempt to configure each Scrum Team to have as many of the team members to be colocated and near-shore as possible. Colocation means that team members are in the same physical location.

Near-shore means that team members are within the same campus or within the same time zone or two. In the same scenario, if you have a project team of 35 and find that 15 are in India, 7 are in Europe, and 13 are in the eastern part of the United States, then it makes sense to have two teams of 7 and 8, respectively, in India, one team of 7 in Europe, and two teams of 6 and 7 in the eastern part of the United States. If you find that, within the United States, five of the team members are colocated in Massachusetts, then it makes sense to have those five on one team.

Agile Roles beyond Team

Although there are core team roles discussed within Agile, engaging the whole organization in applying the values and principles helps with the overall business success. Aside from the Scrum Master, Product Owner, and Development Team, there are the actual customers, executives, senior management, middle management, sales and marketing, finance, human resources, and other roles that must change to allow for an inspect-and-adapt approach to building software. For a refreshed understanding of Agile core and beyond roles and responsibilities, revisit Chapter 12.

Scrum of Scrums

When a product team is comprised of two or more Scrum Teams, a *Scrum of Scrums* (SoS) may be established. An SoS is a coordinating body made up of representatives from each of the Scrum Teams to focus on the many cross-team issues and dependencies that need to be resolved and to keep large teams synchronized and operating effectively.

Agile Pit Stop   The acronym of SoS traditionally means "save our ship." In Agile, the Scrum of Scrum acronym SoS also connotes saving through capturing and mitigating cross-team risks that can affect project success.

Most agile processes such as Scrum are ideally suited for colocated team sizes of seven plus or minus two people. When you have a large project team of 35, there needs to be a way to coordinate the work and ensure common issues across those teams get addressed in an effective manner. The benefits of a SoS are that it:

- Enhances communications across teams, so each team knows what the other is doing.
- Avoids duplication of effort across teams.

- Reduces suboptimization, when a team is doing work that is best for them but that negatively affects another team.

- Builds a strong support system for Agile teams because change is hard for one team to manage on their own.

- Helps Scrum Teams prioritize the work because some teams may be dependent on work from others.

The purpose of the SoS helps specify who should represent their team. To start, the common representative from each team is the Scrum Master. Figure 15-1 illustrates the Scrum Master from each Scrum Team meeting to discuss project progress, risks, and more.

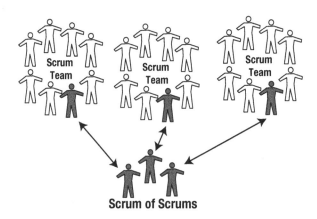

Figure 15-1. Scrum of Scrums includes a representative from each Scrum Team

The generic SoS focuses on project progress, risks, issues, and dependencies. This *Project Progress Scrum of Scrums* is usually comprised of the Scrum Masters, the Product Owners, and an Agile project manager. The Project Progress SoS is responsible for the following:

- Monitors release burn-up with velocity to determine scope to release date and whether adjustments to either scope or schedule need to occur.

- Identifies and mitigates blocking issues that are beyond the scope of a Scrum Team, with the goal of removing the blockage or escalating it to management.

- Discusses story dependencies among Scrum Teams and ensures that the highest priority stories are optimized to the project level.

If there is still a lot of uncertainty regarding customer needs or prioritization of current functionality and user stories, there may be a benefit to convoking a *Product Owner Scrum of Scrums*. The Product Owners from each Scrum Team should attend. A development lead from each Development Team may also attend if technical insight is needed to prioritize the work. The Product Owner SoS is responsible for the following:

- Communicates stories that need to be added to the Product Backlog and negotiates the priority of these stories.

- Explains changes to the backlog—specifically, why stories have been added or removed from the backlog or had their priorities changed.

- Identifies dependencies or overlap of stories between Scrum Teams. Teams can add backlog items for other teams and negotiate priority.

The resulting information helps shape the direction of the product and sprints.

If there is still a lot of technical uncertainty and complexity, then there may be a benefit to initiating a *Technical Scrum of Scrums*. The Technical SoS is comprised of each Scrum Team's lead developer and QA, and the lead architect on the product. The Technical SoS is responsible for the following:

- Evaluates and makes technical decisions that affect Scrum Teams and the overall direction of the product.

- Serves as a working group for solving technical problems across Scrum Teams.

- Establishes code standards by which all the Scrum Teams should operate.

- Identifies new common services to eliminate duplicate coding efforts between teams.

- Identifies and applies the QA vision and the integration (and other) testing needed.

Each SoS may meet as often as every day (but for only 15 minutes) to once a week, depending on various factors. For the Project Progress SoS, the frequency may vary based on the risks, issues, and dependencies that must be addressed. For the Product Owner SoS, the frequency may vary based on the level of uncertainty and the focus on prioritization. For the Technical SoS, the frequency may vary based on the technical complexity.

Scaling toward Larger and More Complex Projects

Some projects are large and complex and represent a challenge irrespective of methodology. Within this section are three scaling ideas that can help teams new to Agile and those with large and complex projects.

Sprint 0

Sprint 0 is a Sprint designed to help teams envision the work ahead. It is primarily used by teams new to Agile to help in their readiness to begin Agile or by teams beginning a complex project that requires thought for visioning and getting organized. Sprint 0 is not a replacement for big up-front activities found within the waterfall and phase-based methods, but instead serves to establish a basic vision of where the project is headed while acknowledging that things will adapt as the team moves forward. The length of this Sprint should be no longer than the standard Sprint length. Here are some tasks that typically occur during a Sprint 0.

- Define teams, including team size, need for multiple teams, and team distribution.
- Define Sprint length.
- Educate teams on agile processes and practices.
- Collect and groom stories within the backlog with an emphasis on prioritization.
- Establish Scrum of Scrums.
- Work on spike solutions per the XP definition.
- Identify project risks, issues, and dependencies.
- Establish the product, technical, QA, and CM visions.

Some may argue that Sprint 0 is not true to Scrum, and they are correct because no working software is produced. However, in some cases, these tasks need to occur prior to Sprint 1, irrespective of what you call this time-boxed period.

■ **Agile Pit Stop**   The key in creating a vision is to envision what is known and enough of a short-term path to provide high-level guidance to share with the team.

For clarity, a vision provides enough detail for team members to understand the general direction of the topic area. It is not meant to be detailed or fixed, because in an Agile mindset you cannot possibly know everything up front, and you expect that it will evolve. Visions should be brief and easily digestible. They may live in the team document repository, such as the wiki. Also, if the vision remains mostly the same from one release to the other, then the vision should primarily include what is changing.

The various visions that can help a team include:

- *Product vision*: provides business context of the product to include business performance, market share, and measures of customer satisfaction, high-level product roadmap, and a prioritized list of business objectives. It may also include an *elevator pitch* encapsulating the project in succinct but compelling terms.

- *Technical vision*: provides the direction of the architecture, including known and emerging elements of the technology stack, frameworks, common infrastructure and operating platforms, needs for refactoring, and system-level nonfunctional requirements such as usability, performance, reliability, security, and any governing regulatory or industry standards that must be followed.

- *QA vision*: provides an overview of the proposed testing framework, testing process and how it interacts with the development process, testing types, test tools, and who may perform the various types of testing.

- *CM vision*: provides an overview of the proposed version control tool, branching and merging processes, and build management tool and process.

It is best to implement Sprint 0 much like any other Sprint. The team starts with a form of Sprint Planning, a Sprint 0 backlog is used to manage the work, and daily stand-ups occur to share progress and roadblocks. Instead of a Sprint Review and retrospective, I recommend that you conclude the Sprint 0 with *Agile Release Planning*. This is a session in which everyone is together (physically or virtually) sharing the results of Sprint 0 at the same time.

Agile Release Planning

Agile Release Planning is an activity that replaces the detailed planning phase in a more traditional waterfall model. It is made up of a session, often two or three days, where all Agile Team members are involved, including management, and anyone else who can materially participate. A major part of Agile Release

Planning is grooming the backlog as a team (or as individual Scrum Teams) to gain an understanding of the breadth of the work ahead. The benefits of the Agile Release Planning are:

- Shares the release and Sprint schedule.

- Gains team insight into the product vision and business context for the release.

- Informs the team on the latest on technical, QA, and CM within their respective visions.

- Provides overview of who will be on which team and who are on other teams.

- Shares structure and participants of Scrum of Scrums.

- Provides the team with clarifications of the objectives, epics, and stories.

- Gains team commitment (a critical factor).

- Helps resolve conflicts of vision (what we would like to accomplish) versus reality (what we can accomplish).

- Raises dependencies and risks early.

This is done to ensure the whole team participates, gains insight into the work ahead, and promotes an initial commitment to the work. An example agenda of a two-day Agile Release Planning may look like this:

- Introduction of attendees and agenda: facilitator (may be a Scrum Master).

- Welcome address: executive.

- Product vision: Product Owner.

- Technical, QA, CM visions: respective leads in these areas.

- Backlog grooming: team(s)—this is the biggest part of the two days.

- Sharing results from grooming: common themes, risks, issues, and dependencies.

- Retrospective: facilitator (similar to a Sprint Retrospective)

- Wrap-up: executive, product owner—next steps and thank you.

There are two approaches to timing Agile Release Planning. The first is at the beginning of a project, in a Sprint 0 context or otherwise. The second is that it occurs every 90 days to periodically visit the visions and direction of the product.

Automation

One aspect of scaling is reducing manual steps and automating the necessary steps. Eliminating and automating provides the team an opportunity to scale and increase their velocity. It is recommended to automate any process that is repeated by enough people for which the team will see a cost and time benefit in doing so. Because the team can focus less on the manual steps of a process and more on the work of building product, they have a real opportunity of increasing their team velocity.

As an Agile Team gets up and running, given the continuous nature of building, migrating, and testing code and the increasing size of the code base with new functionality, a lack or minimal amount of automation may start to affect velocity fairly quickly in a negative way. Please understand that at a certain point velocity may remain constant even with automation, but you can be certain that without automation or with minimal automation the team's velocity will plateau.

Resources That Can Help You Scale

There are many resources that can help you scale your Agile implementation. The key is to get all roles involved while continuing to align with Agile values and principles. The resources include:

- *The Enterprise and Scrum.* In this book, Ken Schwaber takes you through change management—for your organizational and interpersonal processes—explaining how to successfully adopt Scrum across your entire organization.[1]

- *Practices for Scaling Lean & Agile Development.* In this book, Craig Larman and Bas Vodde draw on their experience leading and guiding lean and Agile adoptions for large, multisite, and offshore product development provide information on large-scale Scrum that sustainably and quickly delivers value and innovation.[2]

---

[1] Ken Schwaber. *The Enterprise and Scrum.* Microsoft Press, 2007.
[2] Craig Larman and Bas Vodde. *Practices for Scaling Lean & Agile Development,* Addison-Wesley Professional, 2010.

- *Scaled Agile Framework (SAFe)*. In this interactive knowledge base for implementing agile practices at enterprise scale, Dean Leffingwell highlights individual roles, teams, activities, and artifacts necessary to scale Agile from the team to program to the enterprise level.[3]

- *Disciplined Agile Delivery* (aka DAD). In this book, Scott Ambler and Mark Lines introduce IBM's process framework, a disciplined approach to agile development which acknowledges and deals with the realities and complexities of a portfolio of interdependent program initiatives.[4]

Scaling Up

As Agile gains adoption within your product team and outward into your organization, you may need to consider how to scale your implementation. This chapter has suggested some ways you can enhance your agile framework for larger and more complex teams. It is not however meant to be exhaustive. The key takeaway is that as you scale, you should seek out information and make sure that you are continuing to promote the spirit of the Agile values and principles as you do so.

---

[3]See Dean Leffingwell, http://scaledagileframework.com.
[4]Scott Ambler and Mark Lines. *Disciplined Agile Delivery*. IBM Press, 2012.

Establishing an Agile Education Program

Education is the most powerful weapon which you can use to change the world.

—Nelson Mandela

Does your company education begin and end with training? Will this suffice for a change to Agile? Agile is a mindset that signifies a change to the culture. Because of this, we cannot think that reading a book or taking a training class will suffice and provide enough knowledge to cause a shift in thinking to be Agile. There is more to ramping up with Agile then just training. It takes a repertoire of educational elements. Training is just one of those educational elements.

The goal of this chapter is to make you aware that it takes a variety of educational elements within an agile context to help your organization come up to speed with Agile. No one element is sufficient; it is instead the accumulation of education elements at different points in time that will provide the comprehensive focus to help you, your team, and your organization. As you read the information, the objective is for you to construct an *education plan* that best serves your goal of an Agile transformation. Ultimately you want to create a self-organizing educational culture with many elements and the most mature level is when employees are willing to give back to their community.

Path to Making Education Matter

Training is a basic educational element and is best applied when an organization wants to build employee skills. When you want to adapt your organizational culture, however, you need an education plan that includes much more than just skill building. As discussed in Chapter 2, culture change is a transformation that involves the most change and requires the most time for an organization to adjust. To support that change, there are certain educational levels that are suited for skills, procedure, and achieving an Agile culture. These are training, coaching, mentoring, and giving back (Figure 16-1).

Figure 16-1. Path of educational levels that can support a transformation to a new culture

Here is a closer look at the educational levels:

- *Training* helps you build skills in a process. Its benefits can be undone the moment the trainee moves back into their existing culture. This is where coaching helps.

- *Coaching* helps a team adopt a process or procedure and lays the groundwork for transforming the culture. The coach is able to guide a team in adopting a process. If you do not have a coach, it is very easy to apply a process incorrectly or give up and revert to the old process. A coach can help you course-correct until you are enacting the process or practice correctly.

- *Mentoring* focuses on relationships and building self-confidence and self-perception. The person being mentored (*mentee*) advances the topics to be treated in the relationship. Deep learning can occur because the mentee is asking questions and seeking answers without being prompted. Mentoring allows people within the organization to start owning the culture.

- *Giving back* occurs when the employee has gained enough skills, experience, and confidence to start giving back. When employees have reached this level and are committed to giving back, they start helping others. A broader group of people who are committed to the transformation to Agile self-organizes to enhance the culture that they feel they own.

Educational Elements

There are many education elements that can help you get to an Agile culture. Within the levels of education described in the previous section are various additive education elements that contribute to the next level of education. As you move up the education levels, the education moves from formal to informal elements of education. Here is one perspective on educational elements within a level:

- *Awareness* may be considered the first step in the education process. This element calls attention to the new Agile initiative, may include the objectives and motivations, and may provide an overview of the initiative or of the topic such as a 30-minute Agile overview. Awareness elements may also be in the form of a brochure, flyer, or short presentation. This element prepares the mind to become open and attentive to subsequent educational elements.

- *Skills training* provides soft or hard skills to the attendee. This may come in the form of an instructor-led seminar or a virtual webinar. An example of this type of training is a course on agile planning tools or how to write user stories.

- *Role training* provides education on a person's role in relation to the process, practices, and methods being taught. An example is a Scrum Master's role for Sprint Planning.

- *Community sharing* includes items within a shared environment. This may take form of agile practices within a website, and recorded seminars and webinars that are hosted and always available for viewing.

- *Process and role coaching* involves in-session education by a coach to a team or an individual. This may include respective Scrum Master and Product Owner Q&A sessions where those playing these roles may ask specific questions regarding the application of the agile process in context to their role. This element helps reinforce a new skill or process to ensure they are being applied as expected.

- *Culture coaching* involves in-session education by a coach to promote Agile principles and values. This may include establishing an apprentice coaching circle to build in-house coaching expertise for Agile Champions ready to give back to the organization. This element helps reinforce the new behavior to ensure it is being applied as expected.

- *Mentoring* involves educating individuals where a mentee or participant leads the conversation to gain ownership and build self-confidence.

- *Community contributing* includes items within a shared environment. This may take the form of blogs and just-in-time seminars and webinars that are given by local Agile Champions giving back to their community.

Agile Pit Stop   Forms of education include instructor-led training and seminars, virtual training and webinars, blog articles, books, video snippets, and practice exercises on websites.

Examples of Common Agile Education

When product teams or organizations move toward Agile, the more common educational elements include role training, coaching teams in long-term Agile usage, establishing an agile community, building an agile website, initiating a blog to capture experience and offer guidance, and launching a seminar or webinar series.

Training Aligned to Roles

Training is often the first visible sign of education. Within an Agile context, training tends to align around roles because each role will be responsible for different areas. Here are examples of training programs by role:

- *Agile Team Foundation* provides guidance for being an effective team. This training steps the team through the agile process and the team's responsibility within each practice (that is, *Sprint Planning*).

- *Scrum Master* provides guidance for being an effective servant leader and facilitator for a team. It steps the Scrum Master through the agile process and their responsibility within each practice.

- *Agile Product Owner* provides guidance on being an effective Product Owner and how to work with customers and the team. It steps the Product Owner through the agile process and their responsibilities.

- *Executive Overview* summarizes Agile principles and values, their business benefits, and executives' role and responsibility within an Agile culture.

Building an Agile Community

Another form of education involves establishing an agile community by such means as the following:

- A *website to share practices with the community*. When an agile framework is established, this information along with the practices, glossary, pointers to education, and more are placed on the company agile website so that teams have ready access to this information moving forward.

- A *venue for agile social collaboration among the community*. This provides an online space for those in the agile journey to pose questions to those outside of their teams to hear thoughts, ideas, and lessons learned, as well as provide answers to others who are posing questions. This space provides an opportunity to discuss and collaborate on a variety of topics.

- *Opportunities for local Agile Champions to give back to the community*. These may include writing internal blog articles and giving seminars and webinars.

Gamification

Gamification adapts game concepts to nongaming situations to engage employees and motivate them to improve their performance and behavior. It rewards employees for completing performance levels with points, badges, privileges, and sometimes monetary incentives. Gamification can be deployed to engage employees in agile educational elements.

The key to gamification is that it must be driven by a clear business objective. With the context of Agile, the goal with gamification is to encourage employees to become Agile Champions and achieve an Agile culture. Although it may start with training, you eventually would like employees acting as Agile Champions to give back to their community.

Here is an example of using gamification to motivate and engage employees to become Agile Champions who give back to the community. Let's posit five levels of Agile Champion and the points needed to achieve each level:

- Steel: 5 points
- Bronze: 25 points
- Silver: 50 points
- Gold: 100 points
- Platinum: 250 points

An agile education plan has been established with the goal of getting employees to give back to the community. The plan lays out the following education elements, together with the points earned by completing each one:

- Take the "Agile Overview" for awareness: 5 points
- Attend Scrum Master, Product Owner, team, or manager training per your role: 20 points
- Take a variety of short online courses such as "How to Write User Stories" to build skills: 5 points each
- Attend a 45-minute seminar/webinar on various Agile topics such as "Lessons Learned from Sprint Retrospective" to understand process: 5 points each
- Write a blog article on giving back: 25 points
- Present a webinar on giving back: 50 points

Notice that by taking the "Agile Overview," the participant immediately becomes Steel level. This gets them into the game and motivates them to keep playing. Also notice that the bigger point items promote giving back to the internal agile community. This preferential valuation aligns with the goal of giving back. If you use gamification, ensure the achievement is real, helps the employee with their work, and is aligned with the objectives.

Are You Getting Educated?

It takes a repertoire of educational elements to achieve an Agile culture. Training is just one educational element that are needed. How will your teams be educated? An accumulation of education elements at different points in time will provide the comprehensive focus to help you, your team, and your organization. Construct an education plan that best serves your goal for an Agile transformation. Ultimately you want to create a self-organizing educational culture where employees are willing and eager to give back to their community.

Creating a Customer Validation Vision

Nothing is as empowering as real-world validation.

—Steven Pressfield

Engaging the customer is one of the most important aspects of building customer value. Gaining continuous customer feedback of working software is an important aspect of the inspect-and-adapt model, which ensures that you are constructing a valuable solution for the customer. Without customer validation, you are not really applying Agile; you are just doing a form of iterative development without aligning your work with customers' need. Although the engineering practices applied within an agile project focus on building the *product right*, the validation practices focus on building the *right product*.

Chapter 4 discusses the importance of customer engagement. This chapter helps you establish the building blocks to achieve continuous customer validation via an approach I call the *Agile Customer Validation Vision*. The notion of thinking through and establishing an authentic validation approach for the product is missing from agile projects and practices. This vision provides a framework for identifying the right customers, constructing customer profiles, identifying personas, establishing continuous validation sessions, motivating the customers to attend the validation sessions, and incorporating their feedback.

A business representative such as the Product Owner is responsible for constructing this vision and characterizing in detail the customers who are valuable to the company. That information helps in identifying who should attend the Sprint Reviews of the working software to supply the most valuable customer feedback. You learned about the PO's role in Chapter 12. This chapter enlarges on that responsibility in regards to customer validation.

Whether or not you formally establish an Agile Customer Validation Vision, consider performing these activities to ensure you are working with the right customers to provide the valuable feedback you need so that you are building the right thing.

Identifying the Right Customers

A precondition of effective continuous customer engagement is identifying your key stakeholders. Stakeholders are those people who have a business interest in your work. They include senior management, sponsors, and customers who have a stake in the success of building customer value.

The key stakeholders are the customers. The primary reason is that without customers perceiving value in your products and buying them, your company will not stay in business. The key to engaging the customer is finding the right customers who can actually help you identify and build customer value. To do this, customers should be segmented into target groups according to their different business needs.

Agile Pit Stop   Your key stakeholders are your customers. If customers don't perceive value in your products and buy them, your company will not stay in business.

You may be saying to yourself that your product management, sales, and marketing groups help you with identifying customers. This is good, and in Agile it is important to foster the team mindset by including their participation and introducing these groups to the engineering teams.

However, you need a single person, such as the Product Owner, to merge customer needs and decide on which customers will be the focus for requirements gathering and validation events. The ultimate goal is to bring the customers to your Sprint Reviews of your working software to prove value or adapt according to their feedback. Someone needs to be responsible for identifying the right customers and for all the activities involved with continuous customer engagement. You need a dedicated business representative on your team who is focused on building customer value within your products.

Customer Target Groups

Customers come in a variety of forms and may be identified and categorized in a variety of ways. The key is to establish your customer segments or target groups. At the broadest level, customer target groups include:

- Current customers
- Potential customers
- Past customers

The challenge with identifying the elusive customer value is that potential customers often see value differently than do current customers. More challenging is that even current customers may see customer value differently. Identifying target groups help you understand what they need and what they don't need.

Agile Pit Stop   The challenge with identifying the elusive customer value is that different customer target groups see customer value differently.

It is important to know that your current customers are the real buyers of your product, must be treated well, and are your highest priority. The potential customer group represents an opportunity to grow your revenue. Potential customers represent both potential buyers and browsers. Although it is hard to differentiate between potential buyers versus browsers, it can affect their priority within the overall customer pool. If you have past customers, it is important to keep track of who they are in case you want to revisit them. You can often glean important information from a past customer from the perspective of what they did not like about the product and what it might take to bring them back into the fold again.

Within the current customer group, it is important to identify which customers are leaders and which ones are followers. A leader is a customer who embraces your product, is willing to speak positively about it, has the cachet to attract other customers, and is eager to discuss requirements. A follower might use the product but not necessarily advocate for it. You want to identify the leaders. In some cases, with the right grooming, you can convert a follower into a leader. Grooming may entail engaging them in your requirements discussions and Sprint Reviews.

Identify Personas

Personas represent specific users of a product and act as examples of the types of users who would interact with it. Most products have several personas that use the product in different ways. Examples of three personas for a product are the regular user, power user, and administrator.

- The *regular user* uses only the basic user interface functionality.

- The *power user* needs more detailed interface functionality to handle more sophisticated work.

- The *administrator* needs back-end installation and maintenance functionality.

All three use the product differently, and different features are built for their respective needs. Personas are a powerful way to guide your decisions about functionality and ensure that you are, in fact, building functionality for each persona.

Personas should be identified early on in the development of the product. Often personas are discovered within the user story collection or grooming activities. Personas are a key ingredient in the way that user stories can be presented. Including the persona in a story description provides you the *point of view* (POV) of a user story and defines who that user story is for. Chapter 18 offers more insights into the importance of including personas in user story writing. A persona glossary should be shared with the developers so they understand for whom they are building the user stories and so QA understands the POV for testing the user story.

Agile Pit Stop Personas provide three distinct advantages. The team understands the users better, which helps guide decisions about functionality. The user stories are written to support and build functionality for personas. Based on their personas, the Product Owner knows who can give the best feedback and therefore whom to invite to the Sprint Reviews.

I recommend that you establish a description for each persona. This description is typically illustrated as a fictitious person that represents a real role. It will include the knowledge, experience, and activities of that role. By writing a persona as a fictitious person with a name, this makes the persona easier to imagine and relate to, as in the following examples.

- Eric is a regular user of the product and primarily uses it to take courses. He has a bachelor's degree in communications. He has little time to take online courses but is interested in doing so. He works from home on occasion and uses his tablet for work-related matters as well as taking courses.

- Iman is a power user and supports the executives within her company. She uses the product to run reports to understand if regular users are taking courses and which courses are most popular. She likes to make her management happy by producing easy-to-read dashboards.

- Sherris is an administrator for the company. She has a bachelor's degree in IT and five years of experience in the product support field. She enjoys supporting products and has taken additional technical skills training in the maintenance and support area.

Personas are beneficial to the Sprint Review context. When a team is demonstrating a feature, invite customers from the persona target group for that feature so you get the right feedback. If personas are part of the written user story, then you know which persona should be reviewing the working software of that demonstrated user story. For example, when you are demonstrating a feature that focuses on administration tasks, then the best feedback comes from having a customer who represents the administrator.

Establish Customer Profiles

Now that you have sorted your customers into current, potential, and past customers and established product-specific personas, you should construct profiles for each customer, giving priority to your current and then your potential customers. Each customer profile paints a picture of the company and the customers therein. It can help you make a range of business decisions. The two key decisions are which customers are best suited to provide user stories, and which are best suited to attend customer validation events and provide the valuable customer feedback.

Just as with the agile inspect-and-adapt model, you need to adapt your customer profiles to their changing business posture and needs. A customer profile identifies common traits in your target customers and may include:

- Demographics
- Buying patterns
- Areas of interest regarding functionality

- Personas of the product they represent
- Whether the customer is perceived as a leader or follower
- What value they are receiving from your product

Within the context of customer validation, the goal is to identify and select customers who meet the profile you are looking for and who are willing to provide feedback.

Customer Demonstrations

The primary way to be continually in touch with your customers and ensure you are building customer value is to provide customers with the opportunity to validate the working software. This engagement is critical to inspect-and-adapt model to ensure the narrowest possible gap between what is delivered and what the customer needs at the time of delivery. Studies show that customer validation opportunities are fewer than expected.

According to a self-reported survey, only 57 percent of the respondents affirmed that "at the end of each iteration, we demo our work.[1]" Worse, only 38 percent say, "We demo the solution to stakeholders every iteration." These results are sobering. They indicate a widespread lack of understanding of Agile values and principles and particularly in the importance of the inspect-and-adapt model with the customer.

The key to Agile is not just to adapt but to do so in the direction that closes in on business value. It is challenging to do this when stakeholders—particularly the customers—are not attending the continuous demonstrations of working software. The goal should be to get the customers to the demonstrations.

Types of Customer Validation

The Sprint Review is the gold standard for customer validation events at which the customer gets an opportunity to view the working software. Nonetheless, other validation activities can help you gain insight into what the customer finds valuable. You should describe in your customer vision the types of validation events you plan to have, such as the following:

- *Product vision validation* shares the vision of the release of the product to help you adapt to your customers' needs at a strategic level.

---

[1]Scott Ambler, "How Agile Are You? 2013 Survey Results," http://www.ambysoft.com/surveys/howAgileAreYou2013.html.

- *Sprint Review demos* demonstrate the working software that was completed during the Sprint, shown to customers to highlight progress and gain feedback.

- *Hands-on experience* lets customers exercise the software in a hands-on manner in a simulated or pilot working environment to generate functional usage and usability feedback.

Motivate Customers to Attend

One of the common challenges that teams have when they want to get customers to the Sprint Review is figuring out how to actually get them to the event. Remember, customers are working full-time at another company and their time is precious. The key is to create a scenario that is compelling for the customer to attend and continue attending. So how do you get customers to attend?

Agile Pit Stop   Customers who attend your validation events are working full-time at another company. Their time is precious. Use this time to gain their valuable feedback.

One approach is to start by inviting customers to one demo session and get their input. Customers who have not experienced something like this before typically are impressed to see working software so early in a release life cycle. They especially like to be asked for their feedback. If they like the first validation session, then invite them to the next demo session. If they agree, entice them by building in some of their feedback. If they show up for the second session, excite them by highlighting the points where you've incorporated their input. At this point, ask the customers if they want to participate periodically at a per-Sprint cadence.

As you are working on your Agile Customer Validation Vision, you should include your strategy on how to motivate customers to attend. You will find, however, that customers are motivated by different things, so you will need an array of motivational tactics within your strategy.

Incorporate Customer Feedback

Although it seems self-evident that you should incorporate customer feedback, too often this critical part of the inspect-and-adapt model is overlooked. Capturing customer feedback is important to ensure you are *building the right thing*. I have seen feedback either languish or not even get captured, which defeats the point of customer validation events and adapting to customer needs. It is critical that the feedback get incorporated into the backlog.

The feedback that you gain should be linked to the contributing user's story, either as a change to an existing story or as a new story. You may also want to capture additional information that the customer shares regarding their own vision, strategies, and direction and incorporate it into their customer profile.

What Is Your Vision of Customer Validation?

Do you have a vision for adapting to customer needs? A haphazard approach may not serve you well. Customer validation is the cornerstone to the inspect-and-adapt approach. Otherwise, what are you adapting to? It will benefit you to continuously engage with customers and truly embrace and incorporate customer feedback, resulting in adapting your product based on the customer need. Consider methodically establishing an Agile Customer Validation Vision.

This vision provides a framework to:

- identify the right customers
- construct customer profiles
- identify product personas
- establish continuous validation sessions such as demonstrations
- motivate the customers to attend the validation sessions
- incorporate the feedback into current and new stories

Once you have established this vision, it is important to share it with the team so that everyone is aware of the vision and the importance of the validation activities.

Writing User Stories and Grooming the Backlog

Focus on what can be done rather than be frustrated by what can't be done.

—Ken Schwaber

The key drivers of work within an agile process are the user stories, which are collected from the customers, stored in the backlog, and built by the team. User stories are essentially requirements that are written from the perspective of the user of the product. The backlog is essentially a requirements list that is continuously groomed to understand priority and gain clarity. As a readiness activity within the RICH model, you need to consider the user story language construct you plan to use to help with consistency and comprehension, where you plan to store the Product Backlog for easy access and sorting, and how frequently you plan to groom the backlog.

Hierarchy of Requirements within an Agile Context

User stories are a form of requirements. The challenge with the word *requirement* is that it may indicate requirements at many levels and sizes, such as user requirements, technical requirements, and business objectives. Because of this possibility for confusion, you need to discriminate where any particular requirement belongs by virtue of its scope and size in a hierarchy of requirement types: *themes, epics, user stories,* and *tasks.*

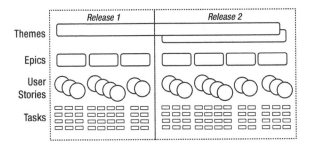

Figure 18-1. Hierarchy of requirement types within an Agile context

Themes are top-level objectives that may span multiple releases and products. Themes should be decomposed into epics that can be applied to a specific product or release. Themes can be used by a solution or product to drive strategic alignment and communicate a clear direction. Examples are:

- Reduce the number of clicks to get to our user functionality within our products and services.

- Improve traffic to the website.

- Apply single sign-on capability to all company products.

Epics are the parent of multiple user stories and are roughly equivalent to a feature or very large story that encapsulates a large piece of functionality. Epics are written by the Product Owner. Epics are helpful when creating a product vision for a release. They should be decomposed into user stories before being introduced into a Sprint. Examples of epics are:

- Administrators can manage users.

- Customer can purchase a ticket.

User stories are equivalent to a business or user requirement and are collected and written by the Product Owner. Stories provide user functionality that represents value to the customer. A user story should be able to be built within a Sprint or, ideally, within half a Sprint. The next section treats user stories at length.

Tasks are the children of user stories and are equivalent to an incremental decomposition of the user story that is defined by the Agile Team. The intent of tasks is to allow the team to incrementally build and test the story so that not all testing occurs at the end. Avoid decomposing stories into stand-alone design, develop, and test tasks, which emphasize a mini-waterfall approach. When a team breaks user stories into tasks, it gains further clarification of the scope of work that needs to be done. For example, a user story that builds a search function can be decomposed into:

- Create static web page.
- Build simple search.
- Add advanced search capabilities.

There are other types of work items that should be captured in the backlog. XP introduces the *spike solution,* which provides a focus on solving a challenging technical, architectural, or design problem. Sometimes known as a *research spike*, this work may seek the answer to a critical business or technical issue. Two examples of research spikes are "What database solution will the team use?" and "What is the product direction in applying forums?" The answers serve to support subsequent epics and user stories.

User Stories

Within an Agile context, user stories are the primary currency used to determine what needs to be built by the team that represents customer value. User stories describe functionality that will be valuable to a user or purchaser of a system (*persona*). User stories are the primary topic discussed in Sprint Planning. The intent of a user story isn't to specify every detail of the need but to provide enough detail to start a healthy conversation about the story to help flesh out the details.

Agile Pit Stop   The user story is the primary requirement building block for specifying the functionality that needs to be built within a Sprint.

The Product Owner is responsible for eliciting user stories from customers and stakeholders. Many others, however, may contribute stories to the Product Owner, including the Agile Team, sales, and marketing. The Product Owner collects and adds the user stories into the Product Backlog. Those user stories that are rank-ordered highest within the backlog get selected and built within a Sprint. The attempt is to build user story functionality within a Sprint time-box.

Canonical Form

There are many ways to write a user story. A *canonical form* is an example of a requirements language construct that is geared toward Agile. This brief statement expresses a user story as *who* wants something, *what* they want from a system, and *why*. The canonical form transcends processes and methodology and works just as well for waterfall as it does for Agile. There are three key elements of a user story in canonical form: the persona, the action, and the business benefit.

- The *persona* represents a particular user of the system, as discussed in Chapter 17. Examples of personas include a buyer who must use the product to purchase items, a power user who uses the product to create quantitative reports, or an administrator who uses the system to manage users and install the most recent patch upgrades.

- The *action* represents what the persona would like to do with the product.

- The *business benefit* provides the value that is gained for the persona. It provides context for the action and helps with testing factors. If I said, "As a user, I can create an account" and leave the business benefit empty, why do you think the user wants an account? The answer can lead you to build very different things if you don't know. If the answer is, "to become a member of the site," you might build a MyPage. If the answer is, "to purchase concert tickets," you might build an order entry system.

Canonical Form Construct and Examples

When establishing a list of user stories, it is strongly recommended to establish a user story language construct that helps you consistently document the stories. The language construct for a user story in canonical form looks like this:

As a <persona>, I want to <action> so that <business benefit>.

The following are examples of user stories in canonical form:

- As a user, I want to create an account so that I can become a member of the site.

- As a learner, I want to set up my profile to include my photo, so that my distributed team members know what I look like.

- As a prospective buyer, I want to search on homes so that I know what properties are available in my price range.

The Product Owner should be trained in writing user stories in the canonical form or whatever form is used to articulate requirements. The Agile Team should be educated in understanding what to look for in a user story and asking questions regarding the elements of the canonical form. The Product Owner may also want to train stakeholders and customers on how to provide their needs in canonical form for consistency and clarity.

Acceptance Criteria and Other Attributes

The *acceptance criteria* are an important attribute of a user story. Each user story should have its own unique set of *acceptance criteria*. Acceptance criteria answer the question, "How will I know when I'm done with the story?" They do this by providing functional and nonfunctional information that helps set boundaries for the work and establishes pass/fail criteria for testers to establish the test cases that are used to test a user story.

Acceptance criteria spell out what the Product Owner expects and what the team needs to accomplish. Ideally, these criteria are provided by the customer at the time they articulate the user story. But they are usually written by the Product Owner acting as the voice of the customer. If the Product Owner is having problems writing effective acceptance criteria, a good resource is the QA team. QA testers can draw from their experience to help the PO.

To write effective acceptance criteria, state the intention, not the solution. In other words, state the "what" not the "how." For example, it is better to write "The user can choose an account" rather than "The user can select the account from a drop-down menu." You want the acceptance criteria to be independent of implementation details.

As an example, if the user story is, "As a user, I want to create an account so that I can become a member of the site," then the acceptance criteria for a user story might include:

- User is presented with an account creation option.

- User must enter an email address and a password.

- The email address must be in a valid format.

- The password must follow the security policy.

- Provide user account confirmation within 5 seconds.

- User lands on the home page after creating the account.

A user story is complemented by several attributes besides the acceptance criteria. Figure 18-2 illustrates a user story card with helpful attributes. These attributes help you understand the scope, ownership, and progress of the story. Each user story should include the following attributes:

- *Description:* a place to add details and decisions.

- *Size:* a place to include the story point number (see Chapter 19).

- *Tasks:* decomposition of the user story into bits of work that represent an incremental build of functionality. They may be nested within a story or linked to the story.

- *Owners:* members of the team working on the story. There should be at least one developer and one QA tester.

- *State:* the status of the work such as *open, in progress, resolved, verified,* or *done.*

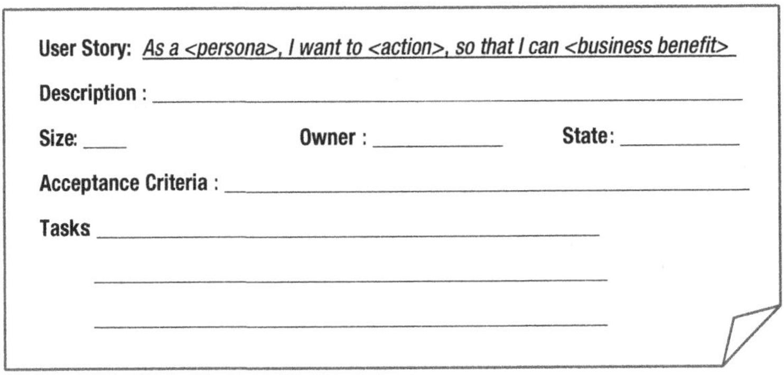

User Story: *As a <persona>, I want to <action>, so that I can <business benefit>*

Description : _____

Size: ____   Owner : _____   State: _____

Acceptance Criteria : _____

Tasks _____

Figure 18-2. User story with attributes to provide a holistic view of the work

Product Backlog

A *Product Backlog* is a repository for user stories and other *Product Backlog Items* (PBIs) such as tasks, epics, and themes. The Product Backlog is the singular place to store all PBIs related to the product. Most Product Backlogs are either a form of document or in an agile planning product that offers automation to manage PBIs.

The Product Backlog is owned and managed by the Product Owner. Others may contribute to the backlog, but the Product Owner controls the prioritization and rank order of the work. The Product Backlog should be readily available to the Scrum Team to view and update, particularly the tasks associated with the user stories.

■ **Agile Pit Stop**   Anyone associated with the product may contribute stories to the backlog. However, only the Product Owner can specify priority or rank order.

The key attributes of the Product Backlog are the priority and rank order (see Figure 18-3). These fields help sort the user stories toward the order of the work. Within an Agile context, the Product Owner and team gain details on the highest priority items, seeking to gain clarity, decomposing epics to user stories and user stories into tasks, and looking for dependencies among stories.

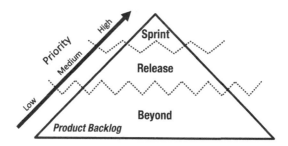

Figure 18-3. Hierarchy of the Product Backlog: highest priority items at the top where Sprint work is occurring

In a traditional waterfall world, the combination of the project plan and the requirements list drives the work. In an Agile world, the Product Backlog drives the work for a team.

Forms of Backlogs

The Product Backlog can be represented in various ways. In its fullest form, it is the location for the whole list of backlog items. There are other forms of backlog. They are the Sprint Backlog and Team Backlog.

The *Sprint Backlog* represents a subset of user stories that are prioritized and rank ordered. Those stories that are highest priority and fit the team velocity or amount of work a team can complete within a Sprint period become the Sprint Backlog. There is a unique Sprint Backlog for each Sprint. The items within it come from the Product Backlog and are identified and added during Sprint Planning. The Sprint Backlog forms the backbone of the work within a Sprint. All stories and tasks within the Sprint are recorded within the Sprint Backlog.

The *Team Backlog* is beneficial when you have multiple Scrum Teams building a product together. The Team Backlog represents a view of the work that is geared toward a particular Scrum Team. During grooming and Sprint Planning, the Scrum Team reviews their prioritized team backlog. From the team backlog, the team can establish a Sprint Backlog of those high-priority stories that the team will work on within a Sprint.

Attributes of a Backlog

A healthy backlog includes attributes that can be associated with the PBIs, such as user stories. It will include the attributes that are associated with a user story, such as a description, size, acceptance criteria, tasks, owner, and progress. In addition, because it is a large list, there are additional attributes that should be included to help you sort the requirements. These attributes include:

- *PBI types*: a way to differentiate between work types such as epic, theme, user stories, tasks, and bugs.
- *ID*: a way to provide a unique identifier for each PBI.
- *Source*: the origin of the PBI, such as customer or stakeholder.
- *Priority*: a way to differentiate the importance of the PBI, often written as high/medium/low, or 1/2/3/4, or must/ should/could/would.
- *Dependencies*: a way to indicate when a PBI is dependent on other PBIs or external functions.
- *Sprint*: the Sprint within which the PBI is built.
- *Comments*: a place to provide additional notes.

Grooming

The primary purpose of *grooming* is to prioritize the backlog so that when you initiate Sprint Planning, you have the stories ready for further refinement, sizing, adding to the Sprint, and gaining commitment to the work that is involved. Grooming may also include ensuring that the user story is in canonical format, details of the story are understood, dependencies are included, and acceptance criteria have been added or clarified. The better you groom the higher priority items within the backlog, the easier and shorter the Sprint Planning event will be.

■ **Agile Pit Stop** The key focus in backlog grooming is to prioritize and rank order the user stories, and then gain more details of those higher priority stories.

The PO is primarily responsible for grooming the backlog. The PO may also invite the full Scrum Team or a select few, such as the lead developer and lead QA team member. There is a great benefit for the PO to invite the Scrum Team. Most important, Scrum Team can ask the PO tough questions regarding specific information and acceptance criteria to gain relevant detail about the story.

Grooming should occur at several different times in your release life cycle: before and during Sprint 0, during Agile Release Planning, during Sprint Planning, and periodically throughout the release.

Before and during Sprint 0

Prior to the project starting, in between one project release and the next, or as a carry-over from the previous release, grooming should start or continue. At the start of any release, grooming should be driven by the PO and include input from the technical leads. If a Sprint 0 exists in the beginning of the project, consider a grooming event at least twice a week of about two hours or more throughout this Sprint.

The purpose of this early grooming is to start or continue collecting user stories to build the Product Backlog. In addition, grooming early helps the team gain an understanding of the work ahead, establishes priority, and helps discover dependencies, risks, and issues early.

Agile Release Planning

If the team applies the Agile Release Planning event toward the beginning of the project, grooming the higher priority stories helps the team appreciate the breadth of work ahead with the understanding that priorities may get adjusted and new user stories may be added (see Chapter 15).

The PO leads the team through the higher priority user stories one by one to accumulate more detail about backlog items; identify additional dependencies, risks, and issues; and potentially "T-shirt size" the stories (small, medium, and large). Ultimately this helps the team gain confidence of the work ahead.

Sprint Planning

The grooming that occurs within Sprint Planning focuses on gaining enough understanding of the user stories to build the functionality within a Sprint. This grooming will include gaining detail about the story, discussing design aspects, decomposing the story into tasks, and sizing the story. If the highest priority user stories are well groomed coming into Sprint Planning, then this event may be shorter than usual.

The grooming within Sprint Planning is performed by the PO and the team. The team should leave the Sprint Planning event with confidence in their knowledge of the user stories that are now part of the sprint backlog.

Periodically throughout the Release

After a release gets started, new user stories may continue to come in or, if there is an abundance of user stories in the backlog, reprioritization will occur. In both cases, those higher priority user stories should be groomed to better understand the potential work ahead. The advantage of having the Product Backlog groomed is that it can avoid disrupting a team's progress if stories are poorly written or not understood.

With that in mind, at regular intervals throughout the Sprint, the PO continues backlog grooming, focusing on the new high-priority stories from customers and includes the team in fleshing out the details of those stories that are candidates for the next Sprint Planning event. The interval within a Sprint can vary depending on the rate of new stories coming into the backlog that are high priority and amount of existing high-priority stories that have not been groomed. As an example, this may occur twice a week, once a Sprint, or somewhere in between. The amount of time may vary from Sprint to Sprint.

The initial grooming of the backlog may occur at the Product Owner Scrum of Scrums if there are multiple teams that make up the release. This gives the PO a chance to discuss prioritization of the work with the other POs before discussing the high-priority stories with their team.

What Is Your Story?

User stories form the backbone of the work on your team. It is important that you consider a requirements language construct such as the canonical form. Including the persona or whom the functionality should be built for helps you understand the point of view of the persona. Including the action helps us understand what is being built. The business benefit provides the value gains and also helps you understand the functionality being built. These elements provide clarity for the team to build what the customer wants.

The Product Backlog provides a single place to store the user stories and other PBIs. It is important to think through whether you want to manually manage the backlog items within a document or in an agile planning product that offers automation to manage PBIs. Finally, ensure there is periodic grooming so you have a prioritized backlog in which the highest priority items have more details. This helps provide a broad view of the work ahead and easier Sprint Planning events. Thinking of these areas early and then sharing them with the team helps provide a framework for collecting, storing, prioritizing, sorting, and better understanding customer needs.

Working with Story Points, Velocity, and Burndowns

The best we can do is size up the chances, calculate the risks involved, estimate our ability to deal with them, and then make our plans with confidence.

—Henry Ford

Within an Agile context, applying story points is an acknowledged way to size user stories. *Story points* are a relative sizing approach that focuses on the scope of work, which is made up of the effort of the work and its complexity. As a readiness activity within the RICH model, it is important to educate team members on the sizing framework you are applying, using Sprint Burndowns to assess progress within a Sprint, and how velocity can help you establish the team pace of work.

Scope versus Schedule Measure

When I help teams implement agile methods, some team members have a hard time getting their head around "estimating" user stories using story points. This has to do with understanding the relative sizing that story points bring. Some team members (including management) ask to align story points with days or hours. I realized that when I use the word estimate it brings the baggage of traditional estimation that uses schedule as a measure (hours, days, weeks, months, years).

With this in mind, I strongly advocate that in Agile it is appropriate to use the term "size" to measure user stories because this relates to the amount of functionality being built. This is more than just semantics. This takes us a step away from the traditional mindset where schedule is king and moves us to the more important focus of scope—because to our customers the functionality is what is valuable and what they pay for. There will always be trade-offs between schedule and scope, but working software that meets the scope of customer needs and provides them value is slightly more important (working software over schedule).

■ **Agile Pit Stop** Story points are an abstract scope measure focusing on the work. It is not wise to apply a schedule measure of hours and days. Instead, use a scope measure like story points to indicate the amount and complexity of the work.

In Agile, the intent is to determine the unit size of work based on the functionality you are building for that story. In effect, *scope* is the measure of progress based on amount of effort and complexity of the work. I realized that there are those who try to apply a schedule measure because of their familiarity with traditional estimation whereas story points are in fact meant to represent the scope of the work. In other words, when you try to apply a schedule measure for scope, it is like trying to fit a square peg in a round hole. Ultimately, you need both scope (story points) and schedule (per Sprint length) to understand your team pace (velocity).

Story Points

Story points are a relative measure that expresses the amount of functionality and the complexity of the work. Every team creates their own story point sizing framework based on the type of work they do, the skills and experience of the team, and what they personally perceive to be a small, medium, or large amount of work. This is why management should not compare the story point velocity of different teams.

This relative sizing framework takes the focus off the actual schedule measure of hours or days and instead puts it on describing the size and complexity of a functionality compared with other functionality. If you are familiar with function points, story points acts as a similar measure that tries to establish a unit size or scope of the work.

■ **Agile Pit Stop**   Story point sizing framework is specific to each team. This is why no one should try to compare the story point sizes from one team to the next.

Fibonacci Sequence

Story points are usually expressed in numeric units. The range of units that is often used within the agile world is the *Fibonacci sequence*. The sequence of Fibonacci numbers provides a numeric distribution that can be used to differentiate between sizes of work (Figure 19-1).

0, 1, 1, 2, 3, 5, 8, 13, 21, 34, 55...

Figure 19-1. Fibonacci sequence that highlights a substantial distribution of numbers

This sequence is established where each subsequent number is the sum of the two numbers immediately before it. The importance of the Fibonacci sequence to the team is that it provides a means for differentiating between unit sizes of functionality being built from the stories within the backlog.

Establishing Relative Story Point Sizing Framework

Story points start as an abstract scope measure until such time as a team establishes a team-based relative sizing framework according to a numerical range, in this case the Fibonacci sequence. The team defines what it means to build the smallest amount of functionality that can stand on its own. For example, the team defines a story point size of a 1 as follows:

- Build a static webpage with fixed content using HTML.

From there, the team can determine what type of work is considered twice as large with minimal functionality or almost twice as large but with slightly more complexity. This would receive a story point size of 2. You may decide up front what work defines a story point size of 3, 5, 8, 13, and 21 to help you size user stories, or you may use what you define as 1 and 2 as the basis for sizing all other work and extrapolating the size from there.

▓ **Agile Pit Stop**   This relative story point sizing framework should be in a readily viewable place for all of the team to see.

This is the beginning of establishing the relative story point sizing framework for your team. Because each Scrum Team may work on different types of functionality (for example, front-end UI versus back-end database), it is critical that each team develop their own sizing framework.

Planning Poker

Planning poker is an instructive and fun consensus-based sizing technique used to size the stories, primarily during Sprint Planning. It is based on *Wideband Delphi*, a consensus-based technique for sizing work. Planning poker starts with placing the Fibonacci sequence numbers from 1 through 55 on the faces of playing cards (Figure 19-2).

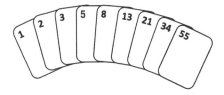

Figure 19-2. Planning poker playing cards used to size user stories

To play planning poker, each team member gets a deck of cards. For this example, Sprint Planning has commenced and the team has discussed the details of a user story. When it is time to size the story:

- Each team member discreetly selects a card from their deck relating to the story points they think reflects the size and complexity of the work for the story and simultaneously displays it to the rest of the team.
- If there is consensus in the size, this becomes the recorded size for the story.
- If there are differences in sizes, then the owners of lowest and highest cards explain their sizing position, and the team briefly discusses the story further.
- Each team member again selects a card based on the new discussion.
- This continues until a consensus on the size is achieved.

Planning poker can be played face to face when all team members are colocated or virtually when team members are distributed. If virtual, then sizes can be instant-messaged to the Scrum Master, who shares the sizes with the team.

Sprint Burndown

A *Sprint Burndown* is used by a team to highlight the amount of work that a team plans to complete, known as the *target velocity*, compared to what work was actually completed and what work is left to do. It is a metric meant only for a particular Scrum Team and is only relevant for a particular Sprint. The benefit is that it is used to provide a team awareness of whether they are on track, predict when all of the work will be completed, and identify roadblocks early.

In Figure 19-3, the *ideal burndown* line starts with the team's target velocity, which is the amount of work a team believes they can do within a Sprint. In this example, the unit of work is called story points and for this Sprint the target velocity is 55. The ideal burndown line is established by starting with the target velocity and then subtracting the average increment each day. You get the daily average increment by dividing the target velocity by the number of days in a Sprint (in this example, 55/10 = 5.5).

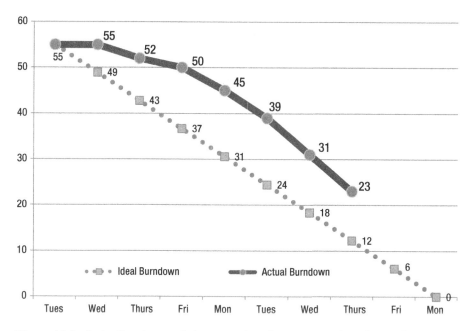

Figure 19-3. Sprint Burndown to help a team view their progress throughout a Sprint

The *actual burndown* line indicates how many story points of work are actually completed from day to day. It starts with the team's target velocity (55), and each day it is subtracted by the amount of work done or completed stories each day. Because each story is a different size, the amount that gets subtracted on each day varies by the number of stories and the unit size of each of those stories. (Don't be surprised if, early in the Sprint, the actual burndown stays flat for a couple of days. Team members are just starting the work and it is not realistic to expect immediate completion of a story.)

Velocity

Velocity is a metric that can help you understand a team's sustainable pace by identifying the amount of stories that represent customer value a team can deliver in a Sprint. Sustainable pace is one of the Agile principles, and the intent is to understand this pace when team members are working 40 hours a week and no more. Sustainable pace allows team members to work indefinitely. A team's Sprint velocity is a representation of how many story points of functionality a team can deliver within a Sprint. At the beginning of a Sprint, it is called the *target velocity*. The *actual velocity* is calculated at the end of each Sprint based on the stories that actually get completed that meet the done criteria (Chapter 20) and the acceptance criteria of each story (Chapter 18).

A team's velocity is commonly represented in graphical form that is used to measure the rate of business value a team can consistently deliver from Sprint to Sprint. Because each team applies its own relative story point sizing framework, this metric is unique and only applicable for a particular team. It must not be used to compare one team to another. The benefit is that over time, it becomes a predictor of the amount of work a team can do in the subsequent Sprint.

In Figure 19-4, the *target velocity* is the team's estimate of how many units of work (or story points) it thinks it can complete within a Sprint. The *actual velocity* is the actual units of work completed in that Sprint. The *average velocity* is the average of the actual velocities accrued divided by the number of Sprints completed.

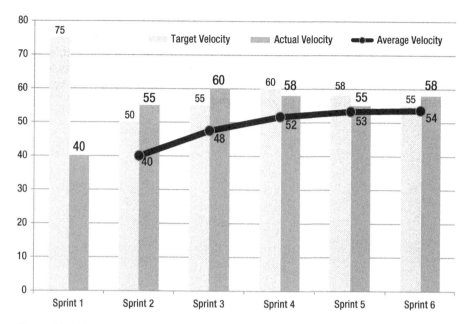

Figure 19-4. Team velocity metrics that a team uses to predict their target velocity (number of story points they can complete in a Sprint)

Notice in the first Sprint that the team estimated a target velocity of 75. Because they did not have any historical data on which to base their velocity, it was a guess. They learned at the end of the Sprint that they actually completed 40 story point units of work. The good news is that at the beginning of the next Sprint, they have a basis of actual work completed as historical data, which can help them predict with more accuracy how many story points of work they can complete. You can see by Sprint 4, the average velocity of 52 story points becomes a fairly accurate predictor of how much work the team can complete in Sprint 5, during which they actually completed 55 units of work. The velocity helps set a realistic target of work for each Sprint and can be used to provide a release burnup for how many story points can be completed for release (see discussion in Chapter 14).

Are You Getting the Point?

As teams get ready to implement Agile, it is important for them to establish a sizing framework they will apply, use Sprint Burndowns to assess progress within a Sprint, and understand how velocity can help them establish a sustainable team pace of work. Story points provide an abstract unit measure of work that becomes specific to a team when they establish their relative story point sizing framework.

This sizing framework is very important for a team to achieve a sustainable pace of work at 40 hours a week and no more to avoid team member burn-out and gain alignment with the Agile principles. To achieve a sustainable pace, you need to track your team velocity, which is the scope quantity (story points) per unit time (Sprint length). Establishing a sizing framework can help a team achieve a sustainable pace throughout the project.

Constructing Done Criteria to Promote Quality

Quality is not an act; it is a habit.

—Aristotle

Done criteria are clearly stated conditions that a user story must meet for the functionality to be deemed complete and shippable for release. Done criteria supports the Agile principle of *technical excellence,* by which team members apply continuous attention to engineering practices and techniques focused on building a quality product.

Done criteria set the tone and create a habit on what it means to be *done.* These criteria should be readily viewable by the team as a reminder as it makes its transition toward Agile. Done criteria confer the following benefits:

- They help set team's expectations of what it means to build the story functionality so that it is potentially shippable.

- They help identify the engineering activities and expectations that must occur to build a quality product.

- They can increase the level of product quality and limit the amount of rework due to defects found in the field.

- They are an input for team sizing user stories during Sprint Planning and ensure all of the work described in the team's done criteria is considered.

This sounds simple enough. But if you are transitioning from a traditional waterfall world, *done* may have meant "I am done with development so therefore the work is done"—and the team now has to expand the meaning to include other engineering disciplines such as testing. In pre-Agile worlds, there is often a separation between development and testing. When you transition to an Agile mindset, done criteria imply that we are bringing development and testing and all of the associated disciplines together.

Agile Pit Stop   There is a difference between *done criteria* and *acceptance criteria*. Acceptance criteria are unique for each user story and answer the question, "How will I know when I'm done with the story?" Done criteria are engineering tasks that apply equally to all user stories within the Sprint and project.

I suggest that done criteria are one of the most critical techniques that must be discussed and implemented to ensure that what gets built is made with quality. You can think of done criteria as a form of team-based quality control applied when a team builds product functionality.

Done Criteria Starter Kit

As a readiness activity within the RICH model, it is critical to establish done criteria prior to building the product. This ensures that the team has the opportunity to discuss the quality steps and understand how they are applied. This also ensures the team begins with done criteria that helps infuse quality into building the product right at the beginning.

I usually bring a starter kit of typical disciplines to get a story to *done*. This helps initiate an active team discussion prior to Sprint 1 so that each team member understands the various elements of the done criteria, what disciplines we expect to follow when building a user story, and what elements we are agreeing to as a team. Here is my done criteria starter kit:

- Design: Specify design tools, design type(s), and modeling the team uses. This extends to practices such as user interface (UI) and user experience (UX). This may include crafting user cases for stories or epics and specifying usability and sustainability goals.

- Development: Specify development programming tools, techniques, and coding standards. This done criterion may include building a story in an incremental manner to allow for iteration between development and testing.

- Documentation: Specify the level of documentation completion we expect when user stories have a documentation component, such as user guides and the nonfunctional requirements associated with them.

- Unit tests: Specify the tools and percentage of unit tests we expect to see executed. When there are no unit tests in place, specify the level of focus on constructing unit tests as part of the story construction.

- Version control: Specify the expected use of version control, private user workspaces (including check-out/check-in), continuous integration needs, and when to branch and when to merge.

- Local builds: Specify the build tools and the expected use of applying incremental local builds, such as continuous builds within the private user workspace.

- Code reviews: Specify when to apply code reviews and the percentage of code reviews being applied (all code changes or a particular type of code change). Discuss if pair programming is being applied and if this displaces code reviews.

- Testing: Specify the test tools and testing types—such as functional, system, integration, performance, or load—being applied to a user story. When there are no tests in place, specify the level of focus on constructing tests as part of the story construction.

- Defects: Specify the appropriate severity-level defects (severity 1 and 2 only or all severities) that must be resolved and verified prior to completing a story.

- Acceptance criteria: Prior to indicating that a story is complete, all acceptance criteria must be complete as well. Although acceptance criteria are separate from done criteria, for a story to be deemed *done*, it must subsume the acceptance criteria (Chapter 18).

At this point, the team discusses these elements, adapts the criteria to their current level of discipline, and establishes a common definition of *done* for the stories. You may need to further adapt your done criteria for the following reasons:

- Align with compliance standards that must be met.

- Enhance with technical best practices of an organization.

- Consider the inclusion of establishing automation activities for streamlining testing and build processes.

Once the team agrees to done criteria, they become a cornerstone for velocity and so have a direct effect on the sizing of stories. During Sprint Planning events, the done criteria should be highlighted as a reminder of the level and detail of work needed to complete the story and as an input to sizing the work. When done criteria are established, post them in a visible place to remind the team.

Agile Pit Stop   You may have variations of done criteria depending on the type of story work occurring. The done criteria described in this chapter focus on user stories. However, you may define a specific done criteria for research spike stories and refactoring stories.

You should expect done criteria to evolve over time. You may want to periodically review them during the Sprint Retrospective events to determine if they need improvement. Also, some of the effort associated with your done criteria is dependent on the tools, infrastructure, and automation that currently exist and on your vision of these areas.

Definition of *Done* and *Done-Done*

You may encounter various synonyms for the term *done criteria*. Some prefer the term *definition of done* (DoD). Others define *done* in Agile as *done-done*. This is meant to imply that you are finished not only with development (the first *done*) but also with testing (the second *done*).

The question is, how many *dones* do you need? Figure 20-1 illustrates the humor of having multiple dones. If your definition of *done* has ten key disciplines, as I outline in the done criteria starter kit, then maybe it should be called *done-done-done-done-done-done-done-done-done-done* criteria. This is why I suggest that just one *done* is enough.

Done   Done   Done
Done

Figure 20-1. How many *dones* do you need to name your done criteria?

Are We Done Yet?

Done criteria are critical to a team following Agile—and indeed to any team that is developing software. They help a team understand the Agile principles of technical excellence and adapt their mindset to what it really means to be complete when building the functionality specified within a user story. It helps ensure that the user stories are built to include the necessary engineering activities and quality criteria to get to an effective and demonstrable piece of functionality ready for release.

Once a team has established its done criteria, the criteria should evolve over time based on what is learned during the retrospective and as the team increases its level of discipline with the benefit of a quality and releasable product. So the next time someone on your team says, "Are we done yet?", make sure that the questioner means, "Have we built our stories with the appropriate engineering disciplines and quality criteria that allow us to build value with high quality?"

Considering Agile Tools within an ALM Framework

Technology is nothing. What's important is that you have faith in people, that they're basically good and smart, and if you give them tools, they'll do wonderful things with them.

—Steve Jobs

I typically do not discuss agile tooling when initially helping teams adopt Agile. I believe the initial focus should be on Agile values and principles and then the processes and practices. Agile tooling discussions should occur as a readiness activity within the RICH deployment model so that it is clear to the team what tools will be used within the project and product context.

From an agile perspective, collocated teams may prefer to work with minimal tooling in the agile space, using spreadsheets, story walls, and whiteboards. As soon as teams become distributed, however, working with online tools becomes beneficial. A team may gain benefits in productivity and transparency from automation that they provide. Details on tools that can help you identify, track, and delivery customer value should be included within the technical vision (Chapter 15).

Application Lifecycle Management

Application lifecycle management (ALM) describes a set of tools and corresponding practices that work together across the release lifecycle to help a team deliver an instance of a product (*release*) from inception to production. A robust ALM framework will include a *metamodel* that defines a common language across the tools and *process engine* that parses and shares information across and among the various tools within the ALM framework.

I have been fortunate enough to have been involved with both ALM and Agile. Unfortunately, there is no one-stop-shop ALM solution because of the breadth and depth that full ALM implies and the fact that software development is more complex and diverse than ever. But the more seamless an integrated tool framework is, the more an Agile Team can focus on building customer value.

There is a need for flexibility and customization so that an ALM tool framework doesn't drive the interaction of the team. This is in support of the Agile principle, "People and their interactions over process and tools." It doesn't say, "You should forgo process and tools"—but it implies that teams should always be aware of what is best for the members based on current and future interactions among the team. More important, teams should not allow tools to drive the process or constrain the interaction possibilities.

ALM Framework for Customer Value

When introducing ALM and the tools it brings to an agile context, it is important to focus on customer value from inception to release. Starting agile ALM as early as inception or business visioning for a specific release helps provide the context for initiating customer value for the project.

■ **Agile Pit Stop**   The tools that you use within an agile context should help you identify, track, and deliver customer value.

Should you pursue an ALM framework to help with an agile deployment, make sure that your main objective is to establish mechanisms that improve your ability to understand and promote customer value throughout the lifecycle. This helps establish traceability of customer value from the beginning of the lifecycle to the end.

The *value chain* is a series of activities focused on delivering value. According to Michael Porter, value "stems from the many discrete activities a firm performs in designing, producing, marketing, delivering, and supporting a product."[1] Figure 21-1 illustrates the notion that just as Agile supports the value chain and the delivery of customer value, ALM should support Agile in reaching this goal. This establishes the basis for an Agile ALM framework.

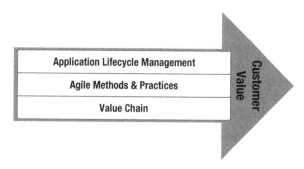

Figure 21-1. Applying application lifecycle management (ALM) tools to support agile methods and practices to build the value chain and the delivery of customer value

Tools to Support Agile

When teams discuss agile tools, the focus tends to fall on Agile Planning. However, Agile can take advantage of tools from a variety of areas across the lifecycle. Besides agile planning tools, a team can take advantage of tools in business visioning, collaboration, defect tracking, configuration management, continuous integration and build, and test automation. ALM can help integrate the tools in a way that benefits the team. The rest of this chapter examines these different tool areas that can benefit Agile and its goal of delivering customer value.

■ **Agile Pit Stop**　Agile Planning is often the first tool thought of for Agile. But business visioning, collaboration, defect tracking, configuration management, continuous integration and build, test automation can also be advantageous.

---

[1]Michael Porter. *Competitive Advantage: Creating and Sustaining Superior Performance.* Free Press, 1985.

Business Visioning: Identifying Customer Value

As teams begin a value delivery lifecycle, they need to provide a means to capture customer ideas and prioritize and rank them to ensure they are building something the customer wants. Ideas primarily come from the customer, but they may be channeled through discussions with sales, presales, marketing, management, and others. With a business visioning idea-capture tool, ideas can come directly from the customer into this customer-facing tool and be sorted out by the Product Owner.

It is advantageous to provide an idea generation and collaboration space with web conferencing that is both threaded and traceable from the source to the idea. This provides customers a place to submit ideas that may evolve into epics or user stories. The latter implies integration between idea generation and user stories in the Product Backlog.

A key to business visioning is having the ability to generate market-level objectives from ideas so that a team has a vision of what they want to build yet remains adaptable to the ever-changing marketplace. Then they should have the ability to generate a business case from the ideas, market objectives, projected return on investment, and market analysis.

Collaboration: Sharing Customer Value

A *collaboration tool* is a virtual replication of an Agile Team room. This is a virtual room that can be viewed from your computer, in which you can see the rest of the team in action. You can "poke" them, have a discussion, break out into individual virtual team rooms, view the story wall, and see your specific work wall.

Team members need to enable continuous communication among themselves with threaded team conversation. These conversations need to be integrated and connected to certain events (such as Sprint Planning and Daily Scrum) or certain work items (such as user stories), so that they can be available for considering context and further detail as needed.

Full project teams and their Scrum Team components also need the ability to support Scrum of Scrums (SoS) for collaboration and discussion. There may be a project SoS (when there are multiple Scrum Teams on a project), Product Owner SoS, and technical SoS. Each may benefit from collaboration space.

From an external perspective, having the ability to initiate virtual customer validation sessions (such as Sprint Reviews) to demonstrate Sprint functionality from the version control or testing environment is enabled by an agile ALM solution. Feedback from virtual attendees can be captured in the collaboration system and agile tools related to specific stories and Sprint. This input should be readily available for the next Sprint Planning session.

Agile Planning: Capturing and Prioritizing Customer Value

A team, led by the Product Owner, needs the ability to establish and manage a Product Backlog to capture epics, user stories, and tasks and then establish relationships among them (from tasks to their parent story, from stories to their parent epic or theme, and so forth). Agile Planning tools must have the ability to capture:

- Product Backlog Item (PBI) types, such as epic, theme, user stories, tasks, and bugs

- unique identifiers for each PBI

- the originator or source of the PBI

- the priority of the PBI

- dependencies the PBI has on other PBIs or external functions

- the Sprint in which the PBI is built

- comments regarding the PBI

Chapter 18 discusses agile planning tool needs in the context of the Product Backlog and attributes.

The good news is that this functionality is readily available in various tools. Within the context of managing a backlog, a team needs the ability to generate Sprint Backlogs from the Product Backlog based on priority—including the ability to capture acceptance criteria related to a story, ensuring that the Sprint story wall is in a visible place.

It is also advantageous for an agile planning tool to capture customer personas. This is useful when a team's requirement language construct (such as the canonical form) captures the persona. You can create the customer personas for your specific product; then, when the Product Owner is writing the user stories, they can be linked to the persona details.

As a result of backlog management, having a means to generate Sprint Burndowns, release burnups, and Sprint and release velocity metrics in an automated manner helps the team track progress. When Agile is being implemented on large project teams with multiple Scrum Teams, it is beneficial to get a cross–Scrum Team view of the Sprint and release progress.

The last session within a Sprint is the *Sprint Retrospective*. It is beneficial to have the ability to support the retrospective process and merge the improvement tasks back into the Product Backlog for Sprint Planning. These tasks can be included in the next Sprint and tracked to closure.

Defect Tracking: Identifying Bugs While Increasing Quality

Defect tracking tools provide a team with the capability of documenting, prioritizing, and tracking defects to closure. As part of the Sprint, teams often incorporate defect work. Because of this, they need the ability to track defects related to the product. In addition, the Product Owner must have the ability to selectively include defects into the Product Backlog as appropriate. This is especially relevant to legacy products.

Teams also need the ability to differentiate clearly among the defects associated with the current Sprint, past Sprints, and past releases. This implies integration between the defect tracking tool and the agile planning backlog management tool.

Version Control: Identifying and Controlling Assets That Form the Basis of Customer Value

A *version control tool* provides the ability to store, manage, and track changes to source code. There is a need for a version control system that can manage any type of element, such as code, documents, test scripts, and executables. These elements form the basis for the assets that must be managed. These code assets require the ability to be tagged to a release of the product.

The version control system should have the ability to form private workspaces so each team member can work securely in a "sandbox," allowing for both creativity and integrity prior to promoting code to the project level or backing stream. To support different code levels and streams, the version control system needs a robust branching and merging process to support different lines of development of working code while the assets that represent customer value can be clearly identified and tracked.

Because assets are important to delivering customer value, the version control system must be regularly backed up, along with a tested disaster recovery process with quick turn-around time for recovery. The version control system forms the basis for the continuous integration and build system so that what is built comes directly from a location of known integrity.

Continuous Integration and Build: Continuously Building Value

Continuous integration and build refers to the process of checking in and merging code from a developer's private workspace to the project stream, thereby immediately initiating a project-level build. Key advantages are that the team learns of merge and build issues right away. Frequent code merging reduces the challenges and pain of large, complex integrations in the future. It also provides team members with immediate feedback on the success or failure of changes in a build and in the subsequent smoke test of the product. The *smoke test* provides a brief test of the functionality to ensure it operates at a basic level.

A continuous integration and build system should be integrated with a version control system that provides effective branching and merging functionality. This includes the ability to initiate merge and build on check-in to the parent branch and to provide information on what was merged and built and their results. In addition, it is beneficial to have an integration with the agile planning tool on one end to make the team aware of the merge and build results and on the other end with the test environment to initiate the next step in testing.

One of the advantages of continuous integration is that the team begins to build the customer value early and often. A very interesting cultural shift occurs when the concept of *continuous* is ingrained into a culture. Agile embraces a mindset of continuous change in which builds move from an event-based integration process to a continuous integration process. In other words, no one needs to hold onto large amounts of changes for a major integration effort. It also promotes more granular user stories and more frequent code changes.

Testing: Verifying and Automating for Quality

Although prioritized scope drives customer value, teams need to ensure that value is of high quality. The test function is important to Agile. Testing comes with a whole range of tools. The ability to run functional tests, system tests, regression tests, performance tests, load tests, and others are critical to ensuring product quality. Integration with the agile planning tool allows the team to be aware of test results, including what tests were successfully run on stories.

In addition, establishing a test automation framework allows for reduced QA and developer involvement and allows for the tests to be continuously run. In Agile, automation helps reduce manual testing, which slows the team down. As automation is added, a focus on quality data can help a team highlight opportunities to increase velocity and improve quality. Details on test tools should be included within the QA vision discussed in Chapter 15.

Do You Have the Right Tools for the Job?

When discussing tools for Agile, planning tools tend to be the focus. But there are many tools across the project lifecycle that can help an Agile Team. These include tools for business visioning, collaboration, defect tracking, configuration management, continuous integration and build, and test automation.

Preparing a technical vision of your tool strategy can help you frame your discussion around the benefits of tools and how the tools can help you identify, track, and delivery customer value.

By fostering integration of tools across the lifecycle, an ALM framework can support both the value chain and Agile in the pursuit of delivering customer value. ALM establishes a tool framework to help a product team establish and manage customer value throughout the lifecycle. It ensures traceability of customer value from one part of the lifecycle area to another. As you consider Agile, remind yourself of the Agile principle: *People and interactions over process and tools*. This doesn't mean that you ignore tools, but that you should employ tools to help you deliver customer value.

Implementing, Coaching, and Honing Activities

You just want to hone your craft, whatever it may be.

—Christopher Cross

The middle part of this book (Chapters 7–21) focuses on the readiness activities described by the RICH model to assist the achievement of the Agile mindset and true agile transformation. *Readiness* is the beginning of conditioning the mind toward the behavior needed to align with Agile values and principles and focuses on making decisions regarding the elements for your implementation. As you incrementally make readiness decisions and continue to focus on the Agile mindset, the implementation process can begin.

Agile Pit Stop The ready, implement, and hone activities of the RICH Deployment Model align with the agile notion of inspect and adapt. Anything that gets deployed should be subject to an opportunity for inspection and adaption.

This chapter highlights the key activities within implement, coach, and hone to achieve an agile state of mind and a transformation to Agile (Figure 22-1).

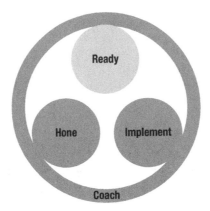

Figure 22-1. RICH model with emphasis on *implement, coach,* and *hone* activities

As the readiness activities are decided, they can be implemented in an incremental or holistic manner. With that in mind, the following sections cover the suggested focus areas for the implement, coach, and hone activities.

Implementing Agile

During readiness activities, there is an ever-growing list of people getting involved in the Agile adoption effort. While the Agile Deployment Team has the primary responsibility, they are incrementally involving new people to gain their input, experience, and awareness. When there is a focus on implementation, the visibility and impact of the agile effort expands to the whole organizational scope.

Implementation activities focus on the timely application of agile elements within a team or organization. With proper conditioning during readiness activities, the participants will understand why they are applying Agile and begin to internalize the values and principles. Although you have made decisions during readiness activities, you may need to adapt approaches and decisions as implementation becomes real.

The primary goal of implementing is to roll out Agile to the organizational scope. There may be emphasis in getting the mechanics in place, but there should also be a strong focus in changing behaviors.

For everything that is implemented, there should be a follow-up to determine whether the team understands why they are adopting, at what level they are mechanically adopting the agile element, and at what level they are making the cultural shift toward an Agile mindset. This reflective follow-up helps with honing. During this time, it is important to infuse implementation activities with appropriate coaching to ensure the agile mechanics and culture begin to stick.

Executing Deployment Backlog and Communication Plan

Commencement of implementation means you have made a decision to initiate the deployment of Agile within your organizational scope. It is time to incrementally begin deployment activities and initiate communication about those activities. As discussed in Chapter 11, a prioritized backlog is beneficial in helping you understand what should be occurring for a successful deployment and to track the progress of the backlog items.

At this point, you should have your objectives and motivations, an understanding of the scope of the effort, a deployment team to help lead and support the effort, a communication plan to help convey progress, suitable teams identified within the organizational scope, the work prioritized in a deployment backlog, and a plan for applying and adapting the agile process and mindset for deployment into the organizational scope.

The communication plan should include how you will encapsulate various messages into various communication types via various communication channels to various audiences with various frequencies. Implementation is a time to communicate progress and expectations frequently. As discussed in Chapter 11, an agile communication plan keeps everyone informed and aware of the continued support for Agile.

Continuing Education

Education for Agile is a long-term venture. The early steps start with promoting awareness and getting the organization trained. Awareness should have begun during readiness to ensure those within the scope are aware of the objective and motivations for moving to Agile.

Promoting Agile Community

Elements of the agile community should now be implemented. This may include launching Agile-related websites and social collaboration venues. The collaboration venue is a place for folks to pose questions to other teams to hear thoughts, share ideas, and discuss lessons learned.

■ **Agile Pit Stop**   The agile community venue provides an opportunity to share, discuss, and collaborate on a variety of topics.

Early on, the members of the Agile Deployment Team may be the biggest responders to questions posed, but they should actively seek contributions from local Agile Champions and other community members. If you have implemented a form of gamification to get people engaged in the community, now is the time to start. Chapter 16 looks at building an agile community and ways to implement gamification.

Initiating Agile Training

The key to implementing training is to conduct the sessions in a just-in-time manner before the people playing agile roles need to apply the agile framework. At this point, whether you have hired external trainers or use your Agile Coach, Agile trainers should be lined up, training materials should be identified, and the training schedule should be executed. Each set of training materials should include a section about the agile framework that will be used. Although most training benefits from being implemented in a just-in-time manner, this may vary slightly by role.

It is highly recommended that the executives and senior management take the executive overview immediately after there is a commitment to Agile. This should have occurred as a readiness activity, but if not it should be the first education activity done when implementing. Executive overview provides executives and senior management with a summary of Agile principles and values, its business benefits, and their role and responsibility within an Agile culture. The key is getting management at this level to understand the important role they play in helping the organization make the cultural shift to Agile.

The Product Owner (PO) should be the one of the folks trained early by taking a role-specific Product Owner workshop or Certified Scrum Product Owner (CSPO) training. As soon as Agile is known to be the approach the team will use, the PO should be trained. This is because the PO has to build the Product Backlog, establish personas, build company profiles, and establish the product vision that helps guide the product direction.

■ **Agile Pit Stop**   Depending on the number of teams needing training, you may consider capturing metrics on *number trained* to gain a sense of training progress.

Next, the Scrum Master should be trained by taking a specific Scrum Master workshop or Certified Scrum Master (CSM) training. This is because the Scrum Master helps set the project up within an agile context, is the facilitator of the agile events, and will act as the guardian and promoter of Agile values and principles.

The members of an Agile Team—specifically the cross-functional team members including developers, QA, and others—should take an Agile Team Foundation course just prior to being asked to use Agile on their new project. This should include training on their role, the Agile values and principles, the agile framework that will be used, and all of the agile events they will participate in. It is beneficial for the Scrum Master and PO to take this training with the team even though they have their own specific training. This promotes team spirit and ties the various roles together.

As a reminder, training is just the beginning of the journey to an Agile culture. Although training can focus on skills and process, its ability to be applied can be undone the moment the trainee moves back into their existing culture. You will need coaching to keep the team on their agile journey and help apply the mindset, process, and skills correctly.

Implementing the Agile Framework

Applying the agile framework takes place the moment that Agile is applied on the project. This isn't a specific activity. Instead, the implementation of the agile framework being used should be initially discussed during training and then applied on the project. For the first three or four Sprints, coaching can be very advantageous for those teams that have not implemented Agile before in ensuring that the processes and team roles are applied properly.

Agile Pit Stop   When implementing an Agile framework, consider following the *Shu Ha Ri* concept of learning (*Shu* - obey the rule, *Ha* - adapt the rule, *Ri* - transcend the rule). First practice by the book. Then you are in a position to adapt and transcend.

Applying Agile Tools

If can be risky to start using a tool right away. A tool often comes with a dictated process. Instead, it is beneficial first to understand the team's interaction and natural process. What a team may first consider doing is to use the physical story wall to display the stories, if the team is collocated, or use a basic online spreadsheet to manage the backlog prior to moving to a more sophisticated infrastructure. This gives the team a tangible idea of how they would like to use a tool before it is applied, in alignment with the Agile value of "people and interactions over process and tools."

A preliminary step to implementing tools is to become aware of the ones that can help you effectively deploy Agile and then identify the appropriate tools for your team's needs. In addition, the tools you use should help you in the pursuit of delivering customer value. Chapter 21 presents the range of tools that can support Agile and details how they can support the value chain of building products customers want.

Implementing a tool infrastructure can take time. As you are planning the installation and set-up of tools, ensure that you provide reasonable lead time between starting the installation and when you would like the team to actually start using the tools. As part of the implementation, ensure that appropriate training and user guides, physical or online, are provided so that users have educational support.

You should have a backlog of tasks that ensures you have considered the tasks for an effective tool deployment. A general outline of tool deployment tasks at an epic level follows:

- Identification and preparation of the environment: involves a server location for the tool to reside and any accompanying needs for storage.

- Installation of the tool: involves physically installing the tool in the prescribed location and installing client software.

- Preparation of your instance of the tool (as appropriate): involves preparing the tool instance and/or configuring in the product to the team's needs and for the process the team intends to use.

- Communication of progress: involves sharing with interested parties via the appropriate communication channel the tool deployment strategy, proposed timeline, and progress along the way.

- Training to support the tool usage you expect: includes sharing the process by which you would like the tool to be used.

The key during implementation is ensuring that the tools serve the needs of the team. This is why it is so important to take the opportunity to hone the tool usage and process. Once a team is using a tool, they may find that the initial process needs to be adapted to better align it with the working interactions and shortcuts that get discovered.

Coaching Agile

Coaching should accompany the readiness, implement, and hone activities. Agile Coaches can provide significant benefit in these areas if they have experience in deploying Agile, are veterans of organizational change, have played Agile roles on a team, and are well versed in working with the business benefits of Agile. Coaching activities focus on helping the team and organization adapt and align to the new culture.

As Agile Coaches help teams toward their goals, they should support and facilitate agile deployment efforts during the readiness, implementation, and hone activities. As discussed in Chapter 12, Agile Coaches can address issues and challenges raised by teams that focus on adoption, culture, effect to customer value, work flow, and quality of the product being built.

Coaching can take many forms. There are executives, managers, and individuals who may be Agile Champions in their own right who have organizational change experience and can help move the organization toward an Agile culture. They may become Agile Coaches and some may remain Agile Champions. Both can provide coaching in their own ways.

Coach as Navigator on the Path to Agile

Think of an Agile Coach as your navigator who can help you move down the best path for your teams and provide course correction when you either regress or move in a less Agile-favorable direction. This is why it is so critical to hire an Agile Coach who has experience in helping at the level of deployment that you are looking for—team, product, or organization. If you do not have a coach, it is very easy to apply a process incorrectly and go down the less favorable path. Without a coach, it is easier to give up and regress back to the old process. The coach provides you with a better opportunity to go down the best path for the team toward Agile (Figure 22-2).

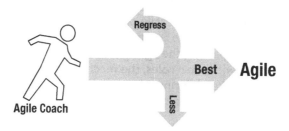

Figure 22-2. An Agile Coach can help you avoid regressing to old practices and taking wrong turns, and instead help you down the best path for your team or organization

Coaching helps a team adopt an agile process and lays the groundwork for transforming the culture. When discussing the path to adoption, coaches help ensure that elements and the Agile culture surrounding the elements stick.

Providing In-Session Coaching

Training can help teams gain understanding of agile processes and mindset, but at some point the team will implement Agile to gain experience. Because many team members have little agile experience or have a different understanding of what Agile is from past experiences, it can be hard to gauge whether a team is implementing Agile correctly. This is where it is very beneficial to have in-session coaching.

In-session coaching is beneficial as teams begin to implement agile processes and for three to four Sprints. In this context, an experienced Agile Coach sits in on the events and helps a team adapt to their new roles and practices. The coach should have the experience of providing teachable moments without unnecessarily interrupting the flow of an event. By the time the team is in Sprint 3 or 4, the coach should disengage and only periodically check in to see how the team is doing.

For example, in the first Sprint, the coach should attend the Sprint Planning, Daily Scrum, Sprint Review, and Sprint Retrospective events. In the early stages, the coach helps the team with event mechanics. By the third or fourth Sprint, the focus should be more on team dynamics and helping the team achieve a self-organizing state. Because of the principle of self-organizing teams, you do not want a coach participating in agile events beyond several Sprints. You do not want the team to become reliant on the coaches and unable to self-organize.

Grooming In-House Talent

As a team is starting to learn their agile process, it is beneficial for a coach to have one-on-one sessions with the Scrum Masters and POs, allowing these two roles charged with championing the agile process to ask specific questions to gain further familiarity with their roles, the mechanics, and the culture that is expected. For the first several Sprints, these sessions can be held weekly, then they should be reduced to once a month or as otherwise appropriate.

If a company is large enough and has several Scrum Masters and POs, another way to groom in-house talent is to hold periodic Q&A sessions for all the exponents of a given role. This is a good way to leverage a coach's time by fielding questions of general application. At the same time, those Scrum Masters or POs who attend can hear each other's challenges and realize that they are not alone. This is also an opportunity for bringing the Scrum Master or PO groups together to form the beginning of an agile community by role.

Building an In-House Coaching Circle

If an organization is large enough, there may be a benefit to grooming internal staff who have an affinity for Agile to become internal Agile Coaches. An experienced Agile Coach is needed to groom internal coaches, because it requires someone with deep knowledge and experience in Agile and the ability to groom enthusiasts to become coaches. This collection of internal Agile Coaches forms the basis for the coaching circle.

An Agile *coaching circle* is a support network of like-minded Agile enthusiasts who are interested in gaining knowledge and hearing others' experiences in readying, implementing, and honing teams in Agile. As an organization implements Agile, some folks will more naturally adapt to it. The pool of potential internal coaches may belong to Agile Team members, Scrum Masters, POs, and local Agile Champions. An organization needs to make a commitment to the internal Agile Coaches to allow them to help teams beyond their current role.

Honing Agile

One of the Agile principles states that "at regular intervals, the team reflects on how to become more effective, then tunes and adjusts its behavior accordingly." Having the opportunity to reflect ensures that the team can continuously hone its agile practice and mindset over time. The event that first comes to mind is the Sprint Retrospective. That is just one opportunity to reflect and adjust at the team level. There also needs to be honing at the product and organizational levels.

Keep in mind that honing can occur the moment any agile element is implemented. Improving the agile mechanics tend to be the early focus of reflecting and honing. However, over time, there should be a strong focus on whether the team is aligning with the Agile values and principles and achieving the transformation an organization or team is looking for.

 Agile Pit Stop   When honing, consider honing the "3 P"s: people, process, and product.

The challenge with reflecting and honing is to identify opportunities for improvement while still staying true to the Agile values and principles. As improvement opportunities are discussed, ask whether they align with Agile values and principles. If they do, this is a good sign and shows that it further supports the transformation toward Agile. The rest of this chapter examines various opportunities for continuously improving over time and achieving an Agile mindset.

Using the Retrospective for Continuous Improvement

The Sprint Retrospective is the first and foremost way to continuously reflect and hone. The goal is to identify what went well in the Sprint and what can be improved. It is an opportunity for the Scrum Team to reflect on the past Sprint's activities, including team dynamics, processes, tools, and culture. It is equally important to discuss what went well and what can be improved.

Once improvement opportunities are identified, they are prioritized by the team. The highest priority improvement opportunities are discussed by the team, and a root-cause analysis should be applied to get to the core of the problem. This ensures the team is providing the right solution to the problem. Then the team commits to those solutions as actions and they become improvement tasks for the next Sprint. This type of reflection and honing occurs on a Sprint-by-Sprint basis.

Using Empirical Data for Improvement Input

As part of honing, it is very useful to use empirical data from meaningful metrics to help a team identify opportunities for improvement. Trend metrics based on empirical data can help you reflect and hone. There are times where team members have a "gut feeling" about something and empirical data can help them take it from instinct to objective fact.

For example, a team is sensing that they are not getting enough time to build their stories during a Sprint. How can they prove this in an empirical manner? To gain empirical data, each team member can review their calendar during the length of a Sprint and see how much of their time is spent in meetings. This empirical data can help someone objectively validate the gut feeling and determine whether a course of action is warranted.

Say, for example, that it is empirically discovered that over 30 percent of the team's total time is spent in non–Agile-related meetings. Now that the team has baseline data to work with, it is possible to determine over successive Sprints if the action of reducing meetings has a positive effect on the amount of time a team has to build stories.

Conducting Periodic Agile Assessments

Agile assessments can provide insight into the level of implementation of the mechanical elements or the cultural and behavioral elements of Agile. The key is to create a baseline with the current level and periodically reassess to determine whether improvement has occurred. Baselining provides visibility into your starting point and information to help you adapt when moving forward. The results of an assessment can provide data points into what areas are thriving and what areas can be honed for improvement.

The Agile Mindset, Values, and Principles (MVP) Advisor is used to answer the question, "How do you know you are Agile?" (see Chapter 13). This assessment may occur at the team or organization level. The results of this survey provide visibility into the behavioral transformation toward the Agile values and principles. This assessment should be first conducted prior to implementation to gauge a team's current alignment to Agile values and principles. This forms the baseline by which subsequent assessments can be compared. Progress can be tracked by comparing the previous assessment and the current one. The results can be reflected on, and improvement opportunities can be identified based on the results. This honing activity may occur every three to six months depending on how regularly you would like to track your behavioral alignment to Agile.

Agile Pit Stop   The Agile MVP Advisor focuses on the transformation toward the Agile values and principles, whereas the Agile Practices Adoption survey focuses on a team's mechanical adoption level of an agile process.

The Agile Practices Adoption survey is used to answer the question, "How do you know you have adopted the agile processes and practices?" (see Chapter 13). The results of this team-level survey provide visibility into a team's mechanical adoption level of the agile process and practices that are being applied. This assessment mechanism should be first conducted after a team has had training and has been implementing their agile framework for three or four Sprints or a similar time period. This honing activity may occur every three to six months or pre-release, depending on how regularly you want to track adoption levels.

Improving Velocity

As a team tracks its velocity, members should look for opportunities to improve their pace. Velocity is a measure that can help you understand a team's sustainable pace by tracking the amount of story points of customer value a team can deliver in a Sprint. As new teams get started with Agile, their velocity trend line is initially inconsistent, but it will eventually become stable and reliable. When a team sees its velocity trend line plateau, it may be time to look for improvement opportunities.

Improving velocity is often a long-term exercise. It can start with identifying and removing impediments and dependencies that slow the team down. Although this action may initiate in a Retrospective, it may require further analysis of challenges that may take several Sprints to fully implement. Some techniques for increasing team velocity follow:

- *Look for software reuse opportunities.* Software reuse is a process whereby product teams may use software components that represent standard functionality and incorporate them into their product. Software reuse can significantly decrease effort spent on building the same functionality. It entails an amount of integration work to understand the code, assess its quality, and integrate it with the product's current code base.

- *Increase test automation.* Test automation is a process that takes manual testing routines and applies coding that executes those tests based on a trigger. Automation can result in a significant decrease in effort spent in executing manual tests. There is effort in getting to a level of automation before it reduces team effort.

- *Apply open-source solutions.* Open source provides you the ability to use peer-reviewed, high-quality code instead of building it internally. If there is a well-architected code structure, the ability to insert open-source code can accelerate pace and lower costs. There needs to be an investment to understand the open-source code that is available, assess its quality, and integrate it with the product's current code base.

- *Applying a colocation strategy.* Colocation is a working environment where a team is in one location. This can be challenging for companies that have distributed staff. Colocation promotes face-to-face communication, which is one of the Agile principles. This activity involves determining if a more colocated team is possible. This may become possible if you are working with several sites where each has seven or more team members. If initially QA was in one location, then QA responsibilities can be distributed. This requires changes for a team, but there can be a benefit to velocity when colocation and face-to-face communication occur.

Promoting Customer Validation

Often forgotten as a honing activity is *customer validation*. Engaging the customer is one of the most effective ways to hone the product toward building customer value. Gaining continuous customer feedback of working software and incorporating that feedback ensures that you are constructing a valuable solution. As discussed in Chapter 17, the Sprint Review is the gold standard for customer validation events at which the customer gets an opportunity to view the working software.

Other validation activities can also help hone the product toward building customer value. Aside from the Sprint Review, you can gain customer feedback in the review of the product vision and in an alpha-type environment where the customer can exercise the software in a hands-on manner. When a customer attends a validation session of working software, what they are really doing is reflecting on the software and determining if it meets their needs. This information allows a team to hone the software to better align with building customer value.

Promoting Giving Back

As you saw in Chapter 16, the notion of giving back applies to employees who have gained enough skills, experience, and confidence that they are capable of giving back to their community. When employees have reached this level of experience and are willing to give back, they start helping others. In relation to Agile, this is a form of self-organization in which a group of local Agile Champions feels ownership of the mission to enhance culture and is willing to support the transformation to Agile.

Equally important, giving back is a form of individual honing for further understanding of agile concepts. To give back to the community, this person must reflect on their own experience to hone his or her thoughts to determine what they contribute back to the community. Honing your thoughts to give back can occur in several ways:

- *Contributing your experiences and providing answers within the local agile social collaboration venues.* Providing answers to a Q&A venue require a reflection and fine-tuning of one's thoughts prior to responding.

- *Writing a blog article on an agile topic or experiences you have had on an Agile Team.* Authoring an article requires reflection and articulation of one's thoughts, knowing that readers will take your writings seriously.

- *Participating as co-lead in agile training.* Preparing for training and being in front of a crowd can motivate a strong need to reflect and hone your understanding of a topic and the delivery approach.

- *Drafting and delivering seminars and webinars.* Creating and delivering information likewise requires reflection and honing.

Are We Adapting and Improving Yet?

The key to the RICH Deployment Model is that you continually hone your product, process, and people. You hone the product by building in validation activities to ensure that the product meets the needs of your customers and provides them with value. You hone your process through reflection activities that allow a team to improve the process by which they work. You hone your people by providing the opportunity to adapt to the Agile culture, become Agile Champions through grooming by Agile Coaches, and by giving them the opportunity to give back to their community.

Ultimately, the goal is adaption toward improvement. Following the Agile values and principles, adaptation becomes a natural part of the process. But to effect this self-transformation, teams must be self-organized and reside in an environment where reflection is allowed and positive change is willingly accepted so that they can home in on their target of building customer value in an effective and high-quality manner.

Adapting Governance and Performance Reviews

The measure of intelligence is the ability to change.

—Albert Einstein

Within an organization, there are many processes beyond the team that can get in the way of a successful transformation to Agile. To achieve an Agile culture, it is recommended that you evaluate these processes to understand their alignment to the Agile values and principles and adapt as appropriate. Two of these processes that I have found can negatively affect an Agile culture are IT governance and performance review processes.

Adapting IT Governance to Agile

Governance and leadership are the yin and the yang of successful organizations. If you have leadership without governance you risk tyranny, fraud, and personal fiefdoms. If you have governance without leadership, you risk atrophy, bureaucracy, and indifference.

—Mark Goyer

Many companies have a form of IT governance that helps them manage the IT aspects of projects toward a successful outcome. IT governance is applied in a variety of ways, many of which include a focus on architecture, development, resource management, and risk management as they relate to the projects within the organizational scope.

The challenge when moving to Agile is that many folks see Agile as a change to only the development organization without seeing that Agile requires a cultural shift throughout the company in order for an Agile transformation to occur. If your governance process still assumes big upfront planning, this will need to be adapted if you hope to gain the business benefits of Agile. Unfortunately, some governance boards are rightly seen as bureaucratic and rigid. These attributes are not aligned with Agile value and principles. When encountering these types of boards, there is a bit of work to do.

The first action with any board is to ask your sponsor, preferably an executive, to share the business benefits of moving to Agile. This readiness activity begins conditioning minds toward Agile. Then it is incumbent to provide awareness of the Agile values and principles along with the objectives and motivations for moving to Agile. This begins the journey to align your IT governance toward an Agile mindset.

Iron Triangle to Flexible Trapezium

Many organizations expect to see the dimensions of scope, schedule, and cost defined and fixed up front in order for the project to be approved and moved forward. This rigid approach to building software is unrealistic because change inevitably occurs in one or more of these dimensions. The software industry is learning that this "iron triangle" constraint is unrealistic and leads to failed projects for two reasons:

- Software development is complex and typically unique. Most software is effectively custom development. This makes it hard to size requirements and predict the schedule.

- Customer value changes over time. To stay competitive in the marketplace, product teams need to adapt to customer value. Because of this, scope should not be locked in.

The natural adaptation is to make the iron triangle flexible, so that if one of the dimensions changes, the other dimensions change with it.

Another challenge with the iron triangle is that "quality" traditionally gets subsumed within the triangle and is subservient to scope, schedule, and cost. This is very problematic, inasmuch as quality practices and effort are often the first to get trimmed when a project is in trouble. To represent properly the proportionate importance of quality within a flexible framework, I recommend taking the three existing corners of scope, schedule, and cost and adding the fourth corner of quality (Figure 23-1).

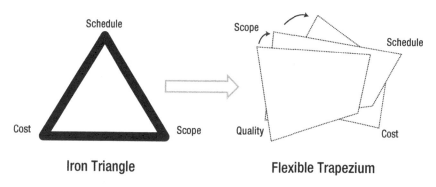

Figure 23-1. Supporting Agile by moving away from the iron triangle to a flexible trapezium

I call this the *flexible trapezium*. (A trapezium is a quadrilateral that has no parallel sides.) The intent is that at any one time on an agile project—and realistically on any project—the relative position of a corner and thus the length of the sides may vary depending on the importance of the dimension at that time (as illustrated by the small arrows in Figure 23-1). Although it is still important to provide a balance of these dimensions so that one is not inappropriately dominant over the others, there is flexibility that allows you to address the customer needs. In too many projects, the schedule becomes the inappropriately dominant dimension to the detriment of quality and scope.

Quality Dimensions Matter

In Agile, there is a strong focus on quality. This is why I strongly recommend that quality be explicitly mentioned. This isn't just the focus on traditional testing but a broader focus on overall quality. This focus allows a team to reduce risk. Quality is made up of practices that emphasize a level of confidence that the software functions in the intended manner and aligns with user stories. There are many ways this can be achieved. The following elements indicate if quality really matters:

- Establishing a mindset that quality is owned by the whole team.

- Constructing done criteria to indicate all engineering elements needed to build quality functionality.

- Establishing acceptance criteria for each user story to answer the question, "How will I know I'm done with the story and meeting customer expectations?"

- Applying testing within an iterative framework so that testing is continuous.

- Embedding testing within the team in order to break down the barriers between development and test.

- Encouraging the notion of test-first and the application of test-driven development.

- Placing a strong focus on unit and regression testing.

- Applying the notion of continuous customer validation of working software with practices such as Sprint Reviews.

- Implementing code reviews or pair programming.

- Incorporating refactoring into the process of updating existing code.

Applying the model of the flexible trapezium emphasizes that quality is an equal member of the dimensions. The question is: What types of changes do you need to make to your IT governance to support quality?

Rank Ordering Dimensions

In much the same way as Agile emphasizes prioritization and rank order of user stories, the four corners of the flexible trapezium should be applied within IT governance. I recommend that there be a discussion to determine a rank ordering for the dimensions and how much flexibility is allowed for one to dominate the other.

For any given project, the IT governance board needs to create a rank order framework for the four project dimensions to inform their decisions for releasing customer value. If scope is the driver, this should be the major factor when discussing missing or hitting the release date. The order of the dimensions should be discussed at the beginning of each project and adapted as appropriate. The gravity of this task cannot be overestimated. How important is the schedule? Is the scope of product functionality the most important? How much of a factor is quality? Can cost along with the people and capital it represents be adjusted? Answering these and other questions ensures that the decision is thought through so that one dimension doesn't get inappropriately selected or neglected, with adverse effects on the success of the product.

Agile Pit Stop   The reason scope is so important is that it asks you whether you think you are building the right product for the customer.

In traditional IT governance, all dimensions are often unrealistically locked in the iron triangle. In agile IT governance, it is important to adapt the dimensions as represented by a flexible trapezium. From an agile view, scope tends to be the highest order dimension because this is the value of functionality that customers purchase. Nonetheless, schedule, quality, and cost all play variably important roles. The trapezium approach provides the board with a more intelligent framework and the flexibility to adapt according to how customers perceive the value.

Collaborative Governance

Collaborative governance unites the brainpower of a governance board and an Agile Team in a collaborative manner. Governance discussions regarding the progress of the project should be a balanced and transparent dialogue between the governance board and the Agile Team. Information, progress, accomplishments, risks, and issues should be candidly and mutually shared toward the common goal of a successful product release. Depending on how rigid or ad hoc your governance is, you may need to adapt it to gain the benefits of Agile.

IT governance boards are often made up of managers who may have thrived on a hierarchical and directive leadership style. Agile requires all levels to share leadership and assume the responsibility that goes with it. Collaborative governance is defined by having the right people making the decisions—not just on the basis of their job titles but because they have the best insights into the change, opportunity, or problem under consideration.

Looking across the governance spectrum in Figure 23-2, on one side is rigid governance where command and control rules and decisions are made at the top. The other side shows no control, where decisions are ad hoc or erratic. Collaborative governance is somewhere in the middle and requires everyone to act like an adult, be responsible and accountable for his or her actions, willing to listen and cooperate, and come to a collaborative decision.

Figure 23-2. The governance spectrum

■ **Agile Pit Stop**   It is strongly recommended that the IT governance board attend the Sprint Reviews for the products in their purview.

If there is a form of IT governance in your organization, make sure they attend the Sprint Review. The Sprint Review supplements the discussion that occurs in an IT governance session with a view of the working software and feedback from the customers. The key to agile IT governance is to ensure that all stakeholders—IT governance board, Agile Team, and customers of the product—are heard and contribute to any go-forward decisions. All stakeholders must acknowledge that customers ultimately have the biggest voice, because they drive the value and buy the product.

Implementing, Coaching, and Honing Governance

After adaptations to the IT governance process occur, they need to be implemented. The implementation should reveal an update to the governance process, including the rank order of the dimensions of the flexible trapezium and alignment toward collaborative governance. The IT governance board should be part of the adaptation process.

During implementation, training should be given to the IT governance team as to the new process so they can gain an understanding of its elements and implementation. A brief form of education should also be given to the Agile Teams to ensure they are aware of the adapted process.

It would benefit the first few governance sessions to have an Agile Coach attend to provide in-session coaching to help adapt the process and, more important, the governance culture. Finally, as part of the Agile mindset, because moving to Agile may be challenging for governance, a periodic retrospective should occur that will allow a continuous improvement of the governance structure.

Adapting Performance Reviews

Performance reviews stress individual performance over the teamwork required for a successful quality effort.

—W. Edwards Deming

Moving to Agile can be challenging. Middle managers, who might be challenged by the new culture that Agile brings, are the same folks who traditionally conduct performance reviews. Because we are moving from a hierarchical world to a flat world, this can be particularly disconcerting for some middle managers.

At the same time, there is often a lot of subjectivity in the performance review process. Ranking and rating employees is sometimes not about skills but about how the person is viewed by management. I have witnessed performance reviews that are fairly objective using revenue, customer satisfaction, and goals to evaluate a worker, and I have seen a system in which none of that seemed to matter—individuals were encouraged to compete and outperform each other at the expense of the team and overall project success. Subjective performance reviews focusing on the individual are two impediments in achieving an Agile mindset.

Agile Pit Stop   If performance reviews are so critical, why does the average employee have to adhere to performance reviews and the executive level doesn't? How can some executives get large bonuses as their company fails? This inequity is another factor that damages the value of performance reviews.

If you insist on having performance reviews, the key is to promote team-based goals, written as objectively as possible, and then move to a continuous review process. How do you go from a world where performance reviews are king to a more meaningful world where performance is a continuous team-based process?

Move to Team-Based Performance

Because Agile focuses on the team, the performance objectives and the evaluation should be team-based. In traditional performance review models, upward of 100 percent of the objectives are individual-based. Employees with individual goals conduct themselves toward the greatest potential for personal reward and security. This is why individual goals are in polar opposition to the Agile Team mindset. The goal, therefore, is to move to a 100 percent team-based mindset, which can only be accomplished by no longer incentivizing individual members to choose their own success over team success.

It may be difficult to move to team-based objectives immediately for a number of reasons. The performance management system may not be functionally able to accommodate common objectives across multiple people (the team), or you may want to maintain an individual-based component to the objectives, so the exact percentages may need to be determined. You may want to take an incremental approach toward team-based performance. If you think aiming for 100 percent team-based objectives is too difficult, start with 50 percent team-based objectives. This will at least provide some incentive for individuals to work successfully as a team.

Objectives in Canonical Form

Though the performance review may not be objective, it can be advantageous to draft the performance objectives in as objective a manner as possible. With that in mind, consider applying the user story canonical form to specify the performance objective statements.

As discussed in Chapter 18, the canonical form is a language construct that many in the agile community use to document requirements (user stories). This includes the role (persona) you are playing, your action, and the business benefit. Applying the canonical form may help in describing your goal more objectively and effectively. For example:

- As a Scrum Team member, I will size the work using story points with the team during Sprint Planning, so that we gain team buy-in for scope and complexity of the story.

- As a Scrum Master, I will exemplify servant leader attributes to help my team become self-organized.

- As a Product Owner, I will continuously groom and prioritize the Product Backlog so that the Scrum Team has a solid list of user stories in which to work on in a Sprint.

- As an Agile Coach, I will coach and mentor the product team so they can adopt Agile effectively.

Once you have the performance goal written in this form, you can list the tangible tasks that make up the goal. You may consider this another interesting way to use the canonical form and articulate your performance objectives.

Performance Reviews toward Weekly 1:1

Ultimately, I recommend moving away from traditional annual or biannual performance reviews. A good first step is to transform your performance reviews into a weekly or per Sprint *1:1 process*. The goal behind this is that employees should never be surprised by a performance review because there should be continuous feedback from their manager.

Applying a 1:1 process provides a more continuous and collaborative approach in discussing objectives, challenges, progress, and learning. These sessions should be low-key and replaces the "big bang" performance reviews. During the continuous 1:1s, there should be an effort from both management and employee to be transparent, and this should avoid any surprises when ratings or compensation matters are discussed. Ultimately, the performance review process should move away from the stodgy, often negative and intrusive event and evolve into a continuous and collaborative discussion on progress and employee needs.

Management Insight into Employee Progress

When moving to a team empowerment environment that Agile brings, a person acting in the manager role (e.g., functional manager or resource manager) may have a challenging time understanding what an employee is doing. The manager needs to realize that when he or she moves into an agile world, discussion of performance should occur in a more collaborative manner, with a focus on progress and learning.

The challenges are twofold. First, the employee is not (or should not be) taking work orders from the manager any longer; instead, the work should be driven from the product backlog (via the sprint backlog from sprint to sprint). Second, the manager actually does have less visibility into what the employee is doing since the employee should be fully committed to the Agile Scrum Team. How does a manager gain firsthand information? Here are two ideas that can help a manager who has direct reports on an Agile Team.

- During the Daily Scrum, the manager may quietly listen to the progress the Scrum Team members communicate during this brief session. The manager should contact the Scrum Master and verify that this daily stand-up is an open meeting and that they may quietly attend. The manager should be sure to tell employees that he may be sitting in on this session.

- During the Sprint Review, the manager can view employees' progress by seeing what they demonstrate. If a manager learns that an employee is demonstrating working software during the Sprint Review, she can quietly listen in to see what the employee built and how it works. The manager should have contacted the Product Owner and Scrum Master to verify that she might quietly attend the meeting, and she should tell her employee that she might be sitting in on the Sprint Review as an observer.

The word *quietly* bears emphasis. Agile practices are not meant for the manager but for building customer value and making progress through the project. The Daily Scrum is specifically meant for team members to communicate to each other on their progress. The Sprint Review is meant to gain valuable customer and Product Owner feedback so that you can ensure you are building the right product for our customers.

Are You Adapting Organization-Level Processes?

If you begin implementing Agile at just the team level, you will soon find that there are organizational-level processes that are not aligned with Agile. Governance processes may ask for fixed requirements up front with a negative view on change, and performance review processes may emphasize individual success over team success.

Regardless of the process, ensure that you keep your eyes open as Agile is implemented so that you have the possibility of honing and adapting these processes over time. You may need the insight of an Agile Coach and the support of your executive sponsor to promote these cultural changes. To achieve an agile culture, you need to evaluate these processes to assess their alignment to the Agile values and principles and adapt as appropriate.

Three Case Studies in Adopting Agile

Strive not to be a success, but rather to be of value.

—Albert Einstein

Once upon a time, there was this desire to become Agile. This is how your story begins. But giving an account of the achievement of an agile transformation is more complex and challenging than many realize. It is a story that requires a change in culture—one of the hardest things to do. It is a tale beset by many obstacles, including people who either do not try to understand the value Agile brings or who try to impede the effort.

Fear not! The roadmap in this book can proactively guide you and lay the groundwork for delivering value, which is what you are in business to do. The roadmap is for an adaptive path based on your decisions and commitment. So what does your story look like?

In this concluding chapter, I offer three case studies—stories of a smaller colocated project, a medium distributed project, and a large distributed team—to help you understand how the readiness activities, deployment approach, and commitment to Agile lead to different results. What will your Agile case study look like?

Smaller Colocated Project

Once upon a time, there was a small project of 8 people. They were a group working on a new product that was scheduled to take about 6 months to release. Although the PO, along with management, sales, and marketing, established a product vision, they realized that there was quite of bit of uncertainty. Because of this they decided to apply agile processes.

As they were getting started, they were honest with each other and realized that no one on the project team or management really understood Agile or how to deploy it into a team. They felt that training was in order, so they hired an Agile Coach to provide Agile training to the team. The coach recommended an overview for the management team. A couple of the management team members declined the overview invite. The coach asked which of the management will become the sponsor for moving to Agile, and they decided it would be a sponsorship by committee.

The Agile Coach introduced management to the readiness activities to help prepare the team. Management wanted to start the project very soon, so only a few activities were allowed to be focused on. These activities included:

- Identify and establish agile roles and responsibilities
- Determine education needs
- Establish agile frameworks and practices
- Identify agile tooling and infrastructure needs

The good news was that most of the team was colocated. Because there were five developers and only one QA person currently on the team, the coach advised adding two more QA engineers to ensure a healthy balance between building and testing. The team was able to hire only one more QA engineer, but this still provided a better ratio of skills.

Management felt that converting their existing project manager to Scrum Master was a good approach, and this was amenable to the coach. Management identified a PO from the existing pool of product management within the organization. The Agile Coach recommended the Scrum Master and PO be allowed to take the *Certified Scrum Master* (CSM) and *Certified Scrum Product Owner* (CSPO) education, respectively. Management declined, citing budgetary concerns.

Scrum seemed to be the right agile process for this project, so the coach recommended this. Everyone agreed. Because the team was colocated, the coach recommended that they initially start with a physical Sprint Backlog wall where the team members could see the stories in their Sprint on a team wall and physically move the stories and tasks forward during the Daily Scrum. The PO opted initially to use a spreadsheet program as the location for the Product Backlog.

Agile Pit Stop If the first release is successful, a continuous delivery approach can be applied with the goal of deploying functionality incrementally every two Sprints.

The Agile Coach provided a two-day training with a focus on Scrum and use of the physical Sprint Backlog wall for the whole team. Then the coach sat with the Scrum Master and PO separately for an additional two hours to focus specifically on their roles and responsibilities.

Because of the team enthusiasm from the training, management felt that they were ready to apply Scrum. Management continued with the Agile Coach for about three months, and he did the best he could in such a short time—long enough to get Scrum off the ground on the team.

The team began implementing Scrum with three-week Sprints with the help of the Agile Coach. The first three Sprints were fairly successful. Upon reaching the fourth Sprint, the coach's contract expired. Management thought that the teams were engaged in Scrum, so the coach was released.

In Sprint 4, the Scrum Master attempted to keep the team focused on Agile values and principles as well as the Scrum practices. There were several strong personalities on the development team, two of whom were secret Agile Deniers. They were worried that they would not be able to continue to be the senior team leaders and would not be rewarded for problem solving.

During the Sprint Retrospective concluding Sprint 4, the two Deniers teamed up to do away with the Daily Scrum, saying that maybe twice a week was good enough. These two did not like the discipline of having to share their progress. They managed to influence the rest of the team to concur, so the Daily Scrums turned twice-a-week Scrums. They also managed to influence the team into using individual velocity instead of team velocity so that they could show how individually effective they were. The Scrum Master tried to prevent this, citing the Agile principle of the team approach, but the team, led by the two Deniers, overruled the Scrum Master.

Several Sprints latter, the Daily Scrum was occurring once a week and the Retrospective actions were not being completed. The real challenge was that the team didn't like decomposing large requirements into user stories that fit into a Sprint. This was difficult to do. Also, the QA team members weren't receiving completed stories until the very end of the Sprint. This became problematic when a majority of the stories were not getting completed within a Sprint.

Although the Scrum Master tried to mitigate many of these problems, he was not experienced enough with Agile to help the team improve. There was little to no understanding of the Agile values and principles on the team and no experience to reference. Yet management put much of the blame of the team problems on the shoulders of the Scrum Master, even though he was escalating the impediments to management for help. Unfortunately, development had more influence with management than the Scrum Master had, and management wasn't experienced enough to support the Scrum Master or Agile.

Agile Pit Stop   If management does not align with the Agile mindset, it can be very difficult for the Scrum Master to keep the team focused on applying Scrum effectively.

Because the performance review process still operated on individual performance, the senior developers on the team made a strong push in the last Sprint to get a large amount of work done. The team members often worked late into the evening and weekends to achieve some level of success. Even with these heroics, however, management decided that testing had to be shortened to keep the release date from getting pushed too far.

The team released their product about two months late. There was difficulty understanding exactly what scope was delivered, and overall product quality was deficient in many areas. The Scrum Master received the blame for much of this, and two development team members received accolades for their "extra effort."

The company brought the Agile Coach back in to conduct a lessons-learned. When debriefed, the team and management learned the following:

- Insufficient time was spent considering readiness activities and the needs of the team to achieve an effective and sustainable Agile adoption. The team found that they stumbled into many decisions on how to move forward.

- They felt that the Agile Coach should have placed more focus on the Agile values and principles and the cultural aspects of getting to an Agile culture. Most of the team members couldn't recall more than three Agile principles.

- Because the Scrum Master didn't have Scrum-specific training and was inexperienced, it was very hard to support and maintain the Scrum practices once the Agile Coach left.

- The Scrum Master felt he was not supported by management to promote and sustain an Agile culture.

- The team realized that they should have engaged the Agile Coach for at least a couple more months to sustain the mechanics, and maybe needed a more experienced coach who could place more emphasis on the values and principles to change the culture.

- The team thought that the retrospective allowed them to decide to change the Scrum process in whatever way they thought best. They didn't realize that minimizing some of the events affects the whole, because Scrum requires Planning, Daily Scrums, Review, and Retrospective to work in a closed-loop iterative system.

- Whereas an Agile Team applies story points to understand team velocity, this team moved to individual velocities. This quickly took them away from team building and self-organization and instead toward their own individual successes at the expense of the team.

- The performance review system continued to focus on individual goals to gauge success rather than team-based goals. To make matters worse, individual velocities were included into individual performance reviews, and those with higher individual velocities received higher merit increases.

- There were accolades to two of the development team members based on individual heroics, which undermined the goal of team-based achievement.

Unsurprisingly, Agile was not well received by this team. The result was that the team regressed back to more of a hybrid waterfall framework in which heroics were rewarded. The team agreed that if Agile was tried again, there needed to be more of a management commitment to change the culture and a more experienced Agile Coach who better understood Agile and achieving a culture change.

Medium Distributed Project

Once upon a time, there was a group working on significantly improving their portfolio product. Management realized that there was quite a bit of uncertainty in the product direction, which requires new front-ends and much more integration than in the past. As they proposed the 12-month project, management felt that due to the uncertainty, they should apply Agile. Because there was enough disagreement on how to deploy Agile, the management team felt that they would benefit by hiring an Agile Coach.

One of the senior management became the sponsor for the Agile initiative. He was excited about Agile and felt that he had a bit of Agile knowledge due to the Agile books he had read. When he brought the Agile Coach on-board, he shared a lot of his Agile ideas with the coach. In the spirit of learning more, the coach recommended that the sponsor take an Agile overview session. The sponsor felt that he knew enough about Agile already but that other management should take the overview session.

The overall project team size was 32 people with folks in New York City and London. The coach advised them to form four Scrum teams of approximately 8 team members each, which was promptly done. Because there were 15 employees in the London, it was decided that 2 teams would be US-based and 2 would be European-based. Each team's competencies evinced a healthy balance of development, user experience, and QA.

The coach emphasized the importance of the Agile values and principles and shared them with the management team. The coach also suggested hiring experienced Scrum Masters. The sponsor felt that it was best to draw from the existing talent to play the Scrum Masters. The Agile Coach recommended that each of the identified Scrum Masters take CSM education. The sponsor agreed to fund this training.

The existing Product Manager was knowledgeable about the intended product and made a good PO candidate. Several of the functional managers became aware that their role would reduce in scope and responsibilities because the team members would get their work from the backlog. In consequence, three functional managers insisted that they become POs. Although the Agile Coach felt there were risks in taking this approach, it was agreed that between the 1 existing product manager and 3 functional managers that each of the 4 Scrum Teams would have a PO. The coach recommended that each PO take a formal CSPO education. The POs felt that a short training from the Agile Coach was enough.

The Agile Coach introduced the team to the readiness activities, and management cherry-picked several of them to focus on, including:

- Understand the current state of engineering and Agile
- Determine team willingness and capability
- Identify and establish Agile roles and responsibilities
- Determine education needs
- Establish agile framework and practices
- Identify agile tools and infrastructure needs

The coach felt that certain areas should be addressed: establishing a common understanding of Agile; focusing on Agile values and principles; understanding levels of executive and stakeholder buy-in; establishing a strategy and backlog for the Agile transformation; and establishing done criteria and measures of success. But the coach made progress with the agreed-to readiness activities. Against the Agile Coach's advice, the POs felt using hours instead of story points was best for story point sizing.

The team started with a 4-week Sprint 0 to get organized. A Product Owner Scrum of Scrums (SoS) was established so that the POs could collaboratively build and prioritize the Product Backlog and sort user stories to the various team backlogs. The POs became a bit overzealous and attempted to prescribe user stories to Sprints through the end of the proposed schedule.

They began implementing Scrum with 4-week sprints with the help of the Agile Coach. The first two Sprints were focused on the mechanics. A project SoS was initiated in which the Scrum Masters got together to discuss project dependencies and progress.

Starting in Sprint 3, command and control was being exhibited by the POs. The three who had been functional managers were reverting back to their old habits of directing the teams. The teams began having problems with self-organization because they were getting overruled in their decision making by the POs.

In the first three Sprints, the teams mechanically exercised the Sprint Reviews with internal stakeholders focusing on the goal of bringing in existing customers of the old product and potential new customers. By the fourth Sprint, the POs recommended that because they felt that they knew what the customers wanted, that there wasn't a need to bring them in to the Sprint Reviews. The Agile Coach strongly encouraged bringing in customers, and the POs said that they would think about it.

During the Sprint Retrospective concluding Sprint 5, several teams expressed concerns about the command-and-control behavior that was being exhibited by the POs. The team members didn't push it because they were also concerned that their performance reviews would be negatively impacted by the former functional managers who were acting as POs.

The Agile Coach attempted to mitigate this command-and-control problem. The POs were quite certain that they were doing the right thing because they felt that the team wasn't making good decisions. Since the project was challenging, the POs felt they needed to take the reins of the project.

Another problem that occurred was that the POs started to compare the velocity across teams. The message that they were sending was, "Look how many hours of work this team is putting in. How come you aren't putting in those kinds of hours?" This started to have a demoralizing effect on several teams.

Agile Pit Stop   Story points are the recommended measure for sizing user stories. Story points are a scope measure that includes effort, complexity, and uncertainty.

The coach, realizing that comparing velocities was also problematic, discussed the various problems with the Agile sponsor. Unfortunately, the sponsor didn't want to make waves because he was friendly with the former functional managers. He said he would talk to the POs, but after another Sprint it was clear that this wasn't a priority with the sponsor.

By Sprint 8, the Agile Coach's contract ended and he was released on account of budgetary constraints. The sponsor stepped in to provide Agile coaching and mentoring to the teams. Some of his advice seemed to conflict with the Agile Coach's past advice.

The project released within 2 weeks of the schedule. During the last 2 months, the teams were placed into a death march to complete the project on time. A few developers and the POs were praised and rewarded for tirelessly making the project a success. Once the product was released, however, there were many customer concerns regarding the alignment of the functionality to their needs. Few existing customers wanted to upgrade to the new version. This next-generation product was not providing value to the customers and did not do well in the market.

The Scrum Masters asked the sponsor to bring in the Agile Coach to conduct a lessons-learned. The sponsor said that there wasn't budget for it, but they were welcome to conduct a lessons-learned on their own. When debriefed, the team and management learned the following:

- The team liked receiving training, and the Scrum Masters were grateful for receiving the CSM training.

- The project started well, focusing on readiness activities and Sprint 0.

- The first two Sprints were very promising.

- By the third Sprint, the team realized that the former functional managers who were the POs were behaving in a very command-and-control manner.

- The POs, specifically those who were former functional managers, overruled many of the decisions the team made. The result was that the team lost any sense of self-organization and felt demoralized.

- Although Sprint Reviews were occurring, no actual customers were attending. The reviews were for internal stakeholders.

- The POs believed they knew what the customers wanted, but they were incorrect. The product release was not aligned with customer needs.

- There was little mitigation of the PO command and control due to their relationship with the sponsor. This negatively affected any chance of achieving a culture change.

- Product quality was deficient in many areas. There was inadequate testing within each Sprint. Testing was minimized toward the end of the project.

- Once the Agile Coach was released, the Scrum Masters and team didn't feel they had anywhere to escalate their concerns when the issues were beyond their control.

- There was strong sponsor support at the beginning, but the sponsor didn't support the culture change needed for Agile.

Some of the members from the Scrum Teams felt negative about Agile after this experience. Other members understood that the POs were not really working in an agile manner and were not aligned with the Agile values and principle. It was recognized that the project regressed to a more hierarchical command-and-control manner and wasn't really Agile.

Large Distributed Team

Once upon a time, there was a group working on a next-generation *identity and access management* (IAM) product. Management realized that there was quite of bit of uncertainty in the new direction and significant re-engineering of their past product line. One of the senior management, having experienced Agile in another company, knew that because of the uncertainty, that this product should apply Agile. Management knew that it was going to take a while and initially targeted about 12 months to build functionality. They were open to adjusting scope or schedule as the project ramped up.

This same senior manager agreed to be the sponsor for the agile initiative. The sponsor felt that it was important to hire an Agile Coach to help deploy Agile. But because not all coaches are created equal, he wanted to ensure he hired a coach who was an Agile subject matter expert and experienced as a change agent, coach, and trainer. As the first action toward Agile, the sponsor asked the Agile Coach to educate his peers and direct reports on the Agile values and principles. The sponsor knew that some of the involved senior management were in other offices, so he sent the Agile Coach to those sites to educate the management.

The Agile Coach introduced the team to the readiness activities, and management agreed to build an Agile Deployment Team to work through these activities. The readiness activities that were focused on included:

- Establish a common understanding of Agile.

- Provide Agile mindset education on the Agile values and principles and drivers for why we are changing.

- Add "customers and employees really matter" to the company vision and "customer engagement" and "employee engagement" to employee objectives.

- Understand levels of executive and stakeholder buy-in.

- Establish an overall strategy and backlog for the Agile transformation (including mitigation of risks).

- Understand the current state of engineering and Agile.

- Determine team willingness and capability.

- Determine suitability of product.

- Evaluate and adapt to collaborative IT governance.

- Identify and establish Agile roles and responsibilities.

- Determine education needs.

- Establish agile framework and practices.

- Establish done criteria, user story framework, and sizing techniques.

- Craft measures of success and general metrics.

- Identify agile tools and infrastructure needs.

The Agile Coach, with the help of the sponsor, identified local Agile Champions who either had experience with Agile or were enthusiastic about it and who were willing to form the basis of the small Agile deployment team. The coach educated the deployment team on the Agile values and principles and the importance of readiness activities to help condition the product team toward an Agile mindset.

Agile Pit Stop   If two or more large product teams are moving to Agile at the same time, it is highly recommended to use more than one coach.

The Agile deployment team discussed their strategy for deploying Agile and created a backlog of tasks based on the readiness activities. They asked the sponsor to a send out a message sharing the reasons for moving to Agile. The sponsor agreed to share the drivers for organizational change and introduced a common understanding of Agile based on the Agile values and principles. From then on, the sponsor periodically shared the progress and the importance of shifting to the Agile mindset.

To support Agile further, the sponsor recommended that management have performance objectives that focus on employees, customers, and Agile values and principles. He also recommended that employees have team-based objectives with a focus on the Agile values and principles. This set the tone to support self-organizing teams and teamwork.

The Agile Coach introduced himself to the overall team in an email and said he would set up several meetings with the team members from each location: Boston, Prague, and Bangalore. In the spirit of transparency, he asked the team in each location about their level of willingness in moving to Agile and followed this up with a survey. He listened carefully to the team members during the meetings to understand their concerns. The survey included questions to gauge the current level of Agile experience within the teams. Both the level of willingness and experience levels were used as input on how to adapt the Agile deployment effort.

The overall team size was 79 people, with most of the team in three locations. The coach recommended that nine Scrum Teams be formed of approximately 9 team members each. Because there were 35 employees in Boston, 16 in Prague and 28 in Bangalore, it was decided that 4 teams would be set up Boston, 2 in Prague and 3 in Bangalore. Initially, there were a high percentage of QA in Bangalore, so there had to be a rebalancing of development and QA across the teams. This was handled with management approval. It was also recommended that each Scrum Team own an end-to-end piece of functionality. This was handled by identifying the functional areas within the architecture vision and parsing them to the teams.

The coach also suggested hiring at least one experienced Scrum Master at each location. The others could come from the existing organization. The Agile Coach recommended that each of the inexperienced Scrum Masters take CSM education. Management agreed.

It was important to find POs for each team who were knowledgeable in the IAM space. There were 3 existing Product Managers who made good PO candidates: 2 in Boston and 1 in Prague. The most senior Product Manager became the uber-PO who supported 1 Scrum Team and more importantly provided overall product guidance to the other POs. Two of the other existing POs agreed to support 2 Scrum Teams each. This meant that the 2 Prague-based Scrum Teams were set and 3 Boston-based teams were set.

This still left the 1 Scrum Team in Boston and 3 teams in Bangalore. A functional manager who was known to have servant leadership attributes from

Boston agreed to become the final PO to support the remaining Boston Scrum Team. For Bangalore, it was decided to hire a PO who had IAM product experience. This person supported 2 Scrum Teams. An existing functional manager who had product knowledge became the PO to support the remaining Bangalore Scrum Team. The Agile Coach strongly recommended CSPO education for these POs. Management agreed to fund this training.

The Agile Coach recommended starting with a 3-week Sprint 0 to get organized. The first two activities were discussing the use of Agile and managing project risks. The POs got together to build the product vision. Because this project was distributed, the coach suggested collaborative online tools for dialogue across teams. There was also a focus on using an online agile planning tool so that the Product Backlog could be easily instantiated into each individual team and Sprint Backlogs. In addition, a configuration management (CM) vision and QA vision were established to support the code changes and quality of the product.

The POs formed an SoS so they could collaboratively build and prioritize the backlog and sort the user stories to the various team backlogs. The uber-PO provided overall guidance. They decided to use the canonical form for writing user stories and spent a lot of time grooming the backlog together. The POs also agreed that each location would hold joint Sprint Reviews so that current and potential customers and other stakeholders were not being asked to attend multiple Sprint Review sessions.

Agile Pit Stop   If the new release of this on-premise IAM product goes well, the team will focus on building a cloud version offering a SaaS solution.

The Scrum Teams individually focused on establishing done criteria. Each team established their relative sizing framework using story points. Several of the teams began working on research spikes during Sprint 0 to reduce technology uncertainty. During Sprint 0, the Scrum Team members received an intensive Agile training on the Agile framework that was being used—a combination of Scrum and XP engineering practices. A project SoS was initiated in which the Scrum Masters got together to discuss project dependencies and progress.

Sprint 0 ended with a cross–Scrum Team Agile Release Planning session. This session was initiated with a joint video conference session together where each team was introduced and the uber-PO shared the product vision with the teams and then gave everyone a chance for Q&A. The teams had to adapt their working hours to accommodate this session. The QA vision, technical vision, and CM visions were also shared during this session. The continuation of Agile Release Planning involved an all-day team backlog grooming session, which occurred independently within the respective team's time zone. Then another joint effort occurred in which each team shared their findings. Upon conclusion, Sprint 1 commenced.

They began implementing Scrum with 3-week sprints. The Agile Coach brought in a fellow coach, and they shared the load of helping teams come up to speed with Scrum. The first four Sprints went by with some success, and there was a lot of focus on the mechanics. Several of the teams were exhibiting self-organizing attributes and some teams were still getting the hang of it. Each team was honing their relative story point sizing framework and tracking their velocity. The coaches actively discouraged velocity comparisons, and these didn't occur.

In Bangalore, the PO who had been a functional manager had to be further coached to reduce command-and-control attributes. The main Agile Coach flew to Bangalore to work with this PO and support the Scrum Masters and local Scrum Teams. The coach attended many of the teams' events to gauge the adoption-level mechanics. He held periodic check-point calls with all of the Scrum Masters to help them with their challenges.

It was initially challenging to hold joint Sprint Review sessions because there was often much more work that was completed than could be shared. The Agile Coach recommended prioritizing the work based on where feedback was most needed and ensuring each team got a chance to demo at least two or three stories. The first two Sprint Reviews were held with just internal stakeholders to exercise this adaptation. This allowed teams time to get used to demonstrating to people and to figure out the mechanics of the review. By Sprint 3, the POs began inviting a few existing customers to gain their feedback. By the fifth Sprint, the Sprint Review began running effectively. A challenge that was resolved over the next two Sprints was taking the Sprint Review feedback and incorporating it into the Sprint Planning for adaptation of built functionality.

After the first several Sprint Retrospectives, the teams began realizing the importance of carrying out the actions for improvement. Though some teams were more effective at it than others, they began working these actions and seeing the benefit. There were two people in two separate Boston-based Scrum Teams who didn't like the notion of the daily Scrum and tried to get this changed within their retrospective, saying it was affecting their work. They tried to change it to weekly, but the rest of the team members believed it was important to share the daily progress and highlight roadblocks. Two Sprints later, one of the team members who raised this concern said that he didn't like having to share his progress all the time and decided to quit. In talking with this team, the Agile Coach said that, given Agile's continuous nature, it may not be right for everyone, and that's okay. The team promptly replaced this team member with an Agile-minded engineer and the coach helped her come up to speed.

By Sprint 7, the Agile Coach initiated two surveys: the agile practices adoption survey and the Agile Mindset, Values, and Principles Advisor survey (see Chapter 13). The results were shared during the next Sprint Retrospective so each team could decide how to improve. Only with the teams' agreement a summary was shared with management, together with some recommendations as to where management could help.

By Sprint 10, the backlog was well fairly well groomed. Affinity sizing was used to minutely size the remaining stories in the backlog. This allowed the POs to create a minimum viable product (MVP) value line consisting of the stories that were targeted for a viable Release 1 product. Having this empirical data along with the MVP stories provided the basis for an objective discussion with the organizational IT governance board. The IT governance board suggested that scope would be the driver and they wanted to continue tracking the MVP line and the release burnup to see when each team's velocity met their MVP lines. Understanding each team's MVP and velocity provided a means to move stories to other teams to balance the work.

■ **Agile Pit Stop**   Do not think of your MVP line as fixed scope but as a gauge for what may make a viable product. It is subject to change based on the continuous customer validation of the Sprint Reviews and new requirements that come from customers.

As the Scrum Teams' MVP lines were adjusted based on customer feedback, each team's velocity was tracked and it became evident that Sprint 18 would be the last Sprint on the project. An additional Sprint was added for integration, performance, and load testing, as well as finishing the user guides, preparing the release notes, and beginning the marketing campaign. When the product was released, many customers immediately upgraded or purchased this next-generation product.

Each Scrum Team conducted a final retrospective. The Agile Coach collated the results. He also conducted another Agile Mindset, Values, and Principles Advisor survey to compare it to the baseline from the previous survey results. Upon a roll-up of the retrospective and survey results, a debrief occurred with the team and management that included the following items:

- It was great having management support and a sponsor for the move to Agile who really understand the Agile values and principles.

- Everyone appreciated receiving training. The Scrum Masters were grateful for receiving CSM training and the POs for receiving CSPO training.

- The project started well. Focusing on readiness activities and Sprint 0 helped the team get their heads around the move to Agile.

- The teams liked hearing the various visions (product, QA, CM, and so on). These helped them understand the go-forward focus and gave them a sense of security that these areas had proper attention.

- Though initially skeptical, the POs and Scrum Masters found the SoS of great value in collaborating across teams and discussing dependencies and ways to optimize at the overall project level.

- Teams liked having the Agile Coach during the first several Sprints but were relieved to see the coach back off after Sprint 4 so that the team could self-organize.

- The teams were pleased that they could push back on the command-and-control and micromanagement and enlist the support of the coach and especially management to remove these regressive behaviors.

- Everyone really liked getting a chance to demonstrate to customers. The POs like it because this helped them validate their product direction.

- As the team adopted the agile practices, they realized the need of having management and IT governance move toward the Agile mindset in order to transform the culture and adapt to customer needs.

As a side effect of the successful project, two of the Scrum Masters wanted to begin their education in becoming Agile Coaches. The Agile Coach emphasized that being a true coach requires more experience but that their attitudes would help them. Building an internal agile coaching circle helped the organization leverage its local agile talent. Because of this positive experience, several other teams in the company wanted to go Agile.

What Will Your Case Study Look Like?

As you approach your agile adventure, the question is, "What will your case study reveal?" Can others learn from your journey? Have your teams mechanically adopted Agile but not reached a transformation toward Agile values and principles? Have you regressed from Agile to a hybrid waterfall framework? Have some teams adopted Agile while management continues to operate in a traditional manner? Are only the engineering teams doing Agile, while management and IT governance continue to demand a fixed scope, quality, schedule, and cost up front?

It is important to remember that moving to Agile is meant to be a move to a new culture, and this is difficult. Do you see a culture shift occurring? Chapter 2 argues that a skill change is easier than a procedural change, and a procedural change is easier than a culture change. A culture change implies a behavioral change in people, focused on a change in the values within their organization that is expressive of a new way of thinking. It does take time, and this is why it is important to think of a move to Agile as a journey. This is also why the readiness activities of the RICH deployment model (Chapter 7) are meant to ensure that you ask the right questions, help you plan your agile adoption with the goal of a cultural transformation, and condition the mindset toward the Agile values and principles.

Agile is not a silver bullet that will give instant results. If you truly align your culture and all of the people's behaviors to Agile values and principles, then maybe you can gain the benefits sooner rather than later. This is why I provide you with the Agile Mindset, Values and Principles Advisor in Chapter 13. It can help you gauge your alignment to the Agile values and principles along the way.

As you discuss Agile with management, ensure the conversation is driven by the business benefits Agile can provide. Going Agile is not just a cool thing for teams to do—it can help you improve a company's financial strength. Gaining the adaptability of scope that Agile brings can help you achieve an increase in revenue. To make money, however, you need to delight your customers by building customer value and harnessing the brainpower of your employees. What happens when you step up the level of customer engagement? What happens when you step up the level of employee engagement?

The roadmap in this book can help you achieve an agile transformation to the betterment of revenue and customer success. Ultimately, what will be the story that represents your agile journey? Will it be a case study that can be held up as an example of successfully implementing Agile, or will it be a parable of perils and pitfalls to avoid? The answer is up to you.

Index

Other Apress Business Titles You Will Find Useful